The

COMPLETE ELDERCARE PLANNER

· SECOND EDITION ·

The
COMPLETE
ELDERCARE
PLANNER

· SECOND EDITION ·

*Where to Start, Which Questions to Ask,
and How to Find Help*

Joy Loverde

THREE RIVERS PRESS

NEW YORK

Copyright © 2000 by Joy Loverde

Published by Three Rivers Press, New York, New York.
Member of the Crown Publishing Group.

Random House, Inc. New York, Toronto, London, Sydney, Auckland.
www.randomhouse.com

THREE RIVERS PRESS is a registered trademark and the Three Rivers Press colophon
is a trademark of Random House, Inc.

Printed in the United States of America

Design by Helene Berinsky

Library of Congress Cataloging-in-Publication Data

The complete eldercare planner : where to start, which questions to ask, and how to find help / by Joy Loverde.—Rev. ed., 2nd ed.
Includes indexes.
1. Aged—Home care—United States—Planning.   2. Aging parents—Care—United States—Planning.
3. Caregivers—United States—Life skills guides.   I. Title.
HV1461.L6843 2000
362.6—dc21   99-048602
ISBN 0-8129-3278-1

10 9 8 7 6 5 4

Second Edition

This book is dedicated to the memory of my father,
the Honorable Charles M. Loverde,
and to my mother, Alba Wright.
Your love, grace, and wisdom have made this book possible.

ACKNOWLEDGMENTS

This book began when I was fourteen years old, and carries with it the spirit of the elders who welcomed me into their hearts one cold and rainy Thanksgiving morning. I walked into their nursing home as a child and left as a woman with a mission. For this life-altering encounter, I am forever grateful to the Sinsinawa Dominican Sisters of Trinity High School, River Forest, Illinois.

I thank my husband and partner in life, David Schultz, for sharing the journey of this book. My respect for his writing and editing skills is immeasurable, and the experience of finding everlasting love is reflected in the inner peace I feel every moment that I walk beside him.

To my daughter, Bonnie Blackburn, her husband, Joe, my granddaughter, Lanea, and Michael, Trinity, and Emily—they are a source of balance and limitless inspiration for the true meaning of family.

The foundation for writing a book of this nature comes from the unconditional love I receive from my family—James Loverde, Carol Loverde, and Dominic DiFrisco, Peter and Orasa Loverde, Linda and Louis Belpedio, Maxine Weintraub and Family, Shirley Fadim, Bernice Nesti and Family, Iola Nesti and Family, the late Rita Nesti, Frank Loverde, Jr., and Family, Jeff and Amy Schultz, Greg and Kim Schultz, Sharon Arkin and Family, Gardner Stern, Jamey and Melissa Fadim, Charlie and Marion LoVerde, Lisa and Laura Loverde, Ethel Stanton and Family. And to my late cousin, Michelle Nesti Longhofer—thank you for loving me so much.

I believe in angels, and this book reflects a certain depth of insight because I have been blessed with the wisdom, guidance, and friendship of Jack Cullerton, Martin Bayne (Mr. Long-Term Care), Lisa Hudson, Mitch Messer, Kathryn Cunningham, and author, Kent Nurburn.

Special people have been with me every step of the way, and I am grateful to them and for them especially Paul Silverman, Jill and Steve Morris, Sandra Neff, Joanne Desmond, Georgia Evans, Bob Coffel, Bob and Janet Ebel, Nadine and Reece Franklin, Harpo, Jerry, and Lynn Kalish, Martha and Tony Kluk, Jan and Scott Lane, Ben and Mary Magestro, Richard Ofstein, M.D., Bernice Pink, Ruth Podgers, Connie Rivera and Mark McPherson, Carl and Patty Sanders, Deanna Schultz, Michael Scott, Paul and Karen Sullivan, Angie and John Thoburn, Deb Turner, Carmen Trombetta, and Vicki Walker.

To my dear friends and fellow eldercare advocates—Rich and Maureen Gilardi of 2336 On The Main Respite Center, Robert B. Blancato of the White House Conference on Aging, Bill Thomas, M.D., of The Eden Alternative, Jan Strong and the staff of The Center for Older Adults, Alisa Markoff, senior fitness director for the Chicago Department on Aging, Sherrie Pincus of the Chicago Fund on Aging and Disability, Anna Fallon, LCSW for the Council for Jewish Elderly, Thomas Humphrey of Children of Aging Parents, Gerry Keane, special projects director for the Chicago Public Library, Hal Thompson of Seniors Unlimited, Anne E. Thar of the Illinois State Bar Association, Marc J. Lane, elder law attorney, Mark Levin of Mark Financial Consultants, Randy Schools of the National Institutes of Health, Bob Kolatorowicz and Father Jack Wall of Old St. Pat's Church, Dr. Sal Arria of the International Sports Sciences Association, Fran Wersells of the U.S. Department of Health and Human Services, Laura and Darryl Morrison, producers of the Practical Self-Defense for Seniors Videos—their devotion to improve the lives of elderly people knows no boundaries, and to them I express my deep appreciation.

My sincere thanks to the work/life professionals whose confidence in my work has resulted in the integration of employee eldercare programs around the world—Bonnie Michaels, president of Managing Work and Family, Inc., Pat Stinson and the staff of the Employee Services Management Association, the Society for Human Resource Management, Wally Nichols and the staff of the American Compensation Association, ARAG Group's Jim Snyder, Bob and Dinah Pearson of CareQuest, DCC Connection, Elinor Hickman and the staff of the International Association of Administrative Professionals, Dennis Kessler, president of Kessler Management Consulting, L.L.C., Scott Mies, a master work/life professional, Redia Anderson and Jennifer Spitz of Sears, Roebuck and Co., Doug Matthews of TEC International Organization of CEOs, Bob Kurdziel, president of Employee Preferred, Inc., Lee Sola of Work/Life Benefits, Women Employed's Nancy Kreider, Theresa Fjelstad, president of Work Life Systems, Inc., Susan Seitel, editor of Work and Family Connections, Sheila Lyne, RSM, Audrey Lang, and Dr. Shirley Fleming of the Chicago Department of Public Health, and the Center for Work and The Family.

I am deeply appreciative of the global publicity I receive from the Internet network—CareGuide, Dave Baker's BenefitsLink, Harvard Medical School, Beverly Roman's BR Anchor Relocation Experts, Richard Boyd's EC Online, Karen Stevensen's Elderweb, OnHealth Live, Marty Mulligan's Mom N' Pop, WomenConnect, Bankrate, AgeNet, Gregg Kroman's Get LTC Info, and hundreds of other websites and cyber bookstores. To Millennia Internet's Burt Beckman and Dimitare—a sincere thanks for your timely computer-crash rescues.

To the international media community, thank you for helping me to communicate the power of eldercare planning, and for consistently keeping caregiving issues in the limelight—the *Today* show's Susan Dutcher and Andrew Goldstein, NBC's Stuart Dan, *USA*

Today's Karen Petersen, Barbara Buchholtz and Marja Mills of the *Chicago Tribune,* Sherren Leigh, founder and publisher of *Today's Chicago Woman,* Denise Brown, editor of *Caregiving Newsletter, Crain's Chicago Business,* CRIS-Radio's Don Breitfelder, Diocese of St. Augustine's Kathleen Bagg-Morgan, Jim Petersen of Healthy Learning Videos, Diane Summers and Paul Clayton of KFUO-Radio, St. Louis, Missouri, Chris Farrell and the staff of *Right on the Money,* Mike Schwanz editor of *Solutions Benefits and Compensation Magazine,* and Tribune Company's Peter Walker.

To my literary agent and dear friend, Joe Durepos, for his insights, courage, and heart, and to my Times Books editor, Elizabeth Rapoport, whose commitment to my work began long before this book took flight. I am deeply grateful to you both for the opportunity, once again, to shed genuine hope and light on the subject of eldercare.

This book celebrates the lives of those elders who have died, and will forever live in my heart. To H. Bess Silverman, Manny Caplin, and Mary Goldberg—thank you for allowing me the privilege of being at your side as you journeyed toward death's door.

Lastly, I am indebted to the thousands of caregivers and elders who have attended my workshops, and shared their insights on caring for elderly loved ones. You hold a special place in my heart.

PREFACE

Do we choose eldercare, or does eldercare choose us?

When eldercare comes knocking on the door, many people run in the opposite direction; but not you. Whether you assumed the job, sought it, or inherited the responsibility out of obligation, even guilt, chances are if you are holding this book in your hands, you accepted—willingly or otherwise—your role as caregiver.

At first, undertaking eldercare feels as if the rug has been pulled out from under you; you're falling, and grabbing for something—anything—steady to hang on to, and there's nothing there. You never quite touch ground, and you soon realize that life is never going to be the same. People who once took care of you or walked by your side are on another journey. You can walk with them now, for a while longer; then you must let them go the rest of the way alone.

Your caregiving journey will take you to places unimaginable, and in the process you will learn more about yourself than ever before. Each day has the potential to bring to the surface life-altering issues and events that offer you the opportunity to develop skills and talents you never knew you had—resourcefulness, stamina, flexibility, and faith, to name a few. You won't come away from the caregiving experience the same as when you started, nor will you look at life, and death, in the way you did before.

Elders can be difficult and demanding. Ideally, you'll cope with love. Or you may tolerate your elders out of guilt and fear all the burdens they represent, but beware of falling into the pit of pity. Do not be blinded by the problem-solving element of eldercare or you will miss the lessons your elders have to teach.

The simple truth about elders is this: they want their lives to be validated, and they do not want to die alone. Go to them as best you can. This is a small price to pay for the riches you will receive in return for doing this work. Eldercare wakes up the soul and brings us face-to-face with our own mortality. Eldercare teaches us to live in the present, and it is the conduit that serves as a daily reminder of what is ultimately important in our lives. Let your elders lead, for every privileged conversation we share with them brings us closer to who we are and makes us wiser in ways that are eventually revealed to us over time.

We become the beneficiaries of these unique gifts the moment we find the courage to talk with our elders. Discussing eldercare issues and keeping the lines of communication open is never easy; consequently, many family members do not have the endurance to do so. They may forfeit the chance to hear and say the most healing words of all, which can only be spoken after the hard work is done: "Thank you, for all you have done for me," and, "I love you." Knowing how truly difficult the process of talking with elderly people can be, I was compelled to add the numerous conversation tips scattered throughout this edition of *The Complete Eldercare Planner* to give you every chance of experiencing the kinds of meaningful conversations that you can carry in your heart for the rest of your life.

Caregiving may be the hardest family responsibility you'll ever take on. It unquestionably affects our every waking moment—at home, in the workplace, where and how we live, and how we cope. If eldercare has chosen you, I will be with you every step of the way. Every page, every sentence, and every word in this book contain my personal messages to you, and I have the utmost respect for your decision to accept this role as caregiver.

Joy Loverde

ELDER EMERGENCY INFORMATION CHART

Today's date _____

Full name _____

Address _____

City/State/Zip _____

Telephone _____

Date of birth _____

Driver's license number and state issued _____

Auto make, model, and license plate number _____

Social Security number _____

Medicare health insurance/policy number _____

Allergies _____

Blood type _____

Current medications (drug name and purpose) _____
_____

IMPORTANT TELEPHONE NUMBERS

(Call 911 for ambulance, fire, and police emergencies)

HEALTH CARE

Doctor _____

Doctor _____

Dentist _____

Hospital _____

Pharmacy _____

Agency on aging_____

Nursing agency_____

Health insurance _____

_____

_____

_____

_____

_____

_____

NETWORK

Family_____

Family_____

Family_____

Neighbor _____

Neighbor _____

Friend_____

Friend_____

Senior center _____

Social worker _____

Clergy_____

Church group_____

Coworker _____

_____

_____

SERVICES

Electrician _____

Electric co._____

Water co. _____

Gas co. _____

Cable co. _____

Plumber_____

Home care _____

House sitter _____

Pet sitter_____

Landlord _____

Banker _____

Attorney _____

Accountant _____

Insurance agent_____

House alarm _____

Locksmith _____

CONTENTS

The

COMPLETE ELDERCARE PLANNER

· SECOND EDITION ·

· 1 ·

EFFECTIVE PLANNING

A Place to Start

Most of us are inadequately prepared, emotionally and otherwise, to face the complex issue associated with caring for elderly loved ones. Each situation usually involves multiple issues. How one family handles a problem is not necessarily the right approach for another, and what works one day could change drastically, overnight. How then do we proceed under these seemingly chaotic circumstances? The answer lies in planning.

Planning, however, takes on a whole new level of meaning when it comes to eldercare. Existing family decision-making patterns will no longer apply, and we soon realize we will not be returning to our past lifestyles. What we *can* plan on is that ongoing changes in the eldercare process will surely impact the rest of the family, sometimes suddenly, sometimes so gradually that we may not even notice the change.

The true nature of assisting an elderly parent, spouse, or other family member includes a roller coaster of emotional upsets, and consequently the process of caregiving requires constant management of our attitudes and decisions. *The Complete Eldercare Planner* is your road map through this unfamiliar territory. Here are some suggestions to help you make the most of this book:

Read the Introduction and the Objectives section at the beginning of each chapter. Knowing the basis for what you are reading, and *why*, will be especially helpful when the emotional aspect of assisting your loved one threatens to undermine your ability to accomplish what you want.

As you finish reviewing the chapter, set goals with the help of the Eldercare Goals chart found on page 286 in chapter 14. Track your progress by referring to the Action Checklists at the end of each chapter. Effective planning is specific, realistic, and *written*.

Start to fill out the Elder Emergency Information Chart on page xiii today. Finally, for quick reference to eldercare resources, websites, charts, and worksheets listed throughout *The Planner*, turn to the Index sections at the end of the book. You now have the tools you need to get started.

A PLACE TO START

- Planning and preparation are critical for effective eldercare.
- Experts agree that rule number one in thoughtful planning is to use some form of planner to write things down.

Whether you are planning for future eldercare needs or helping an elderly relative in a crisis situation, The Complete Eldercare Planner *will assist you and your family in pulling it all together.*

OBJECTIVES

After completing **A Place to Start,** *you will be able to:*

Create opportunities to open up the lines of communication.

Minimize the number of crisis situations.

Reduce confusion in crisis situations.

Gain greater peace of mind by planning ahead.

PLAN ONE
Don't *read* this book. *Use* it.

This planner is specifically designed and organized to help you understand and manage issues associated with assisting an aging parent, spouse, or other family member or friend. *The Complete Eldercare Planner* offers immediate solutions to common problems by way of timesaving action plans, charts, worksheets, and checklists. Make use of the spaces provided for listing telephone numbers, setting goals, and locating documents. At the end of every chapter you will also find an in-depth list of resources to give you the additional support you will need.

Decide what works best for you. How you use *The Complete Eldercare Planner* depends on the nature of your eldercare situation, your family's decision patterns, the help you receive from others, eligibility into specialized programs, and the availability of financial resources. You may choose to implement one plan, several plans, or even a combination of plans. A plan may work one day and not the next. Flexibility will be one of the keys to your effectiveness as a family caregiver.

The process of assisting an elderly family member requires an ongoing assessment of the situation at hand. Nothing stays the same in eldercare; aging people are constantly in transition. Open up the lines of communication early with elders and family members, and seek the advice of geriatric care professionals when you need additional support. Making assumptions about what is happening instead of talking to each other always does more harm than good. Operate from fact, not fiction.

Keep your planning and time line expectations realistic. Ask yourself on a regular basis these three simple questions: *What can happen? What will my elder be able to do about what happens? What can the rest of the family do to help?*

Plan early. The well-being of the entire family depends on the quantity and quality of your eldercare options, decisions, and plans.

PLAN TWO
Implement planning principles.

Follow these six basic planning principles:

Set goals. Know what you are doing and *why*. Effective goal setting is specific, realistic, and *written*. Make use of the Goals Chart on p. 286.

Create support systems and use them. Surround elderly family members with people both inside and outside the family, as well as community assisted-living resources to share responsibilities and protect against family caregiver stress.

Write everything down. Put dates on all notes. Record plans, goals, ideas, phone numbers, questions, answers, promises, decisions, tasks, and appointments and keep them in a convenient, accessible location. Make good use of the forms in this planner.

Organize information. Keep notes, bills, receipts, contracts, letters, brochures, and all other eldercare-related information in a safe, twenty-four-hour accessible place. Create a system that makes it easy for you to find information and answers when you need them.

Allow sufficient time for research. Gathering information and creating options is critical to thoughtful action. Research more than one option.

Research all costs and who pays.

PLAN THREE
Be prepared for the runaround.

Gathering information, locating resources, making appointments, and getting eldercare services in motion can cause a great deal of stress and anxiety on the part of the family caregiver. Detailed application processes, waiting lists, lengthy interviews, endless document searching, being put on hold, and being given outdated telephone numbers are common. Here are some tips to help you minimize these stressful times:

- Confirm in-person appointments a day in advance.
- Make calls and attend meetings with paper and pen or tape recorder in hand.
- Arrange to have someone accompany your elder to *every* appointment.
- Distribute copies of documents while keeping the originals in a safe place.
- Evaluate the quality of services you receive and report anyone who treats you disrespectfully.

Given the opportunity, most aging people would choose to stay in their own homes. As the aging population grows, so too do the number of assisted-living options that allow them to do so. Assessing and arranging for community and state programs, however, is not an easy task. Here's why:

- Each elder requires a unique combination of eldercare services.
- Eldercare programs are often listed under different names from state to state.
- Eldercare services are rarely available from one source.
- Eligibility for public programs is complicated.

To make the process of researching and securing eldercare services go more smoothly, ask the following questions, where applicable, and keep a *written* record of the answers:

What is your name and your title?

Are you a staff member or a volunteer?

How much do services cost?

What is the average cost for my particular needs?

Are fees or commissions negotiable? Is there a sliding scale?

Are initial consultations available free of charge?

What other costs should I anticipate?

Are payment plans available?

Does insurance cover costs?

Are costs tax deductible?

Will you assign someone to assist me?

What documents are needed? Originals? Copies?

Will you put fees and estimates in writing?

Will you itemize bills?

Do you have brochures or literature you can send me?

Will you provide references? Credentials?

Will you provide <u>written</u> contracts? Regulations?

Are you a member of any professional organization?

Are you certified? Licensed? Bonded?

What free services are available?

Will you put me on your mailing list?

Do you provide pickup and delivery service? Transportation?

Can your office accommodate a wheelchair?

Do you have telecommunication access for hearing- or visually-impaired elders?

Are home visits available?

Are you located near public transportation?

What days/hours are you open for business?

 PLAN FOUR
List and prioritize your eldercare concerns.

To assess and prioritize your elder's needs, refer to the table of contents for a complete overview of the responsibilities associated with caring for an elderly person; then ask yourself which of the issues listed must be addressed immediately. Here is a condensed list of topics:

Chapter One: Effective Planning

Chapter Two: Caregivers

Chapter Three: Communicaring

Chapter Four: Emergency Preparedness

Chapter Five: Money Matters

Chapter Six: Legal Matters

Chapter Seven: Insurance

Chapter Eight: Housing

Chapter Nine: Safe and Secure

Chapter Ten: Transportation

Chapter Eleven: Health and Wellness

Chapter Twelve: Quality of Life

Chapter Thirteen: Death and Dying

Chapter Fourteen: Documents Locator

If you're just getting started and wondering where would be the best place to begin, here are the top three subjects you're most likely to need information on right away (in this order):

- Money Matters
- Housing
- Documents Locator

 PLAN FIVE
Make good use of eldercare resources.

The eldercare service providers and organizations listed at the end of every chapter assist family members in many ways. If you're unsure of the services your elder needs or are searching for a specific service provider, use the list below as a quick guide to find what you're looking for.

If you're providing family caregiving assistance from a neighboring community or from a different state, also obtain copies of your elder's community telephone directories—the White Pages and the Yellow Pages. Update your copies of the telephone books on a yearly basis.

Look under the following headings in the Yellow Pages to get the telephone numbers of these eldercare resources where your aging family member resides:

- Hospitals (ask for the discharge planner)
- Religious congregations
- Senior centers
- Social service organizations

Look under the following headings in the Blue Pages to obtain the telephone numbers of these government offices:

- Area agency on aging/Department for the aging
- Department of insurance (Medicare)
- Department of mental health
- Department of public aid (food stamps, Medicaid)
- Department of public health
- Department of rehabilitation services
- Internal Revenue Service (tax relief)
- Department of transportation (reduced fares, taxi coupons)
- Veteran's Administration/Division of veterans' affairs

Call the local hospital, social service organizations, religious congregations, and senior centers to obtain information regarding:

- Free community eldercare directories
- Books, tapes, and videos on eldercare-related topics
- Caregiver newsletters
- Internet websites
- Physician referrals
- Community education programs
- Prerecorded health information
- Registered nurse telephone advice
- Infusion services
- Hospice programs
- Behavioral health programs
- Home respiratory services
- Nursing and personal care services
- Chronic disease management
- Home medical equipment
- Hot line telephone numbers
- Caregiver support groups
- Parish nurse services
- Volunteer programs
- Benefits eligibility
- Community health fairs
- International eldercare resources
- Foreign language services

Use the following lists to get recommendations on specific eldercare services in your elder's hometown:

Homemaker Services (house cleaning, personal and health care, errands, cooking):
- Area agency on aging
- Church groups
- Civic groups
- Social service organizations
- Home health care agency
- Family and friends' referrals
- Classified newspaper ads

Home Repair/Maintenance Services (upkeep, installations, improvements):

- Area agency on aging
- Social service organizations
- Neighborhood improvement programs
- Church groups

Nutrition Sites/Meals Programs (home-delivered meals, group meals):

- Area agency on aging
- Church groups
- Senior centers
- Hospital discharge planner

Companion Services (friendly visits to homebound elderly):

- Area agency on aging
- Church groups
- Hospital discharge planner
- Neighborhood clubs
- Social service organizations
- Civic groups
- Volunteer organizations
- YMCA/YWCA/YMHA/YWHA
- City recreation department
- Hospice volunteers
- Youth groups

Telephone Reassurance (daily contact for aging people who live alone):

- Police department
- Hospital discharge planner
- Senior centers
- Social service organizations
- Civic groups
- Home health care agency

Observation Programs (letter carriers and utility workers trained to identify signs that an elderly person may need help):

- Public utility office
- Post office

- Area agency on aging
- Community watch programs

Transportation Services (van services available to disabled elderly for medical appointments):
- Area agency on aging
- Home health care agency
- Hospital discharge planner
- Public health department
- Social service organizations
- Church groups
- Civic groups

Housing Options (from retirement communities to skilled nursing care):
- Retirement communities
- Area agency on aging
- State ombudsman
- Senior centers
- Hospital discharge planner

Home Health Care Services (from managing medications to skilled nursing care):
- Visiting nurses association
- Area agency on aging
- Social service organizations
- Home health care agency
- Family services agency
- Hospital discharge planner
- United Way

Hospice Programs (care and counseling for dying patients and their family members):
- Hospital discharge planner
- American Cancer Society
- Visiting nurses association
- Church groups
- Social service organizations

Emergency Response Systems (transmitters to call for help):
- Hospital discharge planner
- Fire department

Respite Care Services (providing time off for family caregivers):
- Hospital discharge planner
- Nursing homes
- Senior centers
- Social service organizations
- Home health care agency

Getting Caught Off Guard

The responsibilities associated with eldercare are often initiated in a crisis and can catch us by surprise whether we anticipate them or not. At any given time, anyone can be on the receiving end of an emergency telephone call informing us that an elderly loved one needs help immediately, momentarily throwing us off balance and leaving us feeling scared and confused. No doubt, the emotional climate surrounding an eldercare emergency is highly charged; it is easy for the suddenly self-appointed caregiver to become overwhelmed.

The advent of an eldercare crisis typically brings strong and sometimes conflicting emotions to the surface. Love and anger, in particular, seem to go hand in hand. These feelings can be so intense that they may temporarily immobilize family caregivers. This is normal. The first course of action in the event of an unexpected eldercare problem is to accept the circumstance as is and focus on creating solutions that address the needs of the entire family. This section of *The Planner* will help you gain a quick understanding of the issues you are facing, generate a personal action plan to help stabilize the crisis, and plan for a more certain future. For best results, make use of the Decision-Making Worksheet provided for you on page 15.

To gain an understanding of the situation, to research options, to be resourceful, to communicate responsibly, and to seek assistance are your immediate goals and the keys to surviving this confusing ordeal. Don't let anyone rush you. Resist the temptation to make quick decisions. Take it one step at a time. You are in more control of the situation than you think.

GETTING CAUGHT OFF GUARD

- Our lives are changing at a faster rate than at any other time in human history.
- Addressing unexpected eldercare problems step-by-step builds a caregiver's skills and confidence in mastering change.
- When it comes to caring for aging family members, the best we can do is build and maintain positive attitudes toward accepting change.

Even in the absence of planning, family caregivers can implement proven strategies that will help them handle eldercare situations effectively.

OBJECTIVES

After completing **Getting Caught Off Guard,** *you will be able to:*

Compile eldercare-planning tools.

Accumulate eldercare resources quickly.

Gather an informal network of support.

Access expert advice on eldercare.

Make informed decisions in the event of an emergency.

 PLAN ONE
Reduce confusion and runaway emotions.

In the absence of eldercare plans and discussions, follow these tips to get you pointed in the right direction:

Get organized. *The Complete Eldercare Planner* offers you immediate assistance. Turn to the table of contents to determine which eldercare issue you are addressing today. Review the chapter's action plans and checklists. If the issue requires securing important or legal documents, for example, you'll find what you need in chapter 14, Documents Locator. Create a file on your elder and begin storing information here. Keep this file in a convenient, twenty-four-hour-accessible location. Make sure you have access to a copy machine, facsimile (fax) service, e-mail, and overnight mail service.

Write everything down. Date your notes. Record conversations (in person and on the telephone), names, addresses, telephone numbers, e-mail addresses, care options, decisions, ideas, questions, answers, promises, instructions, directions, who is doing what—everything.

Obtain copies of telephone directories. Have access to your elder's community telephone books (White Pages and Yellow Pages) and his or her personal address book (this is where you'll find your elder's friends, family, and professional advisers).

Create a helpers list. Make a list of people who can help you. Write down their home and work telephone numbers and e-mail addresses. Make copies of this list and distribute it to family and friends. Keep a copy at home and at work. Call or write to the organizations listed under the Low-Cost and Free Resources section at the end of each chapter if you need additional assistance. Here is your list starter:

other family members	friends
neighbors	coworkers
church members	volunteers
advisers	hired help

Make lists. Keep track of day-to-day caregiving tasks like errands, cooking, housekeeping, and shopping. When people ask how they can help, let them choose from your list. If they don't ask, pick up the telephone and solicit their assistance. You are going to need help now with a multitude of eldercare responsibilities whether you realize it or not.

Access eldercare professionals. Obtain the telephone numbers of those professionals who assist your aging relative, such as doctors, dentist, social worker, nurse, pharmacist, police, insurance agent, lawyer, accountant, and clergy. Look in your elder's personal telephone book.

PLAN TWO
Access expert advice.

Professional eldercare advice, referrals, and assistance are a telephone call away. Contact the local hospital and ask for the **discharge planner.** You also can call the local chapter of the agency on aging for information regarding home health care services and to gain access to even more community resources and service providers. Review the Low-Cost and Free Resources listed at the end of each chapter.

If your elderly family member lives out of town and you need help coordinating services, you can employ the services of a **geriatric case manager.** These experts will make an on-site visit to your relative, assess the situation at hand, then make any necessary care arrangements. Be prepared for steep hourly rates—from $50 to $175 an hour, plus an initial assessment fee that can run as high as $300 an hour. However, hiring these geriatric care professionals for several hours my well be worth the price, especially in an eldercare emergency. Call the hospital discharge planner for referrals.

PLAN THREE
Make informed decisions.

In an emergency situation, we family members can expect to find ourselves in the difficult position of making important decisions on behalf of our elderly loved ones. Do we place Mom in a nursing home? Do we move Aunt Anne in with us? Will Dad be able to manage on his own while I'm away on a business trip?

What's right? What's wrong? In today's fast-paced world, deciding one's course of action is becoming more and more difficult. Before radio, television, and computers, important decisions were based on too little information. Today, knowing too much can just as easily cloud our ability to make the right caregiving choices. To make matters even more confusing, eldercare advisers might offer diverse opinions and conflicting information.

Most of us know how to make rational decisions under predictable circumstances, but when conditions are less than perfect, and we are faced with making gut-wrenching decisions over someone else's life, we want to make every effort to resolve the problem at hand responsibly.

If you are now in the position of having to make an important decision, especially one that is on behalf of your elder, use the Decision-Making Worksheet below as a guide to help you in this difficult process. Being a family caregiver almost *guarantees* that you will be frequently confronted by the questions of what's right and what's wrong. Remember, no decision is ever final, and you may modify your plans at any time.

DECISION-MAKING WORKSHEET

What's Right? What's Wrong? Making Informed Decisions

It's easy to feel overwhelmed when faced with too many options and choices. Use this worksheet to break down the task of making a decision into more manageable parts. First, define the decision you need to make. Then, fill in the pros and cons. Once you see how the benefits and disadvantages add up, your decision becomes a matter of several smaller key issues.

*The decision I am contemplating is:*_____

The pros are: *The cons are:*

_____   _____

_____   _____

_____   _____

_____   _____

Consider these important questions when writing down your pros and cons:

Who else can shed light on this decision (family, friends, doctor, etc.)?

Do I understand the answers offered by the professionals? (If not, say so.)

What are the needs and wants of those who will be affected by this decision?

What are my obligations toward others and their needs?

How might this decision negatively affect my physical and emotional health?

Will I put others at risk or hurt anyone with this decision?

How might my personal relationships change for the worse?

Have I researched all costs and who pays for what?

Is *this* the right time for this decision or is it better to wait?

Follow-up.

Now that you have a list of pros and cons, you can see which points are the most important. Make sure these items are based on facts, not assumptions or wishful (or fearful) thinking. Get legal advice on anything that requires contracts, signatures, or financial investments. Keep your aging family members involved in the decision-making process. Insist on continuous family discussions. Keep everyone involved and responsible.

The two most important facts in the pros column are:

_____

_____

The two most important facts in the cons column are:

_____

_____

Based on the pros and cons, I have decided to: _____

_____

Low-Cost and Free Resources

The local telephone book can be a valuable source of information. The front section of the directory includes resources for community access, emergency preparedness, and government agencies. The Yellow Pages will be useful to locate specific service providers. Also, get a copy of your elder's local telephone books and replace them every year when new editions become available.

Call the **agency on aging** to locate community programs assisting the elderly. The phone number is listed in the White Pages of the telephone directory.

Hospital discharge planners can provide current information and referrals on local eldercare services. Also inquire about a community eldercare resource directory, which is usually free for the asking.

The **public library** is stocked with books on related subjects. Get to know the librarians at the reference desk.

Newspapers and radio and television stations often advertise **free community programs.** Look for events sponsored by law firms, insurance agencies, hospitals, banks, retirement communities, schools, home care agencies, and social and business organizations. Call the **mayor's office** to get the information or help you need.

Rent **videos** on related subjects at the public library. Research websites on the **Internet,** under keywords: eldercare, aging parents, caregivers, aging.

Masonic orders, Rotary clubs, Lions clubs, Odd Fellows lodges, veterans' organizations, unions, business clubs, religious groups, and teachers' associations provide special services and volunteers to members and nonmembers alike. Find what you are looking for under the headings of **Associations** and **Religious Organizations** in the Yellow Pages.

Colleges, universities, and trade schools are a valuable source of information, volunteers, resources, and referrals. See **Schools** in the Yellow Pages. Ask for the adult education and community services programs.

Community action commissions (CAC) and **family service agencies** offer services for low-income, minority, frail, and homebound persons including social, educational, and recreational activities.

Local **senior centers** provide a variety of services and activities to elderly persons, including recreation, social gatherings, meals, transportation, and education.

ORGANIZATIONS

AARP
Fulfillment
601 E Street, NW
Washington, DC 20049
(800) 424-3410
Website: *www.aarp.org*

Administration on Aging
330 Independence Avenue, SW
Washington, DC 20201
(202) 619-7501, Fax: (202) 260-1012, TDD: (202) 401-7575
Website: *www.aoa.dhhs.gov*
Directory of Websites on Aging: *www.aoa.dhhs.gov/aoa/webres/craig.htm*

ElderCare Online
Website: *www.ec-online.net*

Eldercare Web
Website: *www.elderweb.com*

National Association of Area Agencies on Aging
927 15th Street, NW, 6th Floor
Washington, DC 20005
(202) 296-8130, Fax: (202) 296-8134
Website: *www.n4a.org*

Senior Options
Website: *www.senioroptions.com*

Seniors-Site
Website: *http://seniors-site.com/home/sitemap.html*

Action Checklist

A PLACE TO START	To Do By	Completed
Set planning goals		
short-term	_____	❏
long-term	_____	❏
Create a system for duplicating and filing		
eldercare information	_____	❏
notes	_____	❏
questions	_____	❏
goals	_____	❏
lists	_____	❏
documents	_____	❏
phone numbers	_____	❏
agreements	_____	❏
Have access to		
telephone	_____	❏
transportation	_____	❏
copy machine	_____	❏
fax	_____	❏
Internet	_____	❏
e-mail	_____	❏
post office	_____	❏
public library	_____	❏

Review Communicaring chapter	_____	❏
Review eldercare resources	_____	❏
Create a backup plan	_____	❏
Attend community eldercare programs	_____	❏

GETTING CAUGHT OFF GUARD

Get organized

review table of contents	_____	❏
prioritize issues	_____	❏
start a file on elder	_____	❏
locate documents	_____	❏
store originals in safe place	_____	❏

Take notes

names and addresses	_____	❏
telephone numbers	_____	❏
plans	_____	❏
instructions	_____	❏
directions	_____	❏
decisions	_____	❏
promises	_____	❏

Get community telephone books

White Pages	_____	❏
Yellow Pages	_____	❏

Create a helpers list

family	_____	❏
friends	_____	❏
neighbors	_____	❏
coworkers	_____	❏
church members	_____	❏
volunteers	_____	❏

Make a list of help needed	_____	❏
Request and accept help	_____	❏
Create a list of eldercare advisers	_____	❏

Access eldercare experts

    hospital discharge planner   _____ ❏

    local agency on aging   _____ ❏

    geriatric case manager   _____ ❏

Make informed decisions

    questions answered to satisfaction   _____ ❏

    time allowed for research   _____ ❏

    costs investigated   _____ ❏

    references checked   _____ ❏

    legal counsel sought for contracts, signatures,
        financial investments   _____ ❏

    family discussions ongoing   _____ ❏

    elder involved in decisions   _____ ❏

Use the Decision-Making Worksheet to help in the process   _____ ❏

· 2 ·

CAREGIVERS

How to Tell When Your Elder Needs Help

Contrary to the way elderly people are typically portrayed in advertisements and movies, getting old does not generally mean being helpless or losing one's memory. Unnecessary problems in the caregiving process develop when we equate aging with decline and pathology. Eldercare is defined by ability, not age. Inappropriate and inaccurate media messages of incompetence and dementia are so convincing that even our elders sometimes believe the stereotypes to be true.

Aging people are people in transition. The loss of family members and friends, a change in living arrangements, the repositioning of finances, retirement, the loss of driving privileges, even the death of a pet are lifestyle transitions that require the entire family's attention. Ideally, our elders will ask for our help during times like these, but, as family members have learned, this may not happen. In fact, one aging parent might "cover" for the other, or one aging spouse may decline assistance from the other because he or she feels ashamed and powerless.

Remember, most elderly people wish to remain independent and in control of their own lives for as long as possible. This section of *The Planner* suggests ways that caregivers can help their aging family members remain relatively independent, as long as the person's safety is not at risk, by making astute observations, asking revealing questions, and paying attention to telltale signs that indicate that their elder may need assistance now.

HOW TO TELL WHEN YOUR ELDER NEEDS HELP

- Ideally, our elders will accept lifestyle changes and request assistance, but this is very often not the case.
- One elderly spouse may "cover" for the other, and problems may go undetected for years.

If you suspect that your elderly family member is losing the ability to perform basic physical and mental tasks, knowing what to look for will help you determine whether he or she needs immediate attention.

OBJECTIVES

After completing How to Tell When Your Elder Needs Help, you will be able to:

Detect eldercare situations that require immediate attention.

Enlist your elder's help with recognizing lifestyle changes.

Prevent overinvolvement with eldercare issues.

Employ effective communication techniques.

 PLAN ONE
Know what to look for.

Things may seem normal on the outside. Some changes are barely noticeable. Once in a while we all forget details or put things off, but when a *pattern* of neglect develops, it may be serious. Remember, dementia (mental deterioration) is *not* a normal part of aging. Sharpen your observational skills, and look for patterns of consistent neglect within the following contexts:

Basic tasks—difficulty in walking, dressing, talking, eating, cooking, climbing steps, or managing medications.

Hygiene—infrequent bathing, unusually sloppy appearance, foul body and/or mouth odor.

Responsibilities—mail is unopened, papers are piled up, checkbook is unreadable, bills are unpaid, bank account overdraft notices are accumulating, prescriptions are un-filled, phone calls aren't returned, cooking pots and pans look burned, refrigerator interior has foul odor, food supply is low, home interior and/or exterior is unkempt, laundry is piling up, automobile has new dents.

Health—weight loss, changes in appetite, problems swallowing, fatigue, burns, black and blue marks (possible signs of falling), hearing loss (look for signs of lipreading and talking loudly), seems withdrawn without reason, incontinence (bed-wetting), spilling and dropping things (check carpet for stains), complaints of muscle weakness, insomnia or excessive sleeping, dehydration.

Isolation—lack of interest in outside friendships, activities, or hobbies, keeps curtains drawn day and night, has little access to transportation, lives in another city or state and lives alone.

Attitude—sadness, display of verbal or physical abuse, talk of being depressed and feelings of despair, abuse of alcohol or drugs, paranoia, refusal to communicate, unusual argumentativeness, a recent emotional or medical crisis.

Cognitive functions—consistent forgetfulness about where things are, getting lost while walking or driving, confusion, loss of reasoning skills, difficulty answering questions, inability to find the right word, use of repetitive words or phrases, severe personality changes, wandering, inability to recall names of familiar people or objects, inability to complete a sentence, forgetting how to use simple, ordinary things such as a pencil, forgetting to close windows, turn off the stove, and lock doors, loss of sense of time.

If some of these warning signs are present, and you are beginning to question your aging loved one's ability to make choices and decisions, do not scare yourself and other family members into thinking that these are the early stages of dementia. Use common sense before suggesting professional help. Overreacting and jumping to conclusions create communication friction and unfounded anxiety.

When help is clearly needed, consult a doctor about your elder. Describe what you've witnessed and let the professional make a formal diagnosis. Sometimes a physical examination reveals a condition that can be treated. What appears to be dementia may in fact be caused by medications (including over-the-counter drugs), alcohol, depression, tumors, heart problems, head injuries, infections, poor vision, or hearing problems. The earlier you detect a problem, the more likely it can be treated effectively.

 PLAN TWO
Open up a dialogue with elderly family members.

Based upon your observations, if you have concluded that eldercare issues demand immediate attention, it's time to take the next step and talk about it. But "let the caregiver beware." You are about to enter a potential minefield. Without knowing the most effective ways to initiate these very sensitive conversations with your elderly family members, the probability of them telling you to mind your own business, or telling you everything is fine when it is not, is almost guaranteed.

Before you begin such a discussion, turn to chapter 3, Communicaring. Review the communication tips and specific examples, which will allow you to employ a series of probing but respectful questions to get this delicate process started.

Share the Care

The American family has undergone big changes. Medical breakthroughs are making it possible for people to live longer. For the first time in history, families have more parents than kids. Nobody's home anymore. We spend most of our time at work, at school, at play. We have created artificial families; hospitals, schools, churches, and companies have replaced home. There is more physical distance between families; caregivers and elderly family members live an average of a hundred miles from one another.

Because of these modern realities, an important goal of this section of *The Planner* is to expand your definition of care. Too often, family caregivers have a rigid concept of care and make hasty statements such as, "My mother will never go to a nursing home." For other caregivers, it is a point of pride not to ask for help. These kinds of attitudes in the caregiving process are unhealthy and unrealistic.

When we come face-to-face with our own limits and can't provide the care we wish we could, we feel it's our own fault. The truth is that we may not be most qualified to take on certain caregiving responsibilities. Limitations of relationships, time, stamina, and skill dictate how much help we can realistically offer.

SHARE THE CARE

- You cannot assist your elder alone; you will need help.
- Limitations of time, stamina, and skill mean that there is just so much you can do, especially if you are providing care from a distance.
- Dealing with aging family members from a distance may be the same as dealing with strangers; there can be so much you do not know.

One of the most important tasks in helping your elder is finding and creating formal and informal support networks made up of family, friends, volunteers, and professionals.

OBJECTIVES

*After completing **Share the Care**, you will be able to:*
   Create a network of people and community resources.
   Consider cost-effective eldercare options.
   Spend more time with your own family, work, and personal interests.

PLAN ONE
Make a list of the tasks you can do and those you can't do or don't want to do.

If you're assisting an aging relative who's experiencing health care problems, ask the doctor to explain the levels of care your elder will require now and in the future. If your parent, spouse, or other relatives are caring for another aging family member, acknowledge the load they are carrying and offer to help whenever you can. Following are some of the caregiving tasks you may have to address:

Homemaker services—household maintenance, repairs, housekeeping, cleaning, laundry, errands, grocery shopping, cooking, transportation, paying bills, interacting with eldercare advisers.

Personal care—bathing, dressing, feeding, toileting, shaving, grooming, bed and chair transferring.

Home health care—skilled nursing care, hospice aid, medications management, patient instruction, physical therapy, nutrition counseling.

Quality of life—companionship, escort, checking in, social activities, exercise, counseling, civic involvement, reading, religious activities, senior advocacy.

 PLAN TWO
Identify potential helpers and tasks.

The help we caregivers receive from our informal network of support—family members, friends, and volunteers—may be more readily available, reliable, and affordable than paid care providers. Create a list of people who can help you and your elder. Write down their names, addresses, home and work telephone numbers, and e-mail addresses, and be honest with them about the potential for being called anytime of the day or night. Distribute copies of this list to your elder and family members. If *you* are not available, make sure they know they can call upon others for assistance. Keep copies of this list in several convenient locations: near the telephone, on the refrigerator, at work, and in the glove compartment of your car.

Suggested helpers include the following:

mother	children and stepchildren
father	grandchildren
siblings	nephews and nieces

spouse	cousins
elder's friends	coworkers
uncles and aunts	elder's neighbors
neighbors	clergy

You can secure volunteers and low-cost services by contacting these community organizations:

community centers	grade/high school
hospitals	community college
nursing agencies	university
health care providers	fraternal orders
neighborhood groups	business groups
volunteer organizations	advocacy leagues
transportation agencies	department stores
seniors' organizations	support groups
agencies on aging	church groups
government agencies	public libraries
women's groups	youth groups
retirement groups	family services
recreation groups	hospice services
veterans' organizations	charities

Now that you know who can help you, define *how* they can help. Make a list of the kinds of services that are needed—for you and your elder. The next time someone says, "What can I do?" let them pick from your list. Update this list regularly, since your needs and the needs of your elder will certainly change. Here are some tasks that family members can do:

shopping	visiting
cleaning	repairs
walking	making telephone calls
transporting	bookkeeping
reading	checking in
cooking	sewing
yard work	errands
eating out	movies
paying for services	pet care
plant care	housing
managing helpers	child care
laundry	grooming

religious services	opening mail
ironing	attending appointments
research	letter writing

Caring for aging parents is not always a family affair. Denial, sibling rivalry, limited finances, living far away, and many other circumstances tend to place the bulk of the physical, financial, and emotional responsibilities on one or two family members, while an only child has no choice but to go it alone with the help of people outside the family.

It's true that the responsibilities of eldercare within the family may be unevenly and perhaps unfairly distributed. To address this, get in the habit of speaking to other family members about your elder on a regular basis. Compare notes and try to listen with an open mind. If any family member seems reluctant to help with hands-on tasks, ask that person to contribute financially as a way of assisting, then you can decide how to make the best use of the money. Chapter 3 offers many suggestions on how to get siblings to pitch in. Review the chapter before you start a conversation so you'll be ready if they refuse to lend a hand.

PLAN THREE
Establish a network of professional care providers.

Specialized care providers can make home care a preferred alternative to institutionalized care. If you are unsure as to what kind of help is needed, where it will come from, what it will cost, or what entitlement programs are available, you might want to hire a **geriatric case manager.** Case managers are highly trained social workers and nurses who have experience working with older adults and can also help you bridge the geographical gulf if you are assisting your elder from far away. (Note: case management services are not usually covered by insurance.) Call the hospital discharge planner for referrals.

Ask these questions to determine whether a case manager candidate is a qualified professional:

What is your educational background?
What medical and/or educational degrees do you hold?
Where did you work prior to entering private practice? For how many years?
How long have you been in business?
Is this a full-time or part-time practice?
Are you certified by the state?
What are your hours and availability in an emergency?
What are your emergency backup plans if you're unavailable?
Who supervises your work?

How much do you charge for an initial assessment?

What is your hourly fee?

What can I expect to pay?

Which services are arranged outside of your care?

What is your role once a referral is made?

How, and how often, do you keep me informed?

May I have the name of three references who have used your service?

To find other types of reliable, competent in-home helpers, talk to people in your network who have had successful dealings with service providers. Also, ask for recommendations from doctors, licensed homemaker and home care agencies, home health care agencies, the area agency on aging, the hospital discharge planner, social service agencies, licensed nurse agencies, social workers, clergy, and an employment agency.

Another resource is the Situations Wanted section of the classified ads, if you want to hire a private, self-employed home care worker. Independent workers tend to have more flexible schedules and charge less than an agency. If none of these leads proves successful, put an ad in the paper. Rent a post office box and request résumés and references.

 PLAN FOUR
Be prepared with specific questions when hiring in-home helpers.

Before beginning the interview process, think about what specific services you need from the helper. When a job applicant calls, give a short job description, time and day expectations, salary, and benefits. Grant interviews only to those being considered for the position. Ask other family members or a friend to be present during interviews for feedback and support. *Check all references before hiring.*

Ask the applicant:

What makes you interested in this kind of work?

Tell me about your past home care work experience.

Why did you leave your last position?

Have you received any special training?

Do you have any problems that might hinder you in this job?

How do you feel about alcohol, drugs, and smoking?

Is there anything about this job that you would not be willing to do?

What is your time commitment to this position?

Are you willing to do household chores like cooking and light housekeeping?

How flexible is your schedule?

Do you have a current driver's license?

Do you have a car available? Can you drive my car?

What would you do if you were ill and could not come to work?

What would you do in the case of an emergency?

Ask the agency:

Are you licensed and accredited? By whom?

Is your agency bonded? Is your worker bonded?

Who pays insurance, taxes, and handles employer responsibilities?

How long have you been in business?

Do you accept Medicare?

Do you offer sliding-scale fees?

What are the fees for services provided by your worker?

What costs are not covered?

Who pays the worker, you or me?

What are the minimum and maximum hours of service?

Are there limits to services provided?

What is your screening process when hiring workers?

How do you supervise your workers?

Is the worker specially trained to work with older adults?

Do you find a replacement if your worker is ill or on vacation?

Do I continue to pay your worker while my relative is in the hospital?

Can your agency provide me with references on you and your worker?

What is the process when a worker does not show up?

How soon can a worker begin?

Ask the reference:

How long have you known this applicant?

What was the applicant's position and job description?

How well did the applicant get along with others?

What were the applicant's strengths? Weaknesses?

Did you find the applicant trustworthy?

Were you aware of any substance abuse? Smoking?

Would you rehire the applicant?

Why did the applicant leave?

Describe the job. Was the applicant well-suited for it?

Ask yourself:

Do I really believe this person is right for the job?

Will this person take charge and respond quickly in an emergency?

Is this person organized? Neat? Flexible? Energetic? Pleasant?

Does this person have the right training and experience for this job?

Will this person get along with my elder? Family? Others?

Will this person know when to consult the family?

Will this person be sensitive to family traditions?

Does this person like pets?

Do family members like and trust this person?

Do family members believe this person can handle this job?

 PLAN FIVE
Develop a job contract for paid care providers.

Clarify duties with a formalized agreement. Modify the contract as needed. Have your employee sign a contract *before* work begins. Include the following information in the agreement:

- Employer name, address, telephone number
- Employee name, address, telephone number
- Employee Social Security number
- Salary, payment method, terms of payment (weekly, bimonthly)
- Benefits (meals, entertainment allowance, vacation, insurance)
- Expenses, transportation fees, reimbursement procedures
- Record keeping/taxes
- Work schedule/timekeeping
- Length of service
- Illness/absences
- Holidays/make-up time
- Job description
- Emergency procedures
- Worker's emergency contacts (names, day and evening telephone numbers)
- House rules (include policies on smoking, drinking, foul language, tardiness, absence without notice, guests)
- Termination of employment (two weeks, two warnings)
- Reasons for termination (theft, carelessness, failure to carry out duties, violation of house rules, physical or verbal abuse)

- Procedure for quitting job
- Employee signature and date
- Employer signature and date

 PLAN SIX
Take steps to ensure quality service from care providers.

Financial and legal considerations—Social Security contributions (FICA), federal unemployment tax (FUTA), state unemployment tax, and state workmen's compensation contributions—are the responsibility of employers when hiring paid care providers. Review employment regulations by contacting the Social Security office or the IRS office. Getting advice from an accountant or lawyer will also be helpful. Keep careful records. Ask your home insurance agent about proper coverage while employing someone in the home.

The salary range for services begins at minimum wage and depends on the amount of training and experience the worker has and whether or not an agency is involved. Transportation fees may be an extra cost. Medicare, private health insurance, and health maintenance organizations apply restrictions on home care coverage.

Hiring a worker from an agency or business does not guarantee the quality of services provided. In fact, many new eldercare services have become available but do not have government regulation or certification programs. The state long-term care ombudsman and the area agency on aging are reliable resources for doing a background check on care providers.

It is important for the entire family to continuously monitor the quantity and quality of services rendered. Follow these suggestions:

- Make regular contact with your relative's care providers—by phone, mail, and better yet, in person. Exchange telephone numbers and let them know they can call you collect if they need you.
- Hire workers from agencies that are licensed, insured, and bonded. Unfortunate accidents with helpers include physical and verbal abuse and theft.
- Write down and discuss all special instructions. Demonstrate tasks if necessary.
- Provide the care providers with emergency telephone numbers. Post this information near a telephone at your elder's residence. Have the care providers give you the names and telephone numbers of their emergency contacts and health insurance carrier.
- Keep the care providers updated on your relative's health condition and, in turn, have them contact you if they notice any changes.
- Be on the lookout for signs of trouble: the day's work isn't done; the worker doesn't keep track of spending money; your relative complains about the worker's attitude and quality of care; clothes, food, and household items are missing; the worker comes late and leaves early; you feel as though you aren't getting important information. Don't let problems build up. Take the time to discuss and resolve issues as they occur.

- Be aware that if the care provider is from a different cultural background, communication styles may vary from yours. For instance, a worker may believe that asking personal questions and saying no to an authority figure is not acceptable behavior. The worker may therefore not give you clear answers, especially if he or she is reluctant to say or do something you've asked.
- Provide encouragement and support. Let the worker know you appreciate his or her assistance. Thank-you notes, flowers, and favorable reports can really make a difference and may encourage that person to pay even closer attention to your relative's well-being.

PLAN SEVEN
Take formal action if you are dissatisfied with the quality of care.

If your elder is being cared for in a hospital, an assisted-living facility, or a nursing home, you can take action if you are dissatisfied with the quality of care. Many hospitals in the United States have a **patient representative** on staff. This advocate guides the patient through the medical bureaucracy and can ensure that the patient is getting the rights to which he or she is entitled, including respectful care, treatment options, and confidentiality.

An **ombudsman** monitors nursing and board and care facilities. Call this advocate if you suspect your family member is being ill-treated. The ombudsman will investigate and refer the case to the state licensing agent. Refer to the telephone directory White or Blue Pages under long-term care ombudsman.

Complaints about long-term care facilities and residential care facilities can be directed to the state department of social services, department of health services and county licensing offices. Licensing and certification reports are public information.

PLAN EIGHT
Bridge the gap in eldercare by using community programs.

Assisted-living programs keep seniors independent and in contact with others who can monitor their health and safety. Programs include:

Home-delivered meals (also known as **mobile meals** or **meals-on-wheels**)—Meals delivered to the home help homebound elders to eat nutritionally and provide an opportunity to interact with the volunteers who bring the food. Resources for this service are listed at the end of this chapter.

Emergency response devices—Your elderly relative wears a bracelet or necklace equipped with a radio transmitter that's activated by pushing a button. A message is sent to the hospital, police, or an emergency contact. Other programs require your family member to check in by telephone on a daily basis. When no contact is made, a designated person checks on your elder. Ask the hospital discharge planner for referrals.

Carrier Alert (also known as **Postal Alert**)—A mail carrier who notices an unusual accumulation of mail will alert a postal supervisor to designate a person to check on your elder. Call the post office for more details.

Social day care—These community programs provide several hours a day of social interaction, recreation, group meals, and supervision for aging people who cannot be safely left home alone. Call the local area agency on aging to find out more about what the community has to offer.

Adult day health care—Supervised day care for adults is a more specialized kind of program than social day care and may include comprehensive services ranging from health assessment and nursing care to social and recreational activities. Participation in these programs usually requires a physician's prescription. Adult day health care centers are not necessarily federally licensed. To evaluate a facility . . .

- Request a *written* target-enrollment policy statement.
- Ask about its policy vis-à-vis patients who are abusing alcohol or drugs.
- Ask if the facility requests updates on the patient's medical records.
- Find out how the facility provides reports on the patient's activities.
- Review the staff–patient ratio. One staff member for every eight patients is typical. In cases where patients are severely mentally and physically impaired, one staff member for every five patients is an acceptable ratio.
- Ask whether the facility's staff includes a director with a professional degree in the field of health and human services, a social worker, a registered nurse (R.N.), or licensed practical nurse (L.P.N.) supervised by an R.N.

Respite care—The primary caregiver needs to have a resource he or she can call upon as a backup when the situation mandates. Respite care can be for as little as a few hours at a time, or a day, a weekend, or even a month, and can be arranged for in or outside the home. Take advantage of the benefits respite care has to offer when you are unsure of decisions regarding your relative's permanent living arrangements. Optional respite care facilities outside the home include hospitals and nursing homes.

For referrals on these community assisted-living programs, call your local department on aging, the social service agency, the family service agency, and the hospital discharge planner. Look in the Yellow Pages under Nurse and Nurse Registries, Home Health Agencies, Senior Services Organizations, and Adult Day Care Centers. Ask your employer what services are provided through your employee benefits work/life program.

PLAN NINE
Identify volunteer resources.

There are numerous community sources for volunteers who are available to assist family members with eldercare tasks, offering companionship and emotional support. Contact these resources to find out what they have to offer:

community centers	women's clubs
senior centers	neighborhood groups
hospitals	business associations
hospices	retirement organizations
public libraries	volunteer organizations
agencies on aging	advocacy leagues
family service agencies	recreation centers
support groups	grade/high schools
nursing agencies	colleges
charities	universities
church groups	youth groups
seniors' organizations	transportation agencies
religious groups	veterans organizations
medical centers	financial institutions
fraternal orders	legal institutions
homeowners' associations	department stores

Take Care of *You*

Your sister criticizes the kind of care Dad is receiving; your husband is resentful of the amount of time you're spending with an aging aunt; you missed your daughter's school play; your boss is losing patience regarding an overdue report. When we take on family caregiving responsibilities, we often feel as though we are being pulled in a hundred different directions—between our children, job responsibilities, relationships, personal commitments, and the elder who is relying on us for attention and assistance. Our first order of business should be our own physical and emotional well-being; but that's easier said than done.

Certainly, planning will help you avoid a work/life crisis and caregiver burnout. Maintaining a healthy attitude will also help keep your priorities in check. For example, feelings of guilt often override other emotions and, as a result, you may be reluctant to delegate eldercare tasks. Moreover, you may feel as though you're neglecting your responsibilities by allowing someone else to relieve you, even for a short time.

Your own health, the quality of your professional and personal life, and your relationships outside of the one you have with your elder need not suffer as a consequence of providing eldercare. Ask for and accept help from others, even when you're able and available to perform certain caregiving tasks. Make ongoing requests of assistance from other family members, friends, community resources, and volunteers. Get others used to the idea that you'll be needing their help from time to time.

You and your elder also need breathing room. You may need a break from caregiving responsibilities and he or she may need a break from you. If your elderly family member resents having someone else take your place temporarily, resist the temptation to cancel your plans. If you're actively carrying out the responsibilities of family caregiving, this section of *The Planner* will offer tips on how to balance work/life responsibilities and your own personal interests.

TAKE CARE OF YOU

- The effects of eldercare on employees is already being felt in the workplace. One out of every four employees has some level of eldercare responsibility. Half of these caregivers say their involvement is equivalent to another full-time job.
- Eldercare is a work/life issue that affects a wider range of employees—and potentially for longer periods of time—than the issue of where to place young children during working hours.
- Family members provide 80 percent of the care for elderly relatives.
- Family caregivers who do not ask for or accept help from others can become frustrated, develop feelings of isolation, and experience anger toward their elder and other family members.

Everyone can expect to assume the role of caregiver at some time in his or her life, but there are steps one can take that will keep life in balance, at home and at work.

OBJECTIVES

*After completing **Take Care of You**, you will be able to:*
Recognize the mental and physical symptoms of caregiver burnout.
Take necessary precautions to relieve caregiver stress.
Share eldercare responsibilities with others.
Integrate work/life responsibilities.

 PLAN ONE
Take an honest look at yourself.

Ask yourself the following questions to monitor your current caregiver stress level:

Do you . . .
Resent your elder? Other family members?
Find little satisfaction in assisting your elderly relative?

Feel trapped and burdened?

Feel the rest of the family aren't doing their share?

Have thoughts of guilt? Shame? Inadequacy? Helplessness? Hopelessness?

Have frequent feelings of anger or rage?

Maintain unrealistic attitudes? ("I should . . .")

Think about being out of control? Not being in control?

Have difficulty saying no to your aging relatives? To others?

Resist delegating eldercare responsibilities to others?

Are you . . .

Letting your job performance slip? Late for work? Missing work?

Using forms of physical abuse? Verbal abuse?

Overeating? Lacking an appetite? Eating junk food?

Crying frequently?

Depleting your own financial resources?

Not seeking or accepting help?

Not asking questions or gathering information?

Not exercising? Not having fun? Not laughing?

Having fitful sleeping periods? Nightmares?

Not sharing feelings?

Smoking? Drinking? Abusing drugs?

Developing physical symptoms like headaches, backaches, breathing problems, lingering colds?

PLAN TWO
Avoid family caregiver burnout.

When it comes to helping older people, more is not necessarily better. Too much assistance and attention can be harmful for both the giver and the receiver. Although strong support of our elderly family members can produce a positive, tangible boost to the quality of their lives at first, continuing to give a high level of help can bring about a depressive effect over time. Excessive assistance erodes an older person's sense of competence and independence and can diminish his or her life skills.

There are many reasons caregivers fall victim to shouldering too much responsibility and becoming overinvolved in their eldercare responsibilities. Feeling needed and useful are life-enhancing qualities for all of us; but idealists who believe that they have control over much of what happens to them and their elderly loved ones become burnout candidates who find themselves running into chronic situational stresses. Family caregivers who suffer burnout exhibit a variety of symptoms: physical deterioration; feelings of helplessness, hopelessness, and disillusionment.

The key to proper care is knowing just how much to give, especially when seniors are still perfectly capable of making their own decisions and performing day-to-day tasks on their own. Here is an invaluable sixteen-point assessment to help you keep a healthy balance between family caregiving responsibilities and maintaining the quality of your own life.

When it comes to my elderly family members, I . . .
- evaluate their strengths and resources, not limitations and weaknesses.
- keep them involved in their own decision-making processes.
- facilitate dialogues rather than try to solve their problems for them.
- let them do what they can for themselves, as long as their safety is not at risk.
- adhere to their decision-making time frame, rather than my own.
- accept, and deal with what is rather than what I'd like things to be.
- not waste energy worrying about people and circumstances that I cannot control.
- be aware that change can occur (for better or for worse) at any time.
- ask for and accept help from others.
- not deplete my own financial resources.
- seek financial advice from professionals.
- not make ironclad promises to anyone about anything and stay flexible.
- accept that today somebody is likely to be mad at me for something.
- continue to satisfy my own personal, professional, recreational, spiritual, and social needs.
- accept that it is okay not to have all the answers.
- talk about my real feelings to a trusted friend about what is happening.

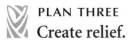 **PLAN THREE**
Create relief.

There are people who will help care for your aging family members and people who will care for you. Ask for help, even if you don't perceive the need yet. The following is a potential network of people and organizations you may want to recruit:

Family, friends, neighbors, volunteers—Let your needs be known. Call them now. Review this chapter's Share the Care section for suggestions.

Employers—Eldercare is fast replacing child care as the number one dependent-care workplace issue. See Plan Four of this section for a multitude of suggestions on keeping a healthy balance of work/life responsibilities.

Personal assistants—If you are time-crunched and drowning in unfinished tasks, household projects, and errands, the services of a personal assistant, concierge, or personal organizer are a telephone call away. Look in the Yellow Pages under Concierge, Home Helpers, and Personal Organizers.

Supportive discussion groups—Join other caregivers to share tips and gain emotional support. Some programs provide education about particular illnesses. You will find referrals for support groups at your local hospital and community senior center.

Cyber community—Talk in real time, or just leave a message; the Internet offers caregiver chat rooms, discussion forums, bulletin boards, and links to other sites. Resources for chat groups are listed at the end of this chapter.

Specific illness associations—Organizations dealing with specific illnesses such as cancer, diabetes, heart disease, arthritis, and Alzheimer's often have programs for family members as well as patients.

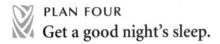 **PLAN FOUR**
Get a good night's sleep.

A good laugh and a long sleep are the two best cures—Irish proverb.

Imagine a full night's sleep with no interruptions, just peace and quiet. In reality, a family caregiver's sleeping patterns are often anything but uninterrupted or peaceful. Your elder may have difficulty sleeping at night or be prone to nocturnal wandering and activity, and you worry about falls, among other mishaps. Although we can't be expected to be on duty 24 hours a day, here are a few tips on solving the challenge of the elderly night owl.

Don't wait. If your elder experiences one sleepless night, your first plan of action is to contact the doctor to determine the cause and make treatment suggestions. Sleeplessness can be due to:

Depression

Medication usage and dosage

Incontinence

Changes in bladder function

Urinary tract infection

Hyperthyroidism

Dementia

Change your elder's daily and evening routine. Recruit other family members and volunteers to help you carry out these activities:

Increase exercise during the day. Even if your elder is bedridden, you can get ideas from a physical therapist, a local nursing home, or a rehabilitation center. Take walks.

Increase day and evening activities. Consider adult day care during the day. Play music, sing songs, and dance together. Play catch with beach balls and balloons. Try shuffleboard or boccie.

Give your elder a job. Offer physical activities that help him or her stretch, bend, grasp, carry, and walk, including setting the table, rearranging the contents of drawers and cabinets, folding laundry, and the like.

Introduce relaxation techniques. Practice breathing exercises together and run a warm bath for your elder at bedtime.

Offer plenty of water throughout the day but begin to limit drinking liquids six hours before bedtime. Set limits to unreasonable, and sometimes manipulative, requests, such as having to fetch a glass of water several times during the night.

Eliminate potential household hazards by following these suggestions:

- Keep certain rooms of the home off-limits at night.
- Set up an activity table either in your elder's bedroom or a room close by.
- Create special areas for items that need to be arranged, sorted, or put away.
- Place a comfortable chair in your elder's bedroom or a room close by.
- Make good use of night-lights, especially in hallways and bathrooms.
- Keep a light on in your elder's favorite room and well-traveled hallways.
- Remove small portable furniture like ottomans, low tables, and all area rugs.
- Label rooms with signs on the doors.
- Rent a bedside commode.
- Provide a call button in the bathroom.
- Install locks and latches on doors, cabinets, and gates.

Hire someone for two or three nights per week so you can go to your own room, close the door, and get a good night's sleep.

See your own doctor.

 PLAN FIVE
Become familiar with your company's work/life policies and programs.

Many of us are trying to achieve a balance among different, but equally important, priorities: the demands of work and home. This isn't an easy thing to do; but it is our responsibility to integrate our personal and professional lives, which includes taking advantage of work/life programs that may be available to us at work.

The work/home gap is narrowing. Today, we have lunch with our kids at the company day care center, pick up our laundry at the employee store, work out at the corporate gym, and have our cars washed and serviced in the company parking lot. Obtaining eldercare advice and assistance from our employers is no different.

Corporate America is beginning to understand that the consequences of avoiding employee eldercare issues in the workplace translate into employees' loss of concentration, higher use of health benefits, lost work time, rising telephone costs, increased absenteeism, and a higher employee turnover rate. The resultant disruption at work is significant, so taking advantage of eldercare work/life benefits can be critical in maintaining workforce productivity and commitment.

Eldercare issues typically surface in two stages: the planning stage and the crisis stage. Either way you will need to know about your company's flextime policy and about the Family and Medical Leave Act (FMLA). If you are a manager or an employer and do not yet have a program in place, or are dissatisfied with your employees' use of your existing eldercare program, seek expert advice from the work/life resources listed at the end of this chapter.

The most effective eldercare work/life programs include:

Intranet resource and referral programs

On-site eldercare planning workshops

On-site work/life fairs

Employee service benefits

Long-term care insurance

Group legal plans

Employee assistance programs (EAP)

Dependent-care tax programs

Contingency care vouchers

Employee store (eldercare books and videos)

Employee newsletter articles

Cosponsored community events

Global relocation strategies

If you are at all concerned about staying productive on the job while balancing family eldercare responsibilities, become proactive and explore the eldercare work/life policies and programs your company has to offer. If your company does not offer any eldercare benefits, ask them to consider doing so, and in the meantime, use *The Planner* to help pull it all together.

These days, a full-time job might also include a company transfer. In an effort to stay connected and interdependent, many employees are moving their elderly relatives with them when they relocate. If your employer asks you to consider a transfer, and you are thinking of moving your relative in the process, here is a quick relocation checklist for you to determine suitable housing for your elder:

Will my elder's health insurance transfer to the new location?

Will my elder be able to afford this home in the long run?

Is this home "high maintenance"?

Are affordable and reliable home maintenance services available?

Does this new location offer my elder plenty of social activity opportunities?

Is the climate suitable?

Is it safe for my elder to take a walk or sit outside?

Does my elder have access to medical care, church, friends, barber/beauty shop, shopping?

Are pets allowed?

Is this place too noisy? Too quiet?

Is there wheelchair access in every room?

Do not consider any particular housing alternative if . . .

There are any stairs (inside or outside) to negotiate.

Building codes will not allow outdoor ramps or first-floor bathrooms.

There are no community in-home care or in-home health care services available.

Transportation services are not available.

The bathtub cannot be removed to install a shower.

Low-Cost and Free Resources

Refer to the telephone directory White Pages for the **Catholic Charities, family service agencies,** and **Jewish Family Services** for additional assistance.

For family caregivers providing home health care, many hospitals and adult education centers offer **home nursing programs.**

The **Eldercare Locator** refers callers to an extensive network of organizations serving older people. Call toll-free (800) 677-1116. When you make your call, be prepared to provide the name, address, and zip code of your elder and a brief description of your problem or the kind of assistance you are seeking.

Florida has a state-sponsored assisted-living program for senior citizens who need help with some tasks but can still remain in their own homes. The program arranges for support services including adult day care, emergency alert response, personal care, homemaker, and respite. Program participants must be over 60 years of age and must meet functional impairment levels to qualify.

ORGANIZATIONS

Access America for Seniors
Website: *www.seniors.gov*

Little Brothers—Friends of the Elderly
954 W. Washington Boulevard, 5th Floor
Chicago, IL 60607
(312) 829-3055, Fax: (312) 829-3077
Website: *www.little-brothers.org*

Meals on Wheels Association of America
1414 Prince Street, Suite 202
Alexandria, VA 22314
(703) 548-5558, Fax: (703) 548-8024
Website: *www.projectmeal.org*

National Adult Day Services Association
c/o The National Council on the Aging, Inc.
409 Third Street, SW
Washington, DC 20024
(202) 479-1200, Fax: (202) 479-0735, TDD: (202) 479-6674
Website: *www.ncoa.org*

National Association for Home Care
228 Seventh Street, SE
Washington, DC 20003
(202) 547-7424, Fax: (202) 547-3540
Website: *www.nahc.org*

National Association of Professional Geriatric Care Managers
1604 N. Country Club Road
Tucson, AZ 85716-3102
(520) 881-8008, Fax: (520) 325-7925
Website: *www.caremanager.org*

National Federation of Interfaith Volunteer Caregivers
368 Broadway Street, Suite 103
Kingston, NY 12401
(914) 331-1358, Fax: (914) 331-4177
Website: *www.nfivc.org*

Volunteers of America
110 South Union Street
Alexandria, VA, 22314-3351
(800) 899-0089, Fax: (703) 684-1972
Website: *www.voa.org*

Work/Life Resources

Benefits Link, Inc.
1014 East Robinson Street
Orlando, FL 32801
(407) 841-3717, Fax: (407) 841-3054
Website: *www.benefitslink.com*

CareQuest, Inc.
583 D'Onofrio Drive, Suite 103
Madison, WI 53719
(800) 833-2524, TTY Relay: (800) 947-3529
Website: *www.carequestplus.com*

Center for Work and The Family
910 Tulare Avenue
Berkeley, CA 94707
(510) 527-0107
Website: *www.centerforworkandfamily.com*

Family and Medical Leave Act (FMLA)
(Employee/Employer Advisor website)
Website: *www.dol.gov/elaws/fmla.htm*

Employee Services Management Association
2211 York Road, Suite 207
Oak Brook, IL 60523
(630) 368-1280, Fax: (630) 368-1286
Website: *www.esmassn.org*

International Foundation of Employee Benefit Plans (IFEBP)
18700 W. Bluemound Road
P. O. Box 69
Brookfield, WI 53008-0069
(262) 786-6710, Fax: (262) 786-8670
Website: *www.ifebp.org*

Managing Work & Family, Inc.
912 Crain Street
Evanston, IL 60202
(847) 864-0916, Fax: (847) 475-2021
Website: *www.mwfam.com*

Silvercare Productions
(Joy Loverde Employee Eldercare Workshops)
1560 N. Sandburg Terrace, Suite 2509
Chicago, IL 60610-7723
(312) 642-3611, Fax: (312) 642-8110
Website: *www.elderindustry.com*

Work & Family Connection, Inc.
(Clearinghouse for work/life issues and practices)
5197 Beachside Drive
Minnetonka, MN 55343
(800) 487-7898, (612) 936-7898, Fax: (612) 935-0122
Website: *www.workfamily.com*

Action Checklist

HOW TO TELL WHEN YOUR ELDER NEEDS HELP	To Do By	Completed
Observe your elder		
performing tasks	_____	❏
physical conditions	_____	❏
environment	_____	❏
mental well-being	_____	❏
Review Communicaring chapter	_____	❏

SHARE THE CARE		
List eldercare tasks		
homemaking	_____	❏
personal care	_____	❏
home health care	_____	❏
quality of life	_____	❏
Set caregiver goals		
short-term	_____	❏
long-term	_____	❏

Create a list of helpers _____ ❏

Make a list of help needed
    short-term _____ ❏
    long-term _____ ❏

Hire caregivers
    create list of questions _____ ❏
    check all references and licenses _____ ❏
    create and sign job contract _____ ❏
    have proper insurance _____ ❏
    look into Social Security taxes _____ ❏

Have a plan to
    oversee quality of care _____ ❏
    request caregiver reports on elder's
      condition regularly _____ ❏
    praise caregivers _____ ❏
    report elder abuse _____ ❏

Review community assisted-living programs
    home-delivered meals _____ ❏
    emergency response devices _____ ❏
    carrier alert _____ ❏
    social day care _____ ❏
    adult day health care _____ ❏
    respite care _____ ❏

Consider volunteers _____ ❏

Obtain a copy of elder's
    telephone directory _____ ❏
    personal address book _____ ❏
    community senior directory _____ ❏

Record emergency telephone numbers _____ ❏

Know phone numbers of
    hospital social services _____ ❏
    family service agency _____ ❏
    area agency on aging _____ ❏
    family members _____ ❏
    elder's neighbors _____ ❏
    elder's friends _____ ❏
    coworkers _____ ❏
    caregivers _____ ❏

geriatric case manager ＿＿＿＿＿ ❏
social worker ＿＿＿＿＿ ❏

Make sure your elder has access to a telephone ＿＿＿＿＿ ❏

Duplicate and post phone numbers; keep copies
at home ＿＿＿＿＿ ❏
at work ＿＿＿＿＿ ❏
in car ＿＿＿＿＿ ❏
in wallet/purse ＿＿＿＿＿ ❏

*Duplicate and distribute phone numbers to
designated persons* ＿＿＿＿＿ ❏

TAKE CARE OF *YOU*

Create self-care goals
short-term ＿＿＿＿＿ ❏
long-term ＿＿＿＿＿ ❏

Monitor caregiver stress ＿＿＿＿＿ ❏

Assess caregiver involvement to avoid burnout ＿＿＿＿＿ ❏

Plan for caregiver relief
schedule days off ＿＿＿＿＿ ❏
join support groups ＿＿＿＿＿ ❏
take vacations ＿＿＿＿＿ ❏
maintain personal interests ＿＿＿＿＿ ❏
use community respite programs ＿＿＿＿＿ ❏

Monitor sleeping patterns ＿＿＿＿＿ ❏

Explore company work/life programs ＿＿＿＿＿ ❏

· 3 ·

COMMUNICARING

Take a Deep Breath, and Jump In

Talking about eldercare issues with elderly relatives isn't easy. Besides, who wants to hash over such unpleasant topics as illness or funeral arrangements while Mom and Dad seem perfectly fine? You may have been avoiding talking altogether, afraid that the process will be tumultuous and probably upsetting for you and your elders. And you're right. However, avoiding conversations between family members about eldercare will ultimately have a negative impact on the economic and emotional stability of the entire family.

When is the best time to initiate conversations about eldercare? *Right now*—while your elder has the ability to make decisions regarding his or her own future, and crises aren't raining down on everyone. People don't realize that many of the "emergencies" they end up confronting could have been avoided by *planning*. Devising an effective caregiving plan requires ongoing, thoughtful communication amongst all family members.

Whether you realize it or not, you already have some of the skills needed for handling eldercare conversations effectively. For example, if you are a parent, think back on the numerous times you created new methods of communicating with your children, at each stage in their lives, in order to encourage them to do what you wanted them to do. To get your point across, you revised your style of conversation as they grew and matured, and as former roles were shed and responsibilities shifted. This same process holds true when it comes to talking with elderly family members.

Proactive conversations, initiated early on, are easier on everybody. This section of *The Planner* will help you take that first communication step, in a nonconfrontational way, toward strengthening family ties and savoring precious moments and, in the process, maximizing your time and energy.

TAKE A DEEP BREATH, AND JUMP IN

- If you are waiting for your elderly family member to announce, "Now's the time to talk," forget it.
- No matter how much love and trust exists, there will be communication pitfalls and obstacles.
- A little empathy goes a long way during eldercare conversations.
- Caregiver guilt is such a powerful force that family members may at times find themselves feeling guilty about not feeling guilty.

Your elder has probably thought a lot more about the future than you realize, even though he or she has never shown any inclination to bring up the subject.

OBJECTIVES

*After completing **Take a Deep Breath, and Jump In**, you will be able to:*

Gain better understanding of how your elder thinks and why.

Maintain a healthy balance of parent-child responsibilities.

Encourage your elder to be accountable for his or her actions.

Use timing to your advantage.

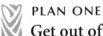 **PLAN ONE**
Get out of your own way.

Surveys of elderly people asked to list their most anxiety-producing problems indicate their chief fears are:

1. Tight budget
2. Purposeless existence
3. Fear of crime
4. Poor health
5. Lack of affordable and trusting home repair services

That the number one problem of elders is trying to live on limited financial resources isn't news; but the second response—having no purpose in life—may come as a surprise to you. No longer feeling needed by somebody for something is one of the greatest losses our elders experience, and is often the root of illness and depression. Fear of becoming a crime victim (number three) will affect an elder's willingness to ask for or accept help from people outside the family, or to stay active outside the home. The onset of an illness (number four) dictates an elder's mobility and freedom; and finally, the inability to meet the demands of home maintenance (number five) will ultimately force an elder into making an unwanted move.

This survey confirms that elders want to be in control of their own lives for as long as possible. The more we family caregivers remain sensitive to this need, the better our odds of keeping the lines of communication open and guiding them in the best interests of themselves and the entire family.

The issue is loss.

With aging comes losses of one kind or another. If you are the caregiver for your parents, both you and your elders will be dealing with loss—your loss of the parents who once took care of you, and their loss of their own independence and former lives. Family eldercare discussions are an outgrowth of the need to adapt to loss. That can be painful.

The word "independence" covers a lot of ground. On a personal level, an independent elder has the ability to manage personal care tasks including basic functions such as dressing, bathing, toileting, feeding oneself, transferring from bed to chair, and walking. Another category of independent living is known as non-personal care, including tasks such as preparing meals, cleaning house, shopping, paying bills, driving, using the telephone, writing, and reading. As an elder's ability to handle these tasks and functions declines, he or she becomes increasingly dependent on others for assistance.

While some elders learn to accept their losses and make necessary adjustments, others may struggle. For those who resist these changes, every conversation *we* initiate—regardless of the subject matter or our apparent motivation—may be interpreted by an elder as a personal threat to his or her already-perceived sense of dwindling independence.

Preserve your elder's autonomy.

Basic personality patterns and traits don't change; they may even intensify or become exaggerated in later years. Consequently, as time passes, elders become more and more who they already are. There is no such thing as an "average" elder. Genetics, experiences, influences, beliefs, and environments—all contribute to making each person unique. Also, people age at different rates.

Grampa may still be able to strive adeptly at ninety, while seventy-five-year-old Aunt Bee requires round-the-clock care. Eldercare is defined by ability, not age. The most effective family discussions focus on what elders *can* do, rather than what they *can't* do. Empowering elders to make good use of every ability they still have lessens the caregiving demands on you.

Making assumptions strains relationships. There is a full life history that goes into each choice or decision our elder makes, and we have no way of plugging into that history. But the more we listen and try to facilitate an elder's wants and needs, the more he or she is assured of our love and that we want what is best. Our goal is to relate to, rather than manipulate, each other. Stay open-minded to *this* particular person's desires and you will have a better chance of averting unnecessary clashes.

Establish trust every time.

Due to the sensitive nature of any eldercare conversation, it is a mistake to rely on past successes to get you through the current talks. Communication breakdowns can happen anytime, when you least expect them. Every conversation with an elder can be a struggle for his or her independence. Keep the trust factor high to assure them your motive is not to "take away." You can accomplish this by listening, asking questions rather than making suggestions, and resisting the temptation to offer unsolicited advice.

Quit scaring yourself.

When Mom forgets your birthday, or Uncle Charlie tells the same joke over and over again, avoid jumping to the conclusion that your relatives are losing their mental capacities. Separate real hazards from your fears of what *could* be happening by seeking information and advice from health care professionals. You might learn that their momentary forgetfulness is a side effect of medications or a symptom of depression. Make no assumptions. Take proper steps to find out.

Educate yourself first.

Before starting any conversations with your elders and other family members, do your homework. The more you know about the family's options, resources, community services, and related costs, the more depth you will add to eldercare discussions, and the better will be your ability to give everyone a realistic idea about how involved you and they might need to become.

 PLAN TWO
Honor thy father and thy mother.

When a discussion between an elderly parent and an adult child takes place, each person enters the conversation from a distinctly different point of view. Being sensitive to these differences will help make your interactions go more smoothly.

Conflicting understanding of responsibilities.

Watching a parent age is a poignant experience. To notice suddenly that Dad's hair is pure white or that Mom is walking ten paces slower triggers fears that significant decline, or even death, is right around the corner. In an attempt to hold back time, we make statements like, "Mom, if you sell your house and move closer, we can spend more time together," or, "Dad, are you sure you're feeling up to mowing the lawn?" Below the surface, however, we are struggling with mortality issues and thinking, "When did you get to be so old?" and, "You're the parent, you're supposed to take care of *me*," and, "I don't want anything to happen to you." These kinds of thoughts race through our minds while we don't want to believe that any of it is true. The perceived role of the adult child when talking to aging parents is to shelter and protect.

Parents, on the other hand, operate from a different set of attitudes. When they make statements such as, "I don't want to be a burden," they sincerely believe that doing whatever it takes to stay out of our way and not be a bother is the *right* thing to do. Unfortunately, our parents are often unaware that maintaining a totally independent lifestyle at an advanced age is an unrealistic goal; as a result, their actions often carve a path of destruction through the rest of the family's well-being. Even so, if you try to talk them out of this mind-set, be prepared to encounter extreme resistance.

Partnering, not parenting.

We have all been raised to prize independence and individualism, yet in a fundamental way we *are* dependent—or more precisely, *interdependent*—on others. We need each other in order to meet our needs. The objective of parent-adult child eldercare conversations is to encourage mutually responsible partnerships. *Partnering with,* rather than *parenting* our parents, is the desired approach.

As long as our parents remain mentally facile and able to make their own decisions, we must appreciate the limits of our own authority. Many adult children have learned the hard way that attempts to impose their ways on their parents will touch off a downward spiral in the communication process, leading to a breakdown in the relationship as a whole.

When we focus our conversation style on influencing parents to seek and accept help from others, and keep them accountable for their own choices, they can remain true to their independent ideals.

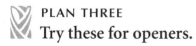 PLAN THREE
Try these for openers.

Now that you have a basic understanding of what your elder's mind-set may be, it's time to take the plunge and open up a dialogue. Feeling scared and uncomfortable is normal and even predictable; you and your elders are just beginning to relearn how to talk to each other.

Seize the moment.

Today's elders are a generation that is not accustomed to asking for help directly and they may mask their problems by dropping hints. For instance, worries about the cost of their own long-term health care may be referenced in statements such as, "My neighbor's paying close to $4,000 a month to keep his wife in a nursing home." Or they may insist they are financially sound, but complain more and more about the cost of groceries. In any case, any conversation *they* initiate—especially when it comes to the subject of their money—presents an opening for you to start talking. The best approach to creating a real dialogue in a nonthreatening fashion is to speak in questions. Here are some examples:

How can your neighbor afford the cost of his wife's care?
How can anyone afford nursing home care these days?
How would you handle the situation if you were in their shoes?
Yes, the cost of groceries sure has me on a pretty tight budget. How about you?

Also, take advantage of family situations that come up naturally—a death in the family, the onset of an illness, a friend's divorce. During these times people are more inclined to be thinking about their own mortality and financial issues, and consequently, such occasions provide a natural opportunity to ask your elders what they are doing, *if anything*, about the particular situations under discussion.

Similarly, an approaching birthday or holiday may be the perfect time to offer the gift of a service an elder needs, but is unwilling to pay for. You might say, "Dad, I'd love to get you a year's worth of lawn service for your birthday. May I?"

Plant the seed.

If the opportunity to start an eldercare conversation doesn't present itself, and you want to get things started, create your own. Clip a current newspaper article that reports a growing eldercare issue, like long-term care. Next time you visit your elder, show him or her the article and say, "Says here that in-home services are not covered by Medicare. What are your thoughts on this?" Clipping articles works especially well if the person you want to talk to is your parent. Remember, in your parents' eyes, you're still "their child," and news articles can well serve as an authority figure when we, by ourselves, are not viewed as such.

Ask for advice.

Soliciting advice from your elder is an effective way to open up a dialogue. It makes them feel needed and appreciated for their years of experience, rather than threatened. You can say, "Dad, I'm just beginning to think about my own retirement, and it looks like you're doing pretty good. Do you have any tips for me?" Here are a few more openers:

I am getting around to creating my will. How did you go about doing yours?

I've always admired the way you . . . Do you have any suggestions for me?

I've been clearing out the basement. What should I give to charity?

Do you think buying life insurance is a good idea?

I want to get your opinion before I start this.

What do you think about . . . ?

How would you do this if you were me?

Fish for information.

Gradually losing the ability to perform basic human functions (buttoning a shirt, opening a jar) brings anxiety to most elders. Because their spouses and friends often cover for each other, we may never really know what's going on. Going "on automatic" and greeting an elder with a mindless "How are you?" will almost guarantee an equally empty "Fine." As a result, we miss out on an opportunity to get some real feedback about any pressing issues or problems that they may be confronting. Next time, try this:

Hello. It's so good to hear from you (see you). What's new?

What have you been up to lately?

What's happening in your neck of the woods?

Turn the tables.

Relationships between adult children and their parents are not static. We adult children may vacillate between a desire for independence and the wish to still be cared for and sheltered by our parents. On the other hand, our parents may see us in one context as advisers, and, in another, as naive children who rely on their infinite wisdom and experience.

Instead of getting defensive when Mom attempts to nurture you in her old familiar ways by saying, "Honey, are you sure you're eating right? You look so thin," think again. Take advantage of this natural bond by asking your elder to help *you*. Appeal to your elder's role as your parent and ask for his or her help:

Dad, there may come a time when I will need to know where you keep your important papers. Just in case something happens, can you help me with this now?

Mom, I don't need to know the details of your life savings, but I should know what you would want me to do in case anything ever happened to you. Can you help me with this?

Dad, I'm pretty exhausted after working all day, and coming here after work is wearing me out. Can we hire someone to help me out with some of these chores, so we can spend time doing the relaxing things we used to do together?

Give your elder an assignment. Maybe Dad doesn't see the need to purchase long-term care insurance, but you are convinced that such coverage will protect his financial stability. One way to get him to consider this option is to ask him to investigate it. Tell him you're swamped at work and ask if he would go to the library or explore the Internet to research insurance carriers and policies on your behalf. When he presents you with his findings, ask him what he would do if he were in your shoes. You're both bound to learn a lot.

Ask a favor. If you are concerned that Mom is letting the yard work slide, and she won't let anybody help her, you can ask, "Mom, I need a favor. Will you let Billy rake the leaves so he'll learn some responsibility?"

Asking our elders to help *us* accomplishes two important goals. It gives them a sense of purpose within the family and makes them feel needed and important, and also creates a nonthreatening approach to talking about potentially explosive subjects. Who knows, you might actually enjoy letting your parents parent you again for a change—and sometimes being cared for by our parents is exactly what *we* need.

 PLAN FOUR
Use surefire talking tips.

You should adjust your communication approach to fit the current situation, but your objective should always be the same: **keep capable elderly loved ones involved in their own decisions, and accountable for their words and actions.** Here are some communication tips to accomplish this goal:

Arrange the best place and time to talk.

When the time is not right, you know it. Nothing you say is well received and nothing you suggest is accepted. You are on the defensive and asking yourself, "How can I get out of this?"

As a rule, holiday family parties are not an ideal time to talk about eldercare. Family gatherings revive old family patterns, and other family members who are present may purposely sabotage your conversations. Also, uninterrupted conversations are practically impossible. Instead, use your time together to look proactively for warning signs that problems may exist, without expecting to *resolve* them. Review the *How to Tell When Your Elder Needs Help* section of *The Planner* starting on page *21.*

If your elder approaches *you,* and you know the timing is not right, postpone the conversation. Listen for a minute, then say, "I'm really glad you're telling me this, and it's important to me, too. Can we continue this when we both have uninterrupted time to talk?" or "I want to give this my full attention. Can we talk about this very soon?" Then set a date so you won't put it off.

Ease into conversations—the more relaxed *you* are, the better. Timing is everything. Before you initiate a conversation with your elders, ask yourself:

Am I overtired or stressed-out right now? (Be sure to get a good night's sleep, first.)

Is it better to separate my parents, or to approach them together?

*Is my elder a morning person or a night owl? Is **this** the best time to approach him or her?*

*Do I have time **now** to get involved in a long and possibly serious discussion?*

*Should I have **this** conversation in person rather than over the phone?*

Do I have enough information on this issue to discuss it intelligently, or do I need to do more homework?

Speak in terms of questions, not answers.

Your being ready to talk about eldercare issues does not mean that your elder is. Growing old, and the problems that go with it, may be scary for our elders, and it may take several attempts before you are able to engage yours in a meaningful conversation. Be patient. If he or she says everything is fine after you've asked a question, or asks to change the subject, let that be okay for now. Don't force issues. Whether your elder lets you know or not, he or she does understand that when you start talking, you want to talk, and that may be all you can accomplish. Sit on it for a week or two, and try again, maybe using a different approach. Here are some general opening lines when you need to probe for new facts and information:

You sound upset. Is something bothering you?

There's something you'd like to talk about, isn't there?

Would you like to talk about it now? Maybe later?

This is important to you, isn't it? Tell me.

Give your elder your full attention.

If your elder does want to talk after you've asked a question, listen patiently. Silence, as Winston Churchill once said, "enhances one's authority." When an elder is responding to your questions, resist interrupting. If he or she feels that you're listening, and understanding, he or she will most likely tell you more. Don't rush to fill in gaps when your elder pauses. **Silence is a powerful communications tool.**

To get into specifics, ask specific questions.

When conversations are in full swing, you will no doubt hear your elder tell you things that will seem impractical, senseless, and even perilous. And in the moment you may feel a strong urge to argue or give suggestions, opinions, and unsolicited advice.

A strong word of warning: Offer suggestions and you're likely to hear the words "You're trying to run my life" sometime in the immediate future. Expect your well-intended advice to get thrown back at you, especially if your elder takes you up on what you said and things don't work out. And your advice will usually be "wrong" because he or she could have done it better, or it was too expensive, it was not what he or she wanted, and so on.

Having a steady stream of suggestions thrown at them can cause elders to feel judged and foolish. They may build up defenses and cut off any further discussions. Worse yet, the trust that took so long to establish may disappear in a flash. Avert these types of breakdowns by phrasing lots of questions.

Trying to talk your elder (who may be testing for your reaction, anyway) out of plans is a waste of time. Get used to saying, "uh-huh." Your objective is not to resolve the problem, but to create a place of inquiry. Instead of trying to control discussions, *facilitate* them. Proceed by asking the kinds of questions that require your elder to think through things:

Can you tell me more about your plans?

What makes you think that?

How do you plan to accomplish what you want?

Isn't this a good time to think about your other options?

Sounds like your plans are going to affect the rest of us, aren't they?

Offer limited assistance.

When elders turn to us for help, our first instinct is to drop everything and take over. While some elders never ask for help, which causes one kind of problem, others may ask for too much assistance as a way of getting attention. Becoming overly involved in their lives, however, establishes an unhealthy dependence and detracts us from other demands that are vying for our attention.

The families that get along best are those in which caregivers keep their elders active in making their own decisions and solving their own problems. Here are some sample questions that can prompt capable elders to do their own research, create interdependent relationships, and encourage elders to take responsibility for their own well-being:

What can you do about this problem?

What have you done so far to solve the problem?

Given what you know now, what do you think is your next step?

Do you have someone to talk to about this?

Who can help you with this?

How do you think I (we) can help?

Where can you get more information?

Would you like me to get you more information on this?

Have you thought about . . . (offer suggestion)?

Communicate caring.

Intelligence is not always what is most needed during eldercare conversations—empathy is. Communicate love and concern, and things may go more smoothly; but this requires time and patience on your part. Take a few moments to listen. Nonverbal messages such as eye contact, touching, speaking slowly and in a soft voice, and a relaxed body posture are helpful. A handful of fresh-cut flowers might warm up an elder's heart.

Let your elders know you care about their well-being:

I worry that something may happen to you when you . . . (drive at night, are home alone)
I've been thinking about you lately.
I love you, and want you to be happy.
You're very special to me.

Turning Conflict into Cooperation

My aunt denies needing help even though I know she does. How do I know if my parents are financially stable? They refuse to talk with me about their money. Even though he can't hear a thing, my husband won't get a hearing aid. What other images come to mind when you think of the times family members won't cooperate? The challenges of present-day family caregiving continue to mount, and so, consequently, do the stressors that tear relationships and families apart.

Talking to each other about eldercare issues is stressful, and not having the skills or the know-how to get what we want can drive a wedge between us and those we love. And when we find ourselves being misunderstood or our motives questioned, the communication process stops, and precious resources of time, energy, and money fly out the window.

Unresolved family issues often play a big part in the breakdown of relating. When we haven't forgiven one another for past hurts, resentment and emotional detachment can override our willingness to see each other's point of view. Also, personalities intensify over the years; negative attitudes, for instance, persist into old age. Personal agendas too can prevent people from getting along. For example, while it may seem obvious to you that Mom can no longer live safely at home, she may refuse your suggestions to consider alternative living arrangements in order to restore her own power within the family, rather than assist you with solving *your* problem. Irrationality, defensiveness, denial, and even outright lying are signals that a personal struggle for power and control is present.

Despite the difficulties, there are solutions. What you will find in this section of *The Planner* are techniques that will help you succeed in persuading others to do what is best. You may even end up being one of the fortunate ones who finally gets to hear the words, "I'm proud of you," "You're doing a great job," and "I love you."

TURNING CONFLICT INTO COOPERATION

- Family caregivers are faced with situations that require negotiation every day.
- A little bargaining know-how can bring you big results.
- The challenges of facing our relatives' old age offer countless opportunities for change and growth within ourselves.

The past doesn't go away, and family members don't change overnight. The quality of family relationships will affect how well the family gets things done.

OBJECTIVES

After completing **Turning Conflict into Cooperation,** *you will be able to:*

Anticipate and respond to arguments.

Manage big issues one small step at a time.

Use techniques that get conversations back on track.

Make your own plans if things don't work out.

 PLAN ONE
Get behind the reason why.

"Mind your own business." "I'm not moving, and that's final." Resistance and defiance during eldercare conversations are common, and conflicts can occur when you least expect them, in spite of how much you love each other.

You most likely had your elder's best intentions in mind when the breakdown occurred, and were probably taken by surprise when he or she resisted your well-intended suggestion. You will often find that what triggers an argument is not even related to the subject matter at hand.

Elders start fights for many reasons, including:

- Lack of trust;
- To restore their power within the family;
- As a stall tactic, to avoid facing a decision they are not yet ready to make;
- As an attention-getting device. Once the problem is solved, you may no longer give them your undivided attention. Arguing, reopening, and rehashing issues that have already been settled are effective ways to keep the focus on themselves.

No one likes to be told what to do by others. When elders feel that they are losing their inherent right to be in charge of their own lives, and perceive that the support of the family unit is slipping away, they will resist your good intentions and go about their plans without seeking the family's further cooperation or approval. They need *constant* reassurance that they are in control.

PLAN TWO
Curb your urge to "take over."

Whose life is it anyway? It doesn't matter if what you have to say is true. It doesn't matter that you are right, and they are wrong. It doesn't matter that you can help them if they would only listen. Imposing your will, offering unsolicited advice, doing things for them that they haven't asked for, enforcing your own values, coming across as the expert on *their* life—will be perceived as manipulative. If your elder's health and safety aren't immediate risks, then do a quick review of your communication approach to help get the relationship back on track. Ask yourself these questions, and review the *Take a Deep Breath, and Jump In* section of this chapter:

> *Am I trying to do for my elder what he or she can still do for himself or herself?*
> *Am I being sympathetic to my elder's issues of loss?*
> *Am I struggling with my own issues of the loss of the person my elder once was?*
> *Am I keeping my elder's uniqueness in mind in solving this problem?*
> *Am I making assumptions about what I think he or she needs?*
> *Am I listening to what my elder says he or she wants?*
> *Am I being open-minded?*
> *Am I asking questions rather than offering unsolicited opinions and advice?*
> *Do I know enough about this subject to make statements instead of ask questions?*
> *Am I empowering my elder to solve his or her own problems?*
> *Am I communicating caring?*

PLAN THREE
Take your elder off the hot seat.

Communication conflicts can occur in the course of eldercare conversations when your elder is made to feel as though he or she is a problem for you to solve. For example, you made the mistake of preaching about his or her far-too-frequent trips to the riverboat casino. Some parents get put out knowing that their children got together and talked about them beforehand. And once their defenses are stirred, they may attempt to halt the discussion altogether.

Profound life events don't just happen to an individual alone, they happen to the entire family. The onset of an elder's chronic illness, for example, will create the need to talk about the many issues that will affect everyone, including the possibility of moving, bringing in outsiders to help, and the costs of long-term care. One strategy for effective communication is to refocus the conversation on the well-being of the entire family, not just on the elder's needs.

Here are some words to say that can help accomplish this goal:

What happens to you, happens to all of us.

We're here to help each other figure this out.

This isn't about you alone; it's a family issue.

Did it ever occur to you that your erratic driving affects all of us?

We're all in this together.

Let's look at the big picture, and how it affects all of us.

By having a housekeeper, you will be helping the whole family with these arrangements.

 PLAN FOUR
Appreciate time zones.

Nobody likes deadlines. Conflicts may arise when you use time as a motivator and your elder doesn't see or agree with your sense of urgency—whether you're dealing with a major, life-altering decision or simply planning a special day outing. For example, you've asked Mom to be ready at a prearranged hour to go someplace special, but find her still in her nightgown when you arrive to pick her up. Expecting your elder to adhere to *your* timetables sets you up for frustration.

To make life easier for everyone, it pays for you to visualize your elder's pace and daily routines. In this way, you'll have a more realistic understanding of how much time it takes to get things done. You may have to tell Mom to be ready an hour or two before the "real" pick-up time to minimize those agonizing, stressful moments when you're running against the clock.

We caregivers lead busy lives and are usually simultaneously juggling work/life responsibilities. Our elders, on the other hand, are often in a "meandering" type of existence. With no bosses to report to or schedules to keep, they may not be the least bit concerned about time: Tuesday could be Friday and April could be September. Forcing our elders to fit their plans into *our* busy schedules probably isn't going to work. Our agendas are not theirs, and boxing them into our time frames may be the impetus they need to dig in their heels and be uncooperative just because they can. Before you bring your time frames into a conversation with your elder, be prepared to live with the consequences should you receive no response by your deadline.

We are a generation of problem-solvers. We want quick answers to resolve all of the family's eldercare issues at once, so we can get on to something else. It really can't work that way. Train yourself to raise one issue at a time, and allow enough time between talks for everyone to adjust and react to the last conversation.

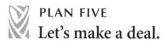 **PLAN FIVE**
Let's make a deal.

You think Mom should get a dishwasher, but she won't spend money on herself; Dad thinks his plans to travel overseas are reasonable, but you know a ten-hour plane ride is far too physically taxing; you know Grandma Elsie is lipreading, yet she refuses even to consider getting a hearing aid; Mom and Pop can no longer live alone, yet they'll still maintain that moving is out of the question.

The situations are endless, but the basis for the conflict is always the same—"you want what you want, and I want what I want." We are *equally* determined to watch out for our own interests.

Not every difference in opinion between you and your elder means that he or she is "losing it" or isn't worthy of your respect. If you and your elder are having trouble seeing eye to eye, then learning the art of negotiating may be what you need to create an *inter*dependent relationship, and perhaps win him or her over to making the changes you believe are necessary.

Be prepared.

Just as you wouldn't start a cross-country car trip without a road map, you can't begin to negotiate with a loved one without knowing your position, and defining the issues that will affect the conversation. Preparing a written list in advance will help you maintain your composure, or keep you from doing or saying something you may later regret. You can also use this list as a yardstick to measure your progress.

Do your homework by taking these steps:

- Think about what you want, and what your elder says he or she wants.
- Define other factors that impact the outcome: money, time, resources, location.
- Gather facts and documentation—the more you know, the more difficult it will be for your elder to argue with you.
- Outline all favorable options you are willing to live with.
- Anticipate resistance—write down how your elder may respond to catch you off guard.

Suggest trial runs.

Explore with your elder what he or she feels he or she *can* do, safely, and for how long. Put a time limit on all trial periods, and follow up when you say you will so your elder knows you're serious. Sometimes, making your elder happy first, for a short while, may open him or her up to accept the alternative plan sooner. Usually, it's a question of dignity. Feedback systems measure change. When the trial period is over, ask your elder and yourself whether the system is working, what changes need to be made, and what could be rearranged or added to make the system work. Here are a few examples:

> *Okay, Mom, I understand you don't want help now. Can we take another look at this situation in two weeks to see how you're doing?*
>
> *Let's move this chair into the other room for a week and see how you like it.*

Give your elder the power to choose.

Choices put most people in a more agreeable mood. When it's time to present alternatives, ask questions that offer choices that are all acceptable to you. For example:

> *Mom, do you want me or Jimmy to drive you there?*
>
> *Should we buy senior taxi discount coupons or give the bus a try?*
>
> *Is it better for you if Mary cleans on Tuesday or Saturday?*

At the same time, be careful not to inundate your elder with suggestions. For example, a question like, "Mom, why don't you go to the senior center today?" will communicate to her that you are trying to control her activities. Instead, offer a subtle suggestion that makes her feel as though she has a choice, such as, "Mom, I'll be happy to drive you to the center if you want."

 PLAN SIX
Inch your elder closer to your goal.

Gently ease into action if your elder isn't willing to do something (e.g., see a doctor). Suggest a less-threatening environment such as a health fair or pharmacy where your elder can be tested for cholesterol and blood pressure. The local library might conduct lectures on diet and exercise. Keep your eyes open for community events, and suggest you attend them together.

PLAN SEVEN
Validate your elder's feelings.

Trying to talk anyone out of the way he or she feels almost always creates distance and conflict between people. Everyone feels better when his or her point of view is understood. Yes, it may be emotionally draining to subject ourselves to our elder's negative thoughts, anger, and criticisms toward us and others, but any attempt to discount his or her inherent right to express any and all feelings will initiate and sustain conflict.

Dad hates the new housekeeper, your cooking is terrible, Mom dislikes her roommate, your spouse doesn't like how you drive, Aunt Liz feels sick and tired all the time—the situations are endless. Underneath it all, given the losses of aging our elders face every day, they are more often than not frightened, and fear they will be abandoned; lashing out at those closest to them sometimes is their only outlet.

When our elders express anger at a situation, or at others' behavior, we may be tempted to respond with questions like "Why are you so angry?" or, "Why do you talk that way?" Or we might offer the false comfort of the cliché, "Things will be better tomorrow," or the cajoling response of "Now, now, quiet down, I'll bring you some tea," making them angrier still that they have been deprived of righteous anger.

Expression relieves the mind, and true caring during times like these shows itself in silence, the quality of our listening, an exchange of glances between two people who understand each other, and some small gesture of love, like holding hands. Talking without words offers a tonic effect and a healing grace.

If you wish to say something during times like these, validate what your elder is feeling—sympathetically. Validating does not mean you agree with what is being said, it simply means that you understand what your loved one is experiencing in the moment. Even though this can be a difficult process, try not to take what your elder is saying personally. Do what you can to distance yourself from what is being said, and use these effective validation techniques to help defuse and lessen your elder's anxiety:

This has been hard for you hasn't it, Mom?
I'm sorry this is happening to you.
I know you're disappointed.
Yes, Dad, you're alone. And I'm sorry you're so sad.
I can imagine how difficult this is for you.
You must be very angry at . . . I'd be mad too if that happened.
Now I understand what you've been going through.
You might be right about that.
That's upsetting. Tell me, how did this happen?
How terrible this must be.

PLAN EIGHT
Take yourself out of the loop.

Are you the best person for the job? Despite good intentions, your elder may not want to talk with *you* about certain subjects. Here's when the refrain, "Mom always liked you best," will work to your advantage. Admit the limitations of your relationship and enlist the help of those who have more influence with your elder. Perhaps your sister gets along with Mom better than you do.

There may be more serious situations when you may have to overstep your elder's objections to your involvement in his or her daily living activities. Leaving the stove on, living in a high-crime neighborhood, driving under the influence of drugs and alcohol, and a host of other high-risk situations dictate that it's time to call for a family and/or professional intervention. Power struggles of this magnitude will easily wear you out and trying to reason with irrational people will get you nowhere.

Certain people *outside* the family circle (authority figures) may be helpful—for example, parents' friends, a doctor, clergy, geriatric case manager, or attorney. Tell them of your concerns. There is an entire network of potential substitutes who may be able to accomplish what you cannot.

When it's time for you to get back in the conversation, you can ask, "Based on what the doctor says about your hearing, Dad, what's your plan about driving?"

In extreme cases, when elders are hurting themselves, abusing drugs and alcohol, or refusing to cooperate with anyone, family members can obtain a court order to gain guardianship over the elder, or they can call the local adult protection services and ask for the assistance of an intervention professional.

PLAN NINE
Step back if there's a fight.

The content of eldercare conversations is life-altering; it's only natural for tensions to build in the communication process. On a positive note, our elder's resistance reminds us that he or she is the ultimate creator of his or her life. Old family conflicts and "hot buttons" have a way of sneaking into conversations, and it takes a lot of maturity to stick to the present issues.

You don't have to respond to an objection or view it as an attack. Issues are rarely settled in one sitting. If there's a fight, first calm yourself by taking a deep breath. Take a sip of water. This will prevent you from saying anything you'll regret later on. Use nonthreatening body language—sit back, uncross your arms and legs. When you're ready, you can say:

I'm sure we can find a solution to this.

I'm on your side.

Where do you think we should go from here?

What's the next step to make this better?

I'm always available to talk with you and am committed to working this out.

I'd like to give this some thought. Let's discuss this later when the shouting is over.

PLAN TEN
Relationships come first.

You want to create a more compatible relationship with your elder *as a person.* Sometimes we get so bogged down in troubleshooting particular situations or solving specific problems that we forget that it's the family relationship that brought us there in the first place. Taking the time to reinforce the personal bond between you and your elder can ease the conflict more than hard "answers."

Talk about what's going on in *your* world—career, world events, and grandchildren. This is the perfect time to say, "It's great knowing I have you to talk with." Smiles and hugs pay big dividends.

PLAN ELEVEN
Agree to disagree.

For months, you've been initiating conversations with Dad, trying to cajole him into moving into an assisted-living facility. Finally, he's had enough, and flat-out refuses to even discuss it with you anymore. From this point on, you have to accept—at least for the immediate time—that you are powerless. All you can do is hope for the best, and then deal with any unfortunate consequences if and when they present themselves.

Self-Talk: Finding Peace of Mind

Caregiving transforms us. In the beginning, we believe that somehow we should be able to figure it out and handle it all because, after all, our elders took care of *us,* and surely we can do the same for them. It's the least we can do, we think. So when Mom asks us to pick up some milk, or Uncle Jim needs help balancing his checkbook, or Charlie needs a ride to the doctor, we're there to pitch in and be helpful.

But then things change and get more complicated—Mom falls and breaks her hip, Aunt Sally is diagnosed with Alzheimer's, Dad sits home alone night after night, your brother refuses to watch Mom for the weekend, your spouse keeps asking when you're coming home, and there's no relief in sight. From sunup to sundown, you feel guilty most of the time, you're more tired than you ever thought possible, and you constantly worry—am I doing the right things? Am I doing enough? Am I a loving person? Do they appreciate what I'm doing for them? And slowly, it painfully starts to sink in that your life is no longer your own.

Caregiving is the toughest job you'll ever have, and the most rewarding. But you must be willing to do what it takes—including asking for what you want—to maintain the quality of your own life. Each of us has the power to do this, and it starts by paying close attention to our internal thoughts.

We are all natural born self-talkers. As children we talked to ourselves instinctively, and we can use the very same process of self-talk to reap real benefits. This section of *The Planner* will help you take advantage of this powerful tool to solve problems and organize behavior. It's time to regain your self-respect, and get back into life where you belong.

SELF-TALK: FINDING PEACE OF MIND

- You can't "fix" old age.
- Talking to yourself is good for you.
- Elder caregiving is the single most guilt-producing responsibility in our lives.

Most people are just not comfortable talking about old age. Who, then, can we caregivers talk to?

OBJECTIVES

After completing Self-Talk: Finding Piece of Mind, you will be able to:

Establish self-respect.

Reevaluate your own priorities.

Untangle the tight grip of caregiver guilt.

Speak your mind with siblings.

 PLAN ONE
Start by telling yourself the truth.

Caregiving is hard work. Caregiving is unfair; usually one person gets stuck doing everything while others disappear when they are needed. Caregiving is exhausting, feelings of anger, love, sadness, helplessness, and guilt can overwhelm you in a matter of seconds. And caregiving is painful—we know how this story ends.

We are not born caregivers. Many of us who have taken on this role (or inherited it) have never been down this road before. Every elder is unique, and each situation is entirely new. We don't know what we are doing much of the time and from one day to the next. We don't know what eldercare crisis lurks around the next corner, or when it will strike. This is how the real world of eldercare operates.

Along the way, the process of caring for elderly people may bring us in contact with other caregivers. Together we share tales that are funny, sad, heartbreaking, warm, full of anxiety or sometimes even fear. Everybody has a story to tell about what it's like for them to ride the emotional roller coaster that eldercare always brings.

You may notice a subtle difference, at first. Some caregivers seem to do quite well, effectively integrating eldercare responsibilities into their lives, while still managing to have a life of their own. Others tell you they feel trapped and are barely able to make it through another day. What can account for such varying experiences? How can one be doing so well, when another is not? The answer lies mostly in their attitudes about what is happening.

Effective caregivers (those who are not compromising the quality of their own lives in the process) share similar values. Here are some examples of their self-talk:

The only person I have control over is me;
I deserve respect;
I will let others know when I'm angry;
I have limits and I will let others help;
I don't have all the answers;
I have the right to change my mind;
I am grown-up, and I have choices.

The caregivers that find their role most rewarding don't live in a fantasy world about what's happening around them. They see the situation for what it is, they see their elder for who he or she is. They assess their eldercare responsibilities from where they stand, not from how they wish it could be. They accept reality, roll with the punches, and handle it as best they can. They don't expect perfection. Their best is good enough.

Alzheimer's: Role Reversal

Your worst fear has come true. Your family member is diagnosed with Alzheimer's disease, and nursing home care is not an option. Out of necessity, you are now living under the same roof; you have the awesome responsibility of making decisions on his or her behalf—what to wear, when to take away the car keys, when to go to bed, when to bathe—*every* decision is yours. Watching a loved one develop a dependent lifestyle, and caring for that person at the same time, is the granddaddy of all family caregiving challenges. Perhaps the greatest emotional strain lies in accepting the fact that your elder's condition will never be better tomorrow than it is today. You may even have a hard time bringing yourself to say the word, "Alzheimer's."

Over time, this disease takes away an individual's capacity to think, remember, and reason. There is no known cure. Alzheimer's is an unpredictable disease, in terms of its duration, effects, and impact. As the disease progresses, the patient will need round-the-clock supervision. The ravages of the disease will ultimately require that you take charge over this person who, until recently, was in full control of his or her own life.

Choosing to take on this kind of responsibility requires major lifestyle changes on your part, including limited free time, reduced sleep, and having to create an injury-proof home environment. At the same time, friends and family may drop out of sight, and you may spend most of your time "going it alone."

Are you really up to this? If the answer is yes, you are choosing to join the ranks of thousands of family caregivers who wouldn't have it any other way. Your first step is to seek expert advice from the medical community. Find out what's new in the area of dementia. If you would like to join a support group but can't leave your elder alone, join millions of others any time of day or night on Internet chat groups. Get information and tips on:

Communication methods that "get through"

Recreational activities

Discovery of new drugs

Adult day care

Respite centers

Making the home a safe place

Support groups

Tracking systems and bracelets

Volunteer services

Resources for low-cost legal and financial advice

Skilled nursing facilities (in case you change your mind)

Your next move is to seek legal and financial advice. You will need to know how to gain legal authority to make decisions on your elder's behalf, and you will need to create long-term financial plans.

They just don't understand.

Friends tell you you've become completely consumed with Mom's care; the kids don't even ask when you're coming home anymore; your husband is angry about the time you're spending with your parents. They just don't get it—you love your elder and want to be there for him or her; but, do the other people in your life have a point? Caring for elderly family members doesn't *replace* other family responsibilities, it *adds* to them. Many caregivers allow themselves to become overextended, and helping elderly loved ones may be seriously damaging your other significant relationships.

Family members and friends may get jealous of the many things you do for your elder, and you notice that they're losing their patience with you. You are so close to the situation that you may not have the ability to view it objectively. Give your loved ones the benefit of the doubt. This simple exercise will help you see things from their perspective. If you find they're right, you might then decide to delegate more eldercare responsibilities to others, both inside and outside the family:

> With a pencil, divide a sheet of paper into three columns.
>
> Put the words Elder, Family, and Personal Interests each at the top of a column.
>
> Under the "Elder" heading, list the things you did with your elder last week. Number each item.
>
> Under "Family," list the things you did with them in the same week. Number each one.
>
> Under "Personal Interests," list the things you did for yourself in the same week, and number each one.
>
> At the bottom of the page, list the many ways your life has changed in the past six months.

Now take a look, and ask yourself:

> *What effect have these changes had on my family and friends?*
>
> *Is my life unbalanced?*
>
> *Are my family and friends being selfish, or are they concerned about me?*

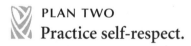

PLAN TWO
Practice self-respect.

At times ornery, rude, and mean, elders can lash out at you with the nastiest one-liners. The triggers for their abusive behavior may have a physical, chemical, or psychological origin. Depression and grief, for example, may be masked by expressions of hostility, impatience, or aggression. A medical examination may reveal a condition that can be treated, even in cases of dementia.

Ask yourself these questions. If the answer to any of them is yes, call the doctor. Be prepared to give a full description of what is happening:

> *Is my elder in physical discomfort or pain?*
>
> *Is my elder forgetful?*
>
> *Has my elder fallen recently?*

Has a close friend or relative died recently?

Is my elder abusing drugs or alcohol?

Is my elder eating properly?

Is my elder having trouble seeing or hearing?

Is my elder mismanaging or reacting to medications? (including over-the-counter drugs)

Take solace in the fact that you are trying to be a caring person. When you are the object of rude and insensitive treatment, understand that your elder may be displacing anger or frustration at the realization of his or her own mortality, or feelings of uselessness to the family or society. Making demands, voicing criticism, or being domineering are other ways that parents try to keep roles from changing and prevent their children taking control over their lives. To prevent further family pain, professional intervention with a trained specialist may be in order.

Self-respecting caregivers get angry.

Caregiving and anger go hand in hand, and the root of anger in the eldercare process comes from a variety of sources:

Unresolved family conflicts

Elders' irritating habits and personality traits

Differences in opinion about what is needed

Feelings of helplessness

Postponing personal agendas

Degrees of difficulty in caregiving

Threats, criticism, guilt-provoking statements, and accusations—elders sometimes employ these actions, and there are limits to what you should tolerate. When we admit to ourselves that we are angry, and acknowledge the right to be angry, we don't compromise our self-worth. If you've decided that you're not going to accept abusive treatment any longer, there are specific steps to take.

Self-respecting caregivers express their anger.

We teach others how we want them to treat us. Suffering in silence after someone says something that makes you angry implies your consent. We cannot change the basic personalities of people, but we must try to stop this behavior toward us. Don't let *any* inappropriate comments slip by; respond to them *all*. Here are a few suggestions:

What you just did (said) made me angry. I do not deserve that.

It makes me angry when you . . . Please stop it.

I feel that my bedroom is private, and it makes me angry when you walk in without knocking first.

I'm angry that you didn't keep your commitment. I rearranged my schedule.

We're all adults now, and your criticism is not appropriate. It would be so much nicer to talk free of that, wouldn't it?

Self-respecting caregivers set boundaries.

Abusers pick on certain people because they are easy targets. Don't make yourself available. There is no disgrace in walking out of a situation that is intolerable or beyond your power to handle; in fact, it is the smart thing to do when you recognize your own limitations. And as you walk out the door, say to yourself, "I've gotten through this before—I will do it again."

Before you enter into a conversation, make a decision ahead of time on what you can and cannot realistically do. Set limits. Screen your calls, and let the answering machine pick up every once in a while. Stick to your plans. Limit your contact. Stay at a hotel rather than at your elder's place. Make visits short. You are not obligated to tell your elder everything you do. If you need time away, tell him or her you're not feeling very well and cannot come over today.

Self-respecting caregivers say "No."

Erroneous self-talk: *If I say yes, they'll love me more.* Truth is, when someone close to us loves us, love doesn't stop because we've said no. People around you will always make requests. They certainly have the right to ask, and you have the right to refuse when the request is inconvenient or unreasonable. You owe it to yourself (eventually you'll believe this), and saying "no" will help you set priorities. Sure, you might feel guilty afterwards; but don't let that stop you. Practice the scenario, and think about your alternatives. Here are some nice ways to say no:

No; *but I could do this . . .* (then say what you will do)

Yes, I'll help; *but here's how (when) I'll help . . .* (describe your terms)

Yes, I can, *however . . .* (describe your terms)

Yes; but all I can spare is an hour of my time. I hope you understand.

No, I can't help now; *but I can do it another time.* (give alternate)

I'm sorry. *I already have plans. If only I had known.*

I'm sorry I can't help; *but let me suggest . . .* (name another person)

Mom, it would help me a lot if you would ask (sibling) to take you shopping.

Self-respecting caregivers allow others to be angry.

As caregivers, we must be prepared for the fact that people around us will get mad at things we do and say. Allow them the opportunity to express their anger. Don't defend. Don't interrupt; let them vent their anger; but don't take it as a personal attack on your own self-worth. Your degree and manner of care may not be perfect, but it is good enough.

During times like these, you might ask your elder's forgiveness. Asking for forgiveness is not an admission of guilt. Here are some words that may be helpful to say:

I'm very sorry I disappointed you.
I know you're upset, and I'm sorry.
I know you're upset. Let's talk things over.

Self-respecting caregivers provide themselves with outlets.

Telephone calls to friends, support groups, keeping a journal, writing angry letters (but not mailing them), physical activity, exercise, respite care, therapy sessions: these are some of the techniques that caregivers can draw upon to express their emotions honestly, without fear of retaliation.

 PLAN THREE
Loosen the grip of caregiver guilt.

I know how busy you are at work; don't bother about me. This calculated comment is an example of a manipulative technique that elders may use when they are scared, lonely, depressed, in pain, or angry, and it can send the rest of the family into an instant frenzy of guilt, hurt, blame, and resentment. Erroneous self-talk: *I'm worthless; I don't do enough.*

If I had taken Mom to the doctor sooner, she wouldn't be so sick now. Total care is unrealistic and unattainable, and when situations fall short of our expectations, we see ourselves as failures. Erroneous self-talk: *I'm not good enough.*

I'm being torn apart. When you're at the gym, you're not with your children. When you're with your friends, you're not with your elder. When you're with your elder, you're not with your spouse. When you're on vacation, you're not visiting your elder. Erroneous self-talk: *I'm bad.*

Guilt is the constant companion. No matter what you do, no matter how much you give, no matter what happens, no matter how much you know, no matter where you are—the guilt is still there. And it's painful. But when you're in pain, you don't just sit there, do you? No, you do something about it. Make a conscious choice to manage the stirring guilt and its negative impact on the quality of life by heeding these suggestions:

Praise yourself.

Erroneous self-talk: *I'm a real jerk for getting mad at Aunt Mary.* When we make a statement like this, we are overidentifying with our perceived shortcomings. Over time, self-attack will wear you down. Step back and ask yourself, "Am I feeling bad about something I *did,* or about *myself?*" Focus on what you *did,* rather than who you *are,* and give yourself full recognition for all that you do for others.

Eliminate "musts," "shoulds," "ought tos," and "have tos."

Erroneous self-talk: *I should be doing more; after all, Mom took care of me.* Take a hard look at everything you've done so far to make this person or situation change. Has spending more time, energy, or money made a difference? Has anything worked? Perhaps it has, but you're still feeling tormented by your perception that it's not enough. Many caregivers attach a lot of fantasies to wishing things were different.

Nothing you do will ever be enough in this situation. Under this layer of guilt is grief. We cannot hide from the fact that we will soon live in a world without a loved one—that is the ultimate reality, and we are powerless to avoid this end. Staying "in the moment"—focusing on maximizing the quality of the time spent together—may be the best you can realistically strive for.

Feel regretful, rather than guilty.

Erroneous self-talk: *I feel so bad about not visiting Mom.* When you feel guilty for things you *aren't* doing, shift the focus from feeling bad to taking action. Ask yourself, "Am I doing the best that I can right now?" If the answer is no, take one small step toward doing something.

Don't take the bait.

An effective response to someone using manipulative behavior is "Are you trying to make me feel guilty?"

Restate your objective.

Self-talk: Do I *have* to do this, or am I *choosing* to do this? There may be several ways to address a situation. Free yourself to explore all the alternatives.

Acknowledge hurt feelings.

In the process of caregiving, we are bound to make somebody mad at us for something. It goes with the territory. Guilt is our conscience's way of letting us know we should make amends after we do something hurtful. Accept responsibility for misdeeds, and say you're sorry.

Learn from your mistakes.

We cannot always undo any harm we may have caused; but we can vow to treat others more thoughtfully in the future. Learn to forgive yourself again and again and again.

In the future

Watch what you say.

Resist the temptation to make open-ended promises. Some caregivers believe that making promises to their elders is a loving, thoughtful thing to do; but this is usually self-destructive in the long run. For example, imagine how guilty you might feel if you promised to visit your aunt every weekend, but last-minute job assignments render your scheduled visits impossible. Or perhaps, Mom once asked you to promise never to put her in a nursing home, yet today, institutionalized care happens to be the very best alternative for her well-being. Too many promises serve as a quick fix to uncomfortable feelings, but can raise our guilt sky-high later on.

To avoid generating this kind of guilt, offer commitments rather than promises. When you speak in terms of commitments, you're giving assurances that you'll be there for the long haul. Here are some words to say when promises cannot, and should not, be offered:

When the time comes, I hope I will be able to do what you wish.
I will always be here to talk with you about solutions to problems.
You're not alone, I'm here for you.
I'll always care about you, and together we'll figure this out.

Prepare and anticipate.

Clear your conscience ahead of time. Do your homework, research options, talk things over, and you'll rest comfortably knowing your decisions were based on the best information available to you at the time.

 PLAN FOUR
Put up a good fight—don't let siblings off the hook.

One unfortunate truth about caregiving is that the responsibilities within the family are often unevenly and unfairly distributed. The amount of assistance we receive from siblings is largely dependent on our willingness and ability to *demand* it. Ask for help from time to time, but move on to something more productive if other family members refuse. Keep this thought in the back of your mind: When you put your head down on your pillow each night knowing that you have done all you can, the rest will fall into place.

Why siblings don't do their share of eldercare is a more complicated issue than you may think. Everyone contributes to the problem:

The Parent . . .

wants only *this* child to care for him or her.

lets sons off the hook and instructs daughters that it's their "duty."

drives wedges between children and plays favorites.

The Caregiver . . .

doesn't ask for help, rather he or she hints or complains.

isn't willing to share the parent's attention with other family members.

wants to prove that he or she is the *good, always-giving* child.

feels he or she can do the best job.

thinks it takes too much time to explain what is needed.

accepts without question that caregiving is "woman's work."

doesn't have any energy left to argue.

The Sibling . . .

denies what's happening and may choose to ignore the situation.

lives far away.

has his or her own major problems and is incapable of being helpful at this time.

wants to get back at you for any number of reasons.

is focused on after-death issues, including inheritance.

Here are a variety of tips to encourage siblings to pitch in. Try several, or just one, but just do it:

Speak up.

Are you *assuming* your siblings know what's going on and *why* you need their help? They may have no idea or understanding of the gravity of a particular situation. Be specific and share details.

Don't complain; request.

Discuss schedules. Set limits on the time and effort you can put in. Give specific assignments. Instead of, "You never help out . . ." say, "I know you have a lot going on at work and it's hard for you, it's hard for me too, and I need help with . . ." (bill paying, grocery shopping, cooking) or "Which one works better with your schedule? Mom needs a ride to the doctor and needs help grocery shopping."

Fill the distance gap.

Be specific with siblings who live far away. Chances are they don't know how to help. Ask them to: call your parents on a regular basis, do research on options and services, send you money as a way of being helpful, have parents visit *them.*

Consult your siblings.

When important decisions need to be made, don't accept "You do what's best" as an answer. The decision-making burden is not entirely yours. Ask for specific involvement on your siblings' part. Instead of saying, "What should we do?" try, "Do you think we should hire a home care nurse or look into an assisted-living facility?"

Call their bluff.

When siblings criticize, don't argue or defend your position about how you're handling your elder's affairs. When they say, "You should take Mom to the doctor more often," agree with them (that lets the air out of their argument) and say, "You may be right, and much better at this than me. Why don't you take over this responsibility?" If the bullying persists, bring in a heavyweight. Ask a geriatric case manager or lawyer to join in the next family discussion.

Stay flexible.

There is more than one single or simple answer to every eldercare problem. People are unique, and bring to the caregiving situation different life experiences, values, abilities, preferences, relationships, and needs. When your siblings do things differently from you, let them do it their way. Give some of their suggestions a try, and let them know when things work for the better.

Stay on them.

When siblings drop the ball, get on the phone immediately and say, "Three weeks ago we agreed that you would help Dad with his laundry, and you have not done so. What will help you keep this commitment?"

Refuse to be anyone's "middleman."

Train parents and siblings to talk with each other directly. You are not a messenger. When parents want another child to call, they may say *to you,* "I haven't heard from Linda. Is she all right?" Or, a sibling may ask you, "How's Dad feeling?" Take yourself out of the middle by saying, "I really can't answer for Dad, it's best if you ask him yourself. Why don't you give him a call?" At the same time, remember that you're not in charge of their relationships. Avoid telling siblings how to act and what to do by saying something like, "Don't upset Mom by talking about moving."

Cut loose.

Don't allow yourself to be drawn back into childhood stereotypes. Be the responsible adult you are in all of your other relationships. When fighting erupts, focus on issues and not people. Don't react when someone else brings up ancient family history; it's not worth your energy. Stop apologizing for having a different opinion.

Let your parents do the talking.

Next time Mom asks you to drive her somewhere, tell her you'd love to but you already have plans with your family. Suggest that she asks (name other sibling) to drive her. Don't make the call for her, let her do it herself. Siblings may have a tougher time rejecting a parent's direct request for help.

Low-Cost and Free Resources

Good communication *can* be learned, and there is an abundance of information available. Consult **communication books** and seek **professional counseling. Assertiveness training programs** can also be helpful.

Contact your local chapters of **Alcoholics Anonymous** and **Al-Anon** to learn more about how to communicate with elders who have drug and drinking problems.

Locate the **Alzheimer's Association** local chapter to find out about support groups and to learn about recent advances in drug therapy and the communication process.

Internet keyword search: communication skills, assertiveness training, psychology, intervention.

ORGANIZATIONS

Alzheimer's Disease Education & Referral Center (ADEAR Center)
P.O. Box 8250
Silver Spring, MD 20907-8250
Website: *www.alzheimers.org*

The American Association for Geriatric Psychiatry
7910 Woodmont Avenue, Suite 1050
Bethesda, MD 20814-3004
(301) 654-7850, Fax: (301) 654-4137
Website: *www.aagpgpa.org*

The American Parkinson Disease Association, Inc.
1250 Hylan Boulevard, Suite 4B
Staten Island, NY 10305-1946
(800) 223-2732, (718) 981-8001, Fax: (718) 981-4399
Website: *www.apdaparkinson.com*

The Anger Clinic
111 N. Wabash, Suite 1702
Chicago, IL 60602
(312) 263-0035
Mitch H. Messer, Director

Well Spouse Foundation
(Help for those who are caring for spouses)
30 East 40th Street, PH
New York, NY 10018
(800) 838-0879, (212) 685-8815, Fax: (212) 685-8676
Website: *www.wellspouse.org*

Action Checklist

TAKE A DEEP BREATH, AND JUMP IN	To Do By	Completed
Do a mental review of your elder's personal issues of loss	_____	❏
Review your elder's current abilities	_____	❏
Preserve your elder's autonomy. Keep these in mind		
basic personality traits	_____	❏
family history	_____	❏
Stay open-minded to this person's particular needs	_____	❏
Establish trust every time		
listen	_____	❏
ask questions	_____	❏

Get professional assessment if your elder is
    consistently forgetful _____ ❏

Do your homework before opening up the dialogue
    resources _____ ❏
    community services _____ ❏
    related costs _____ ❏
    family resources _____ ❏

Review opposing understanding of responsibilities
    between parents and children _____ ❏

Focus conversation style on
    keeping elders involved in own decisions _____ ❏
    creating interdependence

Try a variety of techniques to open up the dialogue
    seize the moment _____ ❏
    plant the seed _____ ❏
    ask for advice _____ ❏
    ask for information _____ ❏

Take advantage of the natural parent-child bond
    ask for help _____ ❏
    ask a favor _____ ❏

Implement surefire talking tips
    arrange best place and time _____ ❏
    speak in terms of questions _____ ❏
    give your full attention _____ ❏
    ask specific questions _____ ❏
    offer limited assistance _____ ❏
    communicate caring _____ ❏

TURNING CONFLICT INTO COOPERATION

Review underlying issues when conflict occurs
    lack of trust _____ ❏
    restore power _____ ❏
    stall tactic _____ ❏
    attention-getting device _____ ❏

Review the Take a Deep Breath, and Jump In
    section of this chapter _____ ❏

Steer conversations back on track
    take elders off the hot seat _____ ❏
    appreciate time zones _____ ❏
    make a deal _____ ❏
    be prepared to negotiate _____ ❏
    suggest trial runs _____ ❏
    offer power of choice _____ ❏

Inch them closer to your goal _____ ❏

Use validation techniques to reduce anxiety _____ ❏

Find others who have more influence _____ ❏

Step back if there's a fight _____ ❏

Reestablish the relationship _____ ❏

Take care of yourself if nothing works _____ ❏

SELF-TALK: FINDING PEACE OF MIND

Stay close to reality _____ ❏

Formulate healthy caregiver attitudes _____ ❏

Know what you're getting into when your elder has dementia _____ ❏

Surround yourself with expert advice _____ ❏
    communication methods _____ ❏
    recreational activities _____ ❏
    new drugs _____ ❏
    adult day care _____ ❏
    respite centers _____ ❏
    home safety _____ ❏
    Internet chat groups _____ ❏
    support groups _____ ❏
    emergency systems and bracelets _____ ❏
    volunteer services _____ ❏
    legal and financial advice _____ ❏
    skilled nursing facilities _____ ❏

*Do a check on relationships outside of the one
   you have with your elder*   _____ ❏

*If your elder is abusive, physically or mentally,
   consider a medical assessment*   _____ ❏

Practice self-respect
   allow anger   _____ ❏
   express anger   _____ ❏
   set boundaries   _____ ❏
   say "No"   _____ ❏
   allow others to be angry   _____ ❏
   create safety outlets   _____ ❏

Manage guilt
   praise yourself   _____ ❏
   limit "should" "could" or "must" words   _____ ❏
   feel regret, not guilt   _____ ❏
   don't take the bait   _____ ❏
   restate your objective   _____ ❏
   acknowledge hurt feelings   _____ ❏
   learn from your mistakes   _____ ❏

Prevent guilt from happening
   watch what you say   _____ ❏
   prepare and anticipate   _____ ❏

Review reasons why siblings aren't helping you   _____ ❏

Don't let siblings off the hook
   speak up   _____ ❏
   replace complaining with requesting   _____ ❏
   fill the distance gap   _____ ❏
   call their bluff   _____ ❏
   stay flexible   _____ ❏
   stay on them   _____ ❏
   refuse to be anyone's "middleman"   _____ ❏
   cut loose   _____ ❏
   let your parent do the talking   _____ ❏

· 4 ·

EMERGENCY PREPAREDNESS

Quick and Easy Access

Planning for quality care does little good if you don't have 24-hour accessibility to your elderly loved ones or haven't made provisions to access their personal property when an unexpected situation creates the need.

Imagine how you would react if you were unable to reach your elder because you didn't have the key to his or her home. Worse yet, what if you meant to give a set of house keys to your elder's neighbor but you never got around to it and then a neighbor heard your elder's cries for help and could do nothing? Have you given any thought to who would call an ambulance if you're unreachable and an eldercare emergency arises?

Family emergencies also have a way of uncovering the absence of legal and important documents and surfacing yet another round of extremely stressful situations for family members. For example, if your elder is hospitalized and his/her household bills are stacking up, you might find yourself paying these debts with your own money because you don't have power of attorney to access his or her checking account. With proper planning, this unfortunate situation is avoidable.

Inaccessibility unnecessarily complicates the caregiving process. This section of *The Planner* will show you the simple steps you can take right now to ensure accessability to those who count on you for care. The process of duplicating keys, creating check-in systems, preparing legal documents, arranging for bookkeeping access, and obtaining emergency telephone numbers are a few of the ways you can be prepared to respond to any unforeseen situation.

QUICK AND EASY ACCESS

- In an emergency, minutes count, and getting help could make the difference between life and death.
- The best way to deal with an emergency is to be prepared.

One of the greatest fears of the elderly is one of being alone and hurt when no one else knows.

OBJECTIVES

*After completing **Quick and Easy Access**, you will be able to:*

Assist elderly family members 24 hours a day, 7 days a week.

Create access to your elder and your elder's property in an emergency.

Have peace of mind knowing someone is always close at hand.

PLAN ONE
Keep important telephone numbers handy.

Obtain the information and telephone numbers listed in the Elder Emergency Information Chart on page xiii. If your time is limited right now, photocopy your elder's personal address book, and get back to the chart when you can. Make copies of this emergency information for your elder, your own family, other family members, and a nearby neighbor.

Keep a copy of the emergency information at home and at work. Post the list near the telephone or on the refrigerator at your home and your elder's home. Keep a copy in your wallet or purse. Update names and phone numbers as needed.

Obtain a copy of your elder's community telephone directories—the White Pages and the Yellow Pages. If your elder lives outside of your 911 emergency district, you must call the police or fire department directly. Look up these numbers ahead of time and write them down.

PLAN TWO
Gain 24-hour access to your elder and elder's property.

Duplicate keys, plastic access cards, electronic openers, and combinations. Label keys and selectively distribute them to family, friends, and neighbors. Maintain 24-hour access to keys and to those having access. Distribute keys in person if possible. If your family member has voice mail on the telephone and e-mail on the computer, learn the access codes in order to retrieve messages.

To draw money from your elder's checking and savings account, most banks require power of attorney prearranged on *their* forms. Another strategy is to set up a second signature on designated accounts. To make either one of these financial arrangements, accompany your elder to the bank and fill out the appropriate forms.

To locate key duplicating services, see the Yellow Pages under Locks and Locksmiths. Duplicate keys for . . .

Residence	Storage
Garage	Bicycle
Gate	Other vehicles
Auto	RV
Boat	Trailer
Office	Mailbox
Desk	Personal/business safe
Trunk	Luggage
Alarm	Locks

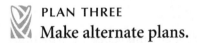

PLAN THREE
Make alternate plans.

If your relative chooses to keep total control of his or her property and money, ask him or her to disclose the names and telephone numbers of those who have access to property and legal documents. Write down this information so you will know whom to call in an emergency.

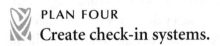

PLAN FOUR
Create check-in systems.

Ideally, your elder will be able to use the telephone to call for help when an emergency occurs. However, this is often not the case. Make a plan for someone to be in contact with your aging family members on a regular basis—by phone, in person, through beepers and e-mail. Create a network of people who agree to stay in touch with your elder. See the *Safe and Secure* chapter of this planner, page 174 for a variety of check-in options.

PLAN FIVE
Consider the protection of a medical alert system.

Identification of hidden medical conditions saves lives in an emergency. Simple options like printed, wallet-sized cards and identification bracelets and necklaces are adequate. Call the agency on aging and the hospital discharge planner for recommendations. Hidden medical conditions include . . .

Diabetes	Hypertension
Asthma	Pacemaker
Emphysema	Angina
Epilepsy	Alzheimer's
Glaucoma	Coronary bypass
Implants	Allergies
Drug usage	Hemodialysis
Cataracts	Organ donor
Hyperthermia	Osteoporosis
Hypoglycemia	Hepatitis
Hemophilia	Osteoarthritis
Contact lenses	Heart disease

PLAN SIX
Keep vital information accessible.

Store information in one safe, accessible place—at home or at work. Update as needed:

Emergency telephone numbers	Durable power of attorney for health care
Blood type	Durable power of attorney
Medical history	Driver's license
Medications	Allergies
Social Security number	Proof of insurance

Managing Medications

Over-the-counter drugs and prescription drugs are both serious medicines. Elderly family members also may be under the care of several different doctors at the same time, each doctor possibly prescribing different medications. Every year close to 125,000 people die from taking the wrong medicine, a wrong dosage, or taking the drugs improperly.

If your elder is taking any medication, this is one caregiving issue that cannot be ignored. This section of *The Planner* offers specific guidelines on becoming familiar with your elder's drug usage, and action plans that prevent deadly medication mishaps.

Self-medication with over-the-counter drugs also has emerged as an important component to health maintenance for older adults, allowing them to take greater control over their own health care. Encourage aging family members to become educated consumers. Reading labels, following directions, asking questions, and taking proper amounts of the drug are essential elements of managing medications responsibly.

MANAGING MEDICATIONS

- A Federal Drug Administration report found people 70 years and older fill an average of thirteen prescriptions per year. Some of these people may fill as many as fourteen to eighteen different prescriptions in a one-year period.
- Studies have indicated that patients in nursing homes have been known to take as many as thirty medications.

If your elderly family members are taking medications, your involvement in fact-finding and safety precautions could very well prevent serious mishaps, including death.

OBJECTIVES

*After completing **Managing Medications,** you will be able to:*
Know what purpose each prescription serves.
Establish a doctor/elder/pharmacist relationship.
Uncover the possibility of mismanagement of drugs.
Assist your elder in managing his or her medications responsibly.

 PLAN ONE
Investigate which drugs your elder is taking and why.

Get involved. It is imperative that your relative's health care providers are aware that others are monitoring his or her medical procedures and prescriptions. Intervention saves lives. If your family member cannot or does not want to answer questions regarding medications to your satisfaction, it is time to step in.

Ask your elder

What medicine(s) are you taking?

What is the medicine supposed to do?

Do some fact-finding, and ask your elder and your elder's physician to review alternative methods of treating your relative's condition without the use of drugs—weight loss, special diet, exercise, massage therapy, bed rest, and ice packs, for example. If you suspect that the physician's prescription policy automatically includes drugs as a way to cope with life's expected conditions, such as bereavement, ask your elder if he or she would consider switching doctors.

 PLAN TWO
Is your elder overmedicated? Find out.

Elderly patients who are attended to by several doctors may neglect telling each one about the drugs being prescribed by the others. To lower potentially dangerous levels of drug usage and to prevent deadly drug combinations, remind your elder to inform each prescriber of all routinely used medications, including over-the-counter drugs and vitamins.

Brown-bag it. Gather your elder's prescription drugs, over-the-counter medications, and other supplements including eye drops, cough syrup, pain relievers, cold pills, vitamins, and herbs and put them in a paper bag. Take them to your elder's next medical exam or show the medications to the pharmacist, and ask for a review.

Have your elder's prescriptions filled at only one pharmacy. The pharmacist will keep track of drug usage by computer and can easily track the possibility of overmedication and dangerous drug combinations.

Create a drug-usage chart (see below) to bring to every appointment. Record current drug and over-the-counter drug usage information. Complete new prescription information in the doctor's office. **NOTE:** If you think this is too much trouble, be assured that interaction saves lives. Any physician or assistant who avoids answering questions or gives family members little time to ask questions should be viewed with suspicion.

DRUG USAGE CHART

Drug name _____

Drug purpose _____

Drug color and shape _____

Amount to take _____

When to take _____

How to take_____

How long to take _____

Possible side effects _____

 PLAN THREE
Learn why elders may not follow prescription directions.

Elders sometimes discontinue, resume, or change medications without the physician's consent which can be quite harmful.

The reasons include
- The drugs make them feel worse than the symptoms of the illness.
- There appears to be no clear evidence that the drug is working.
- Medications are too expensive.
- They would rather spend their money on something else.
- They feel better and don't believe they need to continue the medication.
- Taking drugs gives them a feeling of loss of independence.
- Drugs are a constant reminder of "being sick."
- Short-term memory loss makes it hard to track drug usage.

 PLAN FOUR
Get the most from the pharmacist.

A certified pharmacist, registered with the state pharmaceutical board, is highly trained to answer questions about drugs.

Ask the pharmacist
- any questions regarding drugs
- if generic drugs are available
- for written information about the medicine
- to keep a file on your elder's drug usage and medical history
- for easy-open containers as long as there are no children present
- about senior citizen discounts

- for large-print labels
- about 24-hour telephone and emergency services
- about prescription home-delivery services
- about year-end tax and insurance statements

 PLAN FIVE
Explore the possibility that your elder's medication combination could create deadly side effects.

Make sure that your elder knows the answers to these important questions:

- *What medicines am I taking?*
- *What will the medicine do for me?*
- *How should I take it?*
- *When should I take it?*
- *How will I know the medicine is working?*
- *How long will it take the medicine to work?*
- *How long must I take this drug?*
- *What are the expected side effects?*
- *Can I relieve these side effects?*
- *Is it safe to drink alcohol?*
- *What foods should be avoided?*
- *Will mixing medications be harmful?*
- *Is it okay to crush pills or even dissolve them in water?*
- *Will smoking, coffee, or caffeine beverages cause reactions?*
- *What activities (driving, operating machinery) should be avoided?*
- *Is exposure of the medication to sunlight harmful?*
- *What is the shelf life of the drug?*
- *How should the drug be stored?*
- *Can I switch to generic drugs?*
- *Are there sexual side effects when taking this drug?*
- *Can the medicine cause an allergic reaction?*
- *What should I do if forget to take the medicine?*
- *What will happen if I do not take the medicine?*

PLAN SIX
Implement ongoing drug safety precautions.

Discuss and implement the following options:

- If forgetfulness is a problem for your elder, create a chart. List the days of the week, the name of each medication, and the times to take each drug. Then cross out the drug each time it is taken.
- If your relative plans on using a plastic pillbox (found at most drugstores), keep the original prescription container handy. Keep a sample of each drug in its original container. When traveling, pack the original drug container as well.
- Make sure the prescription labels are clear and in large-print. Keep a magnifying glass near prescription containers. If your elder wears glasses, remind him or her to wear them when reading labels.
- Use pharmacist-provided colored containers for different drugs.
- When filling prescriptions, check the name of the drug on the label before leaving the pharmacy.
- Don't mix alcohol and drugs.
- Consult the doctor before taking over-the-counter drugs or health food store supplements.
- Ask party hosts if the food or beverages they are serving contain alcohol.
- Store drugs as directed. Refrigerate the drug only if told to do so.
- Know the expected side effects of the drugs.
- Never share drugs. Never.
- Keep pills far from the elder's bed. This reduces the possibility of his or her taking the wrong dose or wrong combination when sleepy. Do not take drugs in the dark.
- Read labels in properly lit rooms.
- Discard medicines that have expired or have no labels.
- Ask the doctor or pharmacist if the drug is habit-forming.
- Ask the doctor to order a home visit from a nurse to teach the elder how to manage medications.
- Discuss the fact that rapid movement like standing up too quickly can cause unnecessary falls.
- Ask your elder to keep a list of drugs in use, prescription and over-the-counter, in his or her wallet or purse at all times.
- Keep a list of drugs in use on the refrigerator or by the telephone.
- Do business with just one reliable pharmacy.
- Keep each doctor informed of all prescriptions.

- Share your elder's written medication information with every family member.
- Check with the doctor before asking the pharmacist to substitute the prescription with generic drugs.
- Make use of identification bracelets for allergies and chronic conditions.
- Before purchasing over-the-counter drugs, examine the packages for signs of tampering. If the seal is broken or it looks like the box has been opened, get another package and give the other to the store manager.

If Your Elder Is Hospitalized

Every hospital and medical center has a culture all its own. Family caregivers who have little experience in dealing with health care professionals in these specialized environments too often don't know what to expect, what to do, or what questions to ask. From the moment you arrive at the hospital, feelings of confusion and fear are normal, especially if your relative is taken there unexpectedly.

No matter the circumstance, this section of *The Planner* provides immediate action plans to help you gain control over an eldercare emergency situation. Hospitalization is a traumatic experience for the entire family. Surviving this stressful situation requires asking specific questions and making informed decisions based on facts, not emotions. Veteran caregivers will tell you that a crash course on planning, organizing, and communication skills is in order. The good news is, you're holding the manual in your hands.

IF YOUR ELDER IS HOSPITALIZED

- Asking specific questions and making decisions based on facts, not overwhelming emotions, is the key to managing your elder's hospitalization.
- The law gives patients the right to refuse care or treatment at any time.
- A reality of health care today is that people are whisked in and out of the hospital in record time. A typical stay is under one week.

It is possible to take a proactive stance if your family member is admitted to the hospital, and to be prepared for hasty hospital discharges.

OBJECTIVES

After completing **If Your Elder is Hospitalized**, *you will be able to:*
Ask meaningful questions during times of confusion.
Gather important health care information and legal documents.
Make your elder's hospital stay as comfortable as possible.
Research home and institutional health care options.
Plan ahead for your relative's needs after his or her hospitalization.

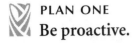

PLAN ONE
Be proactive.

Create an eldercare file on your relative. Include a legal pad in this file to write down questions, answers, phone numbers, and lists of things to do. Put dates on your notes. Save all documentation, reports, lab tests, bills, notes, and other documents related to your family member's hospitalization. Save receipts on money you spend for possible reimbursement from your elder, the insurance company, other family members, settlements, or taxes.

Also, keep copies of your elder's proof of health insurance and the **living will, durable power of attorney,** and **durable power of attorney for health care** in this file. See the **Legal Matters** chapter of this planner starting on page 175 for more information on these documents.

Attach copies of the living will and the durable power of attorney for health care to your **elder's medical chart.**

If your family member is too ill to speak and has not left instructions in a living will regarding medical treatment, the law requires the hospital staff to administer every treatment it deems appropriate to keep the patient alive.

Keep your elder's file folder with you everywhere you go as long as he or she is hospitalized. You may need it at a moment's notice.

PLAN TWO
Take it one step at a time.

With so many questions and so many things to do, you may be overwhelmed to the point of doing nothing, or doing too much with little direction. Follow the action plans in this chapter in the order shown, and go at your own pace.

To begin, make a heading called **Elder Contacts** on the first page of your legal pad or write information down in the space provided here. List the names, addresses, and phone numbers (day and evening) of the individuals suggested in the lists below. Record this information as soon as you make contact with these people.

In case of an accident
police on duty
victims and witnesses
insurance agents
lawyer

Caregiver support
family/friends
neighbors
agency on aging
family service agency
home care agencies
geriatric case manager
assisted-living services

At the hospital
hospital name and address
hospital floor, room, and bed number
head nurse and staff
doctor(s)
specialists
social worker
discharge planner
patient representative
billing director

Home management
housekeeper
house sitter
pet sitter
handyman
home chore services

Post-hospital recovery
assisted-living facility
skilled nursing facility
home hospital equipment
adult day care
pharmacy

Personal
beauty salon or barber
clubs
associations
church
volunteer activities

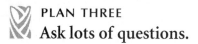 PLAN THREE
Ask lots of questions.

If your family member is unable to communicate and is in serious condition, and a living will or durable power of attorney for health care has been prepared in advance, now is the time to review the contents of those documents. If you are the designated agent who is responsible for deciding your relative's medical treatment, seek the advice of the family doctor, the hospital social worker, and a clergy person. With their help, you can gather the facts about your elder's condition. If health care directives have not been secured in advance, ask to be informed of your rights as a decision-making family member.

As you encounter medical personnel, jot down names, phone numbers, questions, and answers on your legal pad. Don't forget to date your notes.

Ask medical providers
Is my family member in any immediate danger?
What is the medical problem?
What are the short-term effects of this illness?
What are the long-term effects of this illness?
Will my family member stay in the hospital now? How long?
What medications have been prescribed?

If surgery is recommended, ask

What are the possible complications?

What are the short-term expectations?

What are the long-term expectations?

What happens if my elder does not have the surgery?

How often do you perform this procedure?

What is the success rate?

What is the rate of complications from this surgery?

Is surgery needed now or can it wait?

What are the other choices of treatment?

What are the short-term consequences if surgery is not performed?

What are the long-term consequences if surgery is not performed?

(If surgery is recommended, remind yourself of the option to get a second opinion.)

If your elder is to be released from the hospital, ask

Will my elder need home health care assistance? What kind?

Where will this help come from?

What is the expected recovery time?

If your elder is staying overnight in the hospital, ask him or her

Is there anyone specifically you would like me to contact?

Is there anything you would like me to bring you?

 PLAN FOUR
Be prepared for the enormous task of making telephone calls.

There will be many phone calls to make and many questions to answer. You will tell your elder's story over and over again. Friends and family members will want to know every detail. Be prepared to hear some of their own medical experiences—be patient; once they finish with their stories, you can get down to business. There also may be rumors and gossip you have to extinguish.

Don't promise to keep everyone informed of your elder's progress (except a select few). You will have enough to do. Instead, ask people to call you back. Well-meaning family and friends will ask you about telephoning and visiting your relative in the hospital. Give them clear instructions if you or your elder don't want to be disturbed, but don't be surprised if they call and visit anyway.

The task of making telephone calls is extremely overwhelming. It is very important that you delegate and share this responsibility with other reliable people. Don't underestimate the pressures of this task. Locate your elder's personal address book and appointment book. Make copies of both for the purpose of making calls. Calls to make:

Accident-related contacts
police
lawyer and insurance agents
witnesses

Cancel elder's activities at
place of employment
appointments and social commitments
classes and volunteer projects
travel plans (check if insured for cancellation)

Suspend
newspapers and mail pickup

Call
family, friends, and neighbors
banker, accountant, and tax adviser
church group and clergy person
landlord (if renting)
housekeeping services
house sitter and pet sitter

 PLAN FIVE
Take care of business.

Before you leave the hospital, take your elder's valuables (watch, jewelry, wallet, purse) home with you. Store them in a safe place. Review the following suggestions as a way to take care of family business in the meantime.

At your elder's home

- Retrieve messages from the telephone answering machine, voice mail, or e-mail.
- Follow up on important calls.
- Make a list of phone calls to make (See Plan Four).
- Locate your elder's personal address and appointment book and keep it with you, or make a copy of it.
- Find your elder's health insurance policy. Keep a copy of the insurance card with you.
- Go through the mail. Pay urgent bills.
- Keep track of money spent on eldercare for possible reimbursement.
- Notify creditors and let them know your elder is in the hospital.
- Make duplicate keys to the home, property, auto, and mailbox.
- Make bank deposits on your elder's behalf.
- Pack items to bring back with you to the hospital (See Plan Six).
- Go through the refrigerator and throw out spoiled foods. Take home the rest.
- Check and maintain the security of home and auto.

- Store valuables, jewelry, wallet, purse, credit cards, and driver's license in a safe place.
- Make living arrangements for your elder's spouse if necessary.
- If it's near tax time, locate the tax file or contact the accountant for an extension.
- Pack up medications and show them to the doctor at the hospital.
- Have mail picked up regularly or put on hold at the post office.
- Suspend newspapers that are home delivered.
- Have the lawn mowed or snow shoveled.

At your home
- Make phone calls (See Plan Four).
- Get cash and change for the telephone or carry your telephone calling card.
- Pack for overnight visits.
- Make home, work, and personal arrangements.

PLAN SIX
Make your elder's hospital stay as comfortable as possible.

Ask your elder what items you can bring back with you to the hospital. Suggest:

favorite pajamas/robe	hairbrush/comb
slippers	hand/body/face lotion
shaver and shaving lotion	lipstick/makeup
self-standing mirror	nail care kit
deodorant	personal address book
appointment book	handicraft project
laptop games/computer	books/magazines
transistor/walkman radio	hearing aid
glasses/glasses cleaner	crossword puzzles
paper/pen/stationery	stuffed animal
chewing gum/mints	snacks/food (if diet allows)
street clothes/shoes/socks	undergarments
toothbrush	

PLAN SEVEN
Plan ahead as your elder recuperates in the hospital.

You will need to make decisions regarding home or institutionalized health care *before* your elder is released from the hospital. Seek assistance from the hospital discharge planner about home and health care options early on. Hospitals release patients sooner than you think and you will want to start finding out about care options right away.

The law states that patients are free to leave the hospital upon release from their doctor. The hospital is not allowed to detain patients who have outstanding medical expenses and fees not covered by their health insurance carrier.

Ask the doctor
Will home nursing care be needed? Full-time? Part-time?
What other kind of care will be needed? Short-term? Long-term?
What lifestyle changes are expected?
What symptoms could indicate health complications?

Ask the hospital discharge planner
Whom can I call to get home health care assistance?
What are the options for living arrangements during recuperation?
What hospital and home care costs are covered by insurance?

Review elder's living arrangement options at
- your elder's home
- your family's home
- a friend's home
- a board and care facility
- an intermediate care facility
- a skilled nursing facility

Review home care options (See Caregivers chapter)
- visiting nurse
- family
- friends
- homemaker services
- social day care
- adult day health care
- volunteer

Review elder's needs (See Caregivers chapter)

- homemaker services
- personal care
- home health care
- quality of life

 PLAN EIGHT
Use the services of the hospital patient representative.

Patient representatives assist family members of patients with health care problems, concerns, and unmet needs that may have arisen during the hospital stay. Representatives serve as a liaison between patients and the hospital administration.

The patient representative

- evaluates the level of patient satisfaction.
- channels information about care problems to appropriate departments.
- directs inquiries and complaints to appropriate hospital staff.
- refers patients to services and resources.
- investigates patient care complaints.
- assesses responses to incidents.

Low-Cost and Free Resources

More than 5 million people each year receive **CPR (cardiopulmonary resuscitation) training.** The timely application of CPR has been credited with helping save thousands of lives each year in the United States. Persons interested in learning CPR should contact their local American Heart Association or American Red Cross. Check the Yellow Pages under *First Aid Instruction* or on the Internet, keyword search: CPR

Telecommunication Devices for the Deaf (TDD) and **Braille TDD's** are available for telephone customers with hearing and sight disabilities. Contact the special needs center of the telephone company.

Carrier Alert, also known as Postal Alert, is a volunteer program in which letter carriers monitor the possible need of emergency services by examining mail that has not been removed from mailboxes. For more information, contact the agency on aging or the post office.

Emergency preparedness information of all kinds is available by typing "emergency preparedness" in your Internet keyword search.

ORGANIZATIONS

American Heart Association
7272 Greenville Avenue
Dallas, TX 75231
(800) 242-8721
Website: *www.americanheart.org*

American Red Cross
Attn: Public Inquiry Office
1621 N. Kent Street, 11th Floor
Arlington, VA 22209
(703) 248-4222
Website: *www.redcross.org*

American Trauma Society
8903 Presidential Parkway, Suite 512
Upper Marlboro, MD 20772
(800) 556-7890, (301) 420-4189
Website: *www.amtrauma.org*

Council on Family Health
(Consumer information about the proper use of medicines, home safety, and personal health)
1155 Connecticut Avenue, NW, Suite 400
Washington, DC 20036
(202) 429-6600
Website: *www.cfhinfo.org*

Action Checklist

QUICK AND EASY ACCESS	To Do By	Completed
Set elder access goals		
short-term	_____	❑
long-term	_____	❑

Know the 24-hour emergency phone numbers
    doctor(s) _____ ❏
    dentist _____ ❏
    neighbors _____ ❏
    friends _____ ❏
    police _____ ❏
    fire department _____ ❏
    hospital _____ ❏
    hospice _____ ❏
    nurse _____ ❏
    home aide _____ ❏
    pharmacist _____ ❏
    electrician _____ ❏
    plumber _____ ❏
    water company _____ ❏
    gas company _____ ❏
    electric company _____ ❏
    telephone company _____ ❏
    alarm company _____ ❏
    locksmith _____ ❏
    clergy person _____ ❏

Keep copies of emergency phone numbers
    at home _____ ❏
    at work _____ ❏
    in car _____ ❏
    in wallet or purse _____ ❏

Give copies of emergency phone numbers to key people _____ ❏

Duplicate keys _____ ❏

Identify and store keys and openers _____ ❏

Distribute keys to necessary people _____ ❏

Have a plan to access finances in an emergency _____ ❏

Have a backup plan if access to finances is denied _____ ❏

Consider a medical alert system _____ ❏

Create a check-in system _____ ❏

Elder has access to a telephone _____ ❏

MANAGING MEDICATIONS

Discuss medications with
    elder _____ ❏
    doctor _____ ❏
    pharmacist _____ ❏
    family members _____ ❏

Discuss drug
    usage _____ ❏
    purpose _____ ❏
    alternatives _____ ❏
    safety _____ ❏

Create drug usage chart _____ ❏

Take a CPR class _____ ❏

IF YOUR ELDER IS HOSPITALIZED

Start a file folder _____ ❏

Create a system for recording and filing
    phone numbers _____ ❏
    community resources _____ ❏
    helpers _____ ❏
    eldercare receipts _____ ❏
    notes and documentation _____ ❏
    bills _____ ❏
    questions and answers _____ ❏

Create a list of questions for medical providers _____ ❏

Review care options _____ ❏

Make phone calls _____ ❏

Review things to do _____ ❏

Ask what to bring to the hospital _____ ❏

Get additional help from the Hospital Patient Representative _____ ❏

· 5 ·

MONEY MATTERS

The Cost of Caring

The financial considerations of assisting elderly relatives run deep—we spend our own hard-earned money to help loved ones pay for everyday expenses such as home maintenance, groceries, travel, and more. Other family caregivers may find it necessary to take time off from their work schedules to help out, which affects their spending capabilities even more.

At the same time, the decreasing eligibility and benefits of government programs such as Medicare and Medicaid are altering the economic conditions of our elderly for the worse; Medicare does not provide for assisted-living and long-term care, and Medicaid does not kick in until the elder's funds are nearly depleted. Overall, if we family members don't plan for the financial responsibilities associated with aging relatives' care, our personal financial stability may suffer serious consequences.

Consider the hidden costs of eldercare. Long-distance telephone and travel expenses add up quickly. There might be times when we arrive at our relative's home and notice that a leaky faucet needs fixing, the food supply is low, or a prescription needs to be filled. The need for a quick run to the hardware store, grocery store or the pharmacy is an all-too-common economic predicament: the more we dip into our own pockets, the sooner we run out of money.

We want to be helpful, but when we don't budget properly for current and future eldercare-related expenses, we sabotage those good intentions. This section of *The Planner* will help prepare you financially for the cost of caring, and others plans to avert a financial disaster.

THE COST OF CARING

- Long-distance assistance adds up. Family caregivers can expect to spend money on travel, telephone bills, lodging, and much more.
- Aging parents may want their children to believe that their finances are in better shape than they actually are.
- The American Association for Continuity of Care reports that as many as 40 percent of older Americans have annual incomes of less than $6,000, having less—or choosing to spend less—than $25 to $30 per week for food.

The sooner family members understand that the cost of eldercare may eat into their own hard-earned money, the better their chances for long-term financial stability.

OBJECTIVES

*After completing **The Cost of Caring**, you will be able to:*

Get the big picture of what eldercare can cost.

Calculate and budget for short and long-term expenses.

Create opportunities for the entire family to contribute financially.

 PLAN ONE
Pay attention to the business side of caregiving.

We may find ourselves supplementing the cost of a wide variety of products and services needed by our aging family members. Some expenses are quite steep. For instance, monthly in-home care or monthly dues for retirement housing can run to thousands of dollars per month. And there also are hidden costs of caregiving. Those are the "little things" that add up—buying Mom groceries and treating Uncle Bill to a new winter coat. Every unbudgeted dollar that you spend on eldercare is money out of your own retirement savings.

Creating an eldercare budget requires looking at what eldercare entails. Here is a basic guide for calculating expenditures:

Elder's home expenses

- interior and exterior maintenance
- home and appliance repairs
- remodeling (first-floor bathroom, bedroom and closets, entranceways)

- modifications (door widths, outdoor ramps, lighting sources, shelf and counter heights)
- fixtures (handrails, lifting platforms, door levers, locks, window cranks)

Independent-living products

- cordless telephones
- telephone answering machine (voice mail)
- automatic on and off appliances
- adjustable furniture and bed
- remote-controlled devices
- bathroom fixtures (shower stool, raised toilet seat, grab bar)
- nonbreakable glasses and dishware
- computer (Internet access, e-mail)

Basic living expenses

- groceries
- housing (rent, monthly payments)
- utilities (heat, air-conditioning, electricity, water, telephone)
- clothes and footwear
- transportation
- assisted-living services (bathing, dressing, shopping, cooking, errands, transferring)
- personal care (hairdresser, manicure, pedicure)
- travel
- entertainment (cable television)

Health care expenses

- health insurance
- nursing services and in-home care
- medications, prescriptions, and supplements
- special diets
- emergency paging systems (call buttons, beepers)
- home hospital equipment
- hearing aid, eyewear prescriptions
- dental care

In today's mobile society, many of us are assisting elders from far away, and money spent on travel and related costs can quickly make a dent in our pocketbooks. Whether you're traveling from the next town or across the ocean, if assisting your elder means physically being there, these are the expenses to consider for making the trip:

Travel expenses
- airfare (ask each airline about their policy for emergency family travel)
- ground transportation (bus, train, taxi)
- car rental
- car gasoline
- tolls
- costs en route (food, lodging)

Personal expenses
- child care
- house sitter
- pet sitter

Destination expenses
- food
- lodging
- parking
- telephone calls: personal and work-related

PLAN TWO
Can you afford eldercare? Find out.

To budget for short-term and long-term eldercare expenses, consider your personal economic situation, your ability, realistically, to make financial contributions, and your attitude about spending your own money for your elder's care. Ask yourself the following questions:

What is my short-term financial picture? Long-term?
How much can I afford?
How much of my own money am I willing to spend?

To make eldercare financial planning and budgeting more efficient, keep a written record of what you are spending currently, what you are planning to spend, and a list of your assets and liabilities. Your financial plan also should note where you keep your important and legal documents. Complete the **Documents Locator** chapter in *The Planner* beginning on page 261 for yourself, and keep a copy with your financial records. If you are employed outside the home, you also must figure into the equation any lost income from missing work due to eldercare responsibilities. Consider the following for your eldercare budget:

Your current and future assets
- Income (salary, pensions, interest income, IRAs, tax shelters, Social Security)
- Investment income (property, stocks, bonds, mutual funds)
- Assets (property, collectibles, valuables)
- Annuities (surrender value)
- Bank accounts (checking, savings, cash on hand)
- Income tax returns
- Loans receivable ("IOUs")
- Business equity

Your current and future liabilities
- Insurance policies (life, health, disability, home, auto)
- Credit cards
- Mortgages, debts, loans (what is owed, when payments are due)
- Child support/alimony
- Child care
- Education
- Miscellaneous obligations

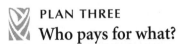

PLAN THREE
Who pays for what?

The question of how much of our own money we're willing to spend is a complicated and difficult one to answer. Some families think they're required to "spend into poverty" to qualify for government programs like Medicaid. Others experience sticker shock at the cost of in-home care, especially if the opportunity to purchase a reasonably priced long-term care insurance policy has long since passed.

Taking on eldercare expenses can be an impossible burden for many. Family members who are already doing their share to help pay for some of their elder's expenses are grappling with their own long-term care and retirement funding. Seek the professional advice of an estate planning attorney, a certified financial planner, and a trusted insurance agent who will assist the family with short- and long-term eldercare financial goals.

PLAN FOUR
Ask for help in terms of time and money.

Develop a family plan to finance eldercare expenses. To get a complete picture of your elder's financial affairs, and to create a budget for current and future expenses, review the next section of this chapter, *Ready Cash,* starting on page 108.

After you have explored the myriad costs associated with your elder's care and examined the family's resources, the next step is to create opportunities for everyone to contribute financially and otherwise to help carry the financial load:

- Company work/life programs may offer long-term care insurance policies to employees and their family members. The same holds true for association members. Find out if this option is available to someone within your family.

- Open savings and checking accounts for eldercare expenditures only. Set aside as much money in these accounts as your budget allows, and ask other family members to do the same.

- Initiate conversations with your family members regarding reimbursement policies. If you buy groceries for Dad on a regular basis, send your siblings a copy of the receipts and ask them to chip in their share.

- Keep all receipts. You may be reimbursed from your elder's estate, insurance company, tax deductions, and any legal settlements.

- Reevaluate your elder's financial needs every three to six months.

- Ask the entire family to give their time and resources for:

  - interior and exterior repairs
  - home maintenance
  - housekeeping
  - laundry
  - heavy lifting
  - shopping and errands
  - transportation
  - cooking
  - personal care
  - paying bills
  - managing medications
  - social activities
  - exercise
  - religious interests

Ready Cash

The high cost of eldercare is on everyone's mind. Daily headlines remind us that people are outliving their savings. The biggest out-of-pocket expenses are for long-term care, pharmacy, and dental expenses, most of which are not covered by Medicare. But we've been taught to respect our elders and to obey the unwritten rule that money is a taboo subject. Many elderly family members take the position that their money is their own business, leaving us to assume that they are living within their means.

So we wonder and worry and wait. Will Mom be able to afford the house on her own? Does Dad's insurance policy cover $80-a-day home care? Does Uncle Frank really understand mutual funds? Unless concerns like these are put out on the table for discussion, we family members won't have any idea as to our elders' true financial stability. We do know that when the money runs out, the rest of the family is often left to pick up the tab.

Today, more people are living to a very advanced age. The costs associated with a longer life can easily wipe out an entire family's financial resources, so it is never too early, or too late, to initiate conversations about money. The most important thing to do is to get started. This section of *The Planner* is designed to help you review, budget, and understand your elder's financial situation and resources. However, before you begin any eldercare conversation with your relatives regarding money, review the contents of the Communicaring chapter of this planner to learn how to talk about sensitive subjects and avert the likelihood of a communication standoff.

READY CASH

- The average life span for men and women has increased. Elders have to support themselves almost a third longer than they thought they would.
- Chronic illnesses are not covered by Medicare.
- Eldercare comprises a complicated set of issues worsened by rising costs of care.

If your elderly family members are financially stretched, you can ease their strain without depriving your own family of financial resources.

OBJECTIVES

After completing **Ready Cash**, *you will be able to:*
Review your elder's present financial status.
Assist in financial planning.
Protect the entire family's finances for the long run.

PLAN ONE
Plan for financial fitness.

Review your elder's current financial state. Use the budget worksheet below to track income and expenses:

AVERAGE MONTHLY INCOME

Salaries/wages/commissions _____

Interest and dividends _____

Social Security _____

IRA/Keogh plan _____

Pension/profit sharing _____

Rental income _____

Other _____

AVERAGE MONTHLY EXPENSES

Housing (rent or mortgage) _____

   Taxes _____

   Insurance _____

   Maintenance/repairs _____

   Utilities _____

Food/tobacco/alcohol _____

Automobile/transportation _____

   Payments _____

   Maintenance/repairs _____

   License/sticker fees _____

   Vehicle insurance _____

Clothing _____

Health care (medical and dental) _____

   Insurance _____

   Assisted-living services _____

   Eyewear, hearing aids, other _____

Personal care	_____
Other insurance	_____
Travel	_____
Gifts/contributions	_____
TOTAL EXPENSES	_____
TOTAL INCOME	_____
SUBTRACT TOTAL EXPENSES	_____
MONTHLY BALANCE	_____

PLAN TWO
Reduce your elder's living expenses.

Here are some ways your elder can reduce living expenses:

- Create a budget and keep a daily written account of any money spent.
- Purchase low-maintenance products.
- Buy sale items.
- Buy nonperishables in bulk and when they're on sale.
- Use money-saving coupons.
- Ask for discounts, especially when paying in full with cash on expensive items.
- Take advantage of senior citizen and group discounts.
- Use 800 toll-free telephone numbers whenever possible.
- Give gifts of time and personal service. Swap skills with others.
- Keep one car and sell the other.
- Look into scaling down your elder's living quarters.
- Avoid buying clothing that requires dry cleaning.
- Ask a family member to manage bill paying and spending.
- Get professional counseling in cases of gambling and credit card abuse.
- Ask a tax adviser about long-range financial and tax strategies.
- Discuss estate planning with an attorney.
- Eat meals at home—restaurants are more expensive.
- Limit impulse purchases—shop with a list and stick to it.
- Check loans, mortgages, and insurance policies for payment waivers.
- Repair air and water leaks.

- Check all bills for errors and overcharges.
- Take advantage of off-hour phone call rates.
- Obtain a benefits eligibility checklist from the local agency on aging.

PLAN THREE
Help reduce your elder's medical costs.

These suggestions, which apply both to you and your elder, help cut the high cost of health care:

- Eat, drink, and exercise wisely.
- Manage medications.
- Get regular medical, dental, and eye checkups.
- Find a doctor who is willing to discuss minor ailments over the telephone, rather than requiring an office visit.
- Avoid hospital emergency rooms for nonemergencies.
- Consider group health insurance.
- Consider long-term care insurance.
- Review health insurance policy for proper procedures *before* receiving treatment.
- Discuss *all* costs with doctor.
- Ask if tests in the doctor's office can be performed without a full office visit charge.
- Bring copies of medical records to every doctor's office visit.
- Get routine tests done before checking into the hospital.
- Avoid filling prescriptions at the expensive hospital pharmacy.
- Check out of the hospital before the check-out hour.
- Keep notes on doctor and hospital visits and medications. Insist on itemized doctor and hospital bills. Review bills and insurance claims for errors.
- Preapprove the costs of hospital medical treatment and equipment.
- File all medical claims.
- Review continuation of medical insurance coverage for the spouse upon your elder's death.

PLAN FOUR
Review insurance policies to uncover room for savings.

To qualify for certain deductions, it is well worth the time to review your elder's insurance papers. If you don't have the policy, call the insurance agent directly. Ask about the following discounts:

Multiple policy discounts may be offered to customers who have two or more policies with the same company.

Smoke and **burglar alarm discounts** may be available for home and office. Ask about security device discounts on dead bolt locks and special window locks.

An accident-free driving record, antitheft equipment, automatic seat belts, air bags, antilock brakes, and **low yearly mileage** may quality you for automobile discounts.

Nonsmoker discounts are often offered to home and auto policyholders. Also look into auto air bag discounts and multi-car discounts.

Home owner discounts for homes and buildings made of special fireproof materials, as well as rebates for attic insulation, are also available.

Mature home owner and **driver discounts** are available for those over 55 years of age.

Long-term policy holder discounts are offered to those who keep a policy with the same company for several years.

NOTE: Do not sign an insurance check until you're satisfied with the settlement.

PLAN FIVE
Discuss ways to reduce travel costs.

The cost of travel doesn't have to be expensive, especially for those who have flexible schedules. To reduce expenses, perhaps your relative will consider the following suggestions:

- Ask about senior citizen and group discounts.
- Travel midweek, off-season.
- Use toll-free 800 phone numbers to make reservations.
- Give consideration to travel cancellation insurance on expensive trips.
- Make friends with a travel agent who can notify you if someone cancels a trip at the last moment and then can resell the trip at a discount.

- Join a last minute travel club.
- Check the Internet for discounted travel fares.
- Check the reputation of all travel outfitters.
- Shop around for traveler's checks. Prices vary.
- Pack for emergencies: nonprescription painkillers, bandages, elastic bandages, thermometer, emergency sting kit, night-light, flashlight, emergency telephone numbers, extra pair of prescription glasses, and an ample supply of prescription medicines.
- Stay at well-known budget-priced motels.
- Know ahead of time how to access emergency money if the need arises.
- Be a savvy shopper.

 PLAN SIX
Plan ahead when considering financial advisers.

Professional financial planners offer a variety of services including budget clarification, stock diversification, and investment recommendations. A good adviser also brings expertise in analyzing insurance policies, identifying risky investments, and understanding estate planning and tax issues. For instance, nursing home and home care costs can be tax deductible if they meet certain requirements of the Internal Revenue Code. But what an adviser cannot do is force anyone to control his or her spending and borrowing.

Finding a good financial planner takes work. A half million people now market themselves as personal advisers in this largely unregulated industry, some of whom are peddling advice that may be inaccurate—or worse.

Start the process of hiring a financial adviser by becoming familiar with their different specialties:

Certified financial planner (CFP) has passed comprehensive examinations on topics including investments and estate planning. CFPs are required to have three years of work experience and participate in continuing education courses.

Certified public accountant (CPA) has passed extensive examinations in taxes and accounting. CPAs must be licensed in the state where they practice.

Personal financial specialist (PFS) is a CPA with training in financial planning. To qualify, the adviser must pass an exam and have three years of work experience in personal finance.

Chartered financial consultant (ChFC) has completed three years of work experience, participated in continuing education courses, and has passed financial exams with an emphasis on life insurance.

Chartered life underwriter (CLU) has in-depth knowledge of life insurance, has three years' work experience, and participates in continuing education courses.

Stockbrokers are trained in the basics and mechanics of buying and selling stocks and related financial products.

Investment adviser is anyone who is paid to offer financial advice such as attorneys, graduates of business schools (MBAs), or individuals who possess a master of financial planning degree (MFP).

To find referrals for financial advisers, begin by soliciting recommendations from trusted sources such as relatives, friends, colleagues, attorneys, and accountants who have firsthand experience working with an adviser. Or turn to the professional groups listed in the resource section at the end of this chapter. Organizations that will help you do background checks on advisers are also listed in this section.

Interview prospective advisers by asking these questions:

Is there a charge for the initial visit?

What training and experience have you had?

Have you worked with clients whose family financial picture is similar to mine?

How are your fees determined? (If hourly, get an estimate of the total.)

What are the ongoing costs of working with you?

What can I expect to pay for the services I need?

Exactly what services are provided?

Will you provide written reports?

Are you available throughout the year or just during tax season?

Who will do the work? An accountant? An assistant?

What methods do you use to keep abreast of new tax developments and laws?

How will I be kept informed of new tax regulations?

Will you represent me if I'm called in for an audit?

Are you easily accessible?

Will you provide names of three recent clients for references?

 PLAN SEVEN
Explore additional sources of benefits, rebates, and reductions.

Tap into financial resources that are set aside specifically to help the elderly:

Social Security is a federal income program offered to individuals upon retirement age or upon becoming disabled. Social Security laws will move up the age of eligibility for full retirement benefits to 66 years of age starting in the year 2005. At this printing, elders are eligible for Social Security benefits at the age of 65. The laws governing Social Security eligibility change from time to time and could mean extra income. Review your elder's benefits at least every two years. Apply for Social Security by telephone or by going to the local Social Security office.

General relief is allocated to elders of very low income who are not eligible for federally funded assistance. General relief may be obtained from the department of social and health services.

Benefits eligibility lists are available through the local agency on aging and the department of social and health services. Services include: adult day care, adult education, community care, consumer fraud protection, property tax assistance, denture referral programs, driver's license discount, elder abuse protection, emergency assistance, food stamps, home-delivered meals and nutrition sites, housing, utility bills assistance, Medicaid, Medicare, ombudsman programs, pharmaceutical services, supplemental insurance, travel and tourism, and access to volunteers.

Veterans' benefits and pensions are available for eligible veterans and their dependents. Call the local Veteran's Administration office.

Supplemental security income (SSI) provides monthly benefits to those with very low income, the aged, and persons with disabilities. SSI is available through the Social Security office. If your elder cannot visit the office, ask for a home visit.

Elders aged 62 and older with disabilities may qualify for tax postponement, home owner's assistance, and renter's assistance. Contact the state tax office.

Grandparents raising grandchildren may qualify for a host of government programs. Contact the local department of social and health services. The Internet has a wealth of information on the many laws that are in place to protect grandparents' rights. Keyword search: grandparenting.

Numerous **state and community programs** offer tax breaks, utility payment assistance, rent relief, public transportation fare discounts, and taxi coupons. Call city hall to get started.

Workers' **unions** and **fraternal organizations** also may offer benefits. Call them directly.

PLAN EIGHT
Accumulate cash through life insurance.

Some insurance companies offer life insurance policies that allow elders to pay for long-term care by using the death benefit to withdraw tax-free cash. This approach avoids the issue of paying premiums for a long-term care insurance policy that might never be used. When purchasing a life insurance policy, be aware that companies reserve the right to lower the benefits if interest rates fall significantly and stay low for several years. Any death benefit that is not used to pay for care is left to heirs. To collect early, obtain a letter from the doctor stating that the insured has fewer than six months to live.

Another option is selling a life insurance policy to an outside company, known as a **viatical settlement company.** In return for naming the viatical company as the sole beneficiary of a given policy, the patient receives an immediate payment of up to 85 percent of the policy's face value, thus allowing him or her to pay for the mounting costs of comfort care in the later stages of life. When the patient dies, the viatical company collects the policy's death benefit.

But beware. There are tax questions, commission claims, and other concerns that need to be clarified before you sign anything. It is imperative that you consult a certified financial adviser or elder law attorney before considering this option. Viatical settlement company advertisements may leave out important facts or use language that implies banklike safety, which may not necessarily be the case.

 PLAN NINE
Retrieve cash through the benefits of owning a house.

Any one of the following financial strategies may be all you need to keep your elder financially independent:

> If your house-rich, cash-poor elder is willing to move, trading down to a smaller place may be a smart strategy. A onetime exclusion that exempts from taxes some of the capital gain from the sale of a house is available to individuals 55 years or older if they have lived in the house for at least three of the past five years.

> If moving is not an option and the house appeals to you as an investment, you could buy the home and lease it back to your relative. The property then becomes a source of income for the seller (your elder) and gives the buyer (you) the tax advantages of rental property. Another option allows an outside investor to buy the home on a sale/lease-back or life tenancy legalized agreement.

> If you have neither the money nor the desire to buy your family member's home and the mortgage is paid, a reverse mortgage allows residents to occupy the home while receiving income. The home owner borrows against the value of the home and receives monthly or line of credit payments from a mortgage lender. The lender charges interest on the payments. No repayment of the interest or principal is required, unless the home is sold or is no longer occupied by the owner. **NOTE:** Reverse mortgages do not assure home owners lifelong income or the right to remain in the home. Be fully informed.

A deferred payment loan from the government can be provided to low-income persons at a low-interest rate. The loan permits home owners to defer payments of all principal interest until the home owner dies or when the house is sold.

Home owner equity accounts are offered by brokerage firms and banks that allow home owners to set up a line of credit secured by the value of the home. Terms vary, as do interest rates. Shop around.

Your relative may choose to gift his or her home to a person or an institution. The gift recipient then agrees to pay the home owner a set monthly or yearly income for so long as he or she is alive.

 PLAN TEN
Make cash gifts to your elder.

Gifts of money to older relatives can help make ends meet, and can enhance their quality of life. However, you should be careful about how much you give, especially if your elder already qualifies for government benefit programs. Open up an interest-bearing checking account for the purpose of supplementing:

transportation	telephone calls
groceries	house maintenance
cable television service	travel
clothing purchases	personal care
lawn care	home decorating
house renovating	health care
household appliances	laundry and dry cleaning

 PLAN ELEVEN
Avoid unwelcome emotional complications when giving cash directly.

Even under the worst of financial conditions, our elders can, at times, be too proud to accept money from anyone. Creating formalized agreements can make such transactions go more smoothly.

Consider a split-interest purchase. Under this joint purchase agreement, you and your elder divide the cost of an investment and agree that he or she gets all of the income while living. You receive the assets and any capital gain after your elder dies.

Give your relative a loan. Legalize the agreement and memorialize the loan in your elder's will. After your relative dies, the money can be repaid from the estate, probably when the assets are sold.

Gifts and services can take the place of money:

a new winter coat	airline tickets
postage stamps	gift certificates
house cleaning services	prepaid phone cards
convenience items	grocery store
restaurant gift certificates	house maintenance
cable television service	personal care services
lawn care	home decorating
house renovating	household appliances
club memberships	magazine subscriptions
entertainment	furniture

PLAN TWELVE
Investigate the advantages of a part-time job.

Employment opportunities aren't limited by experience or age. Many businesses welcome older people as employees. Review the *Quality of Life* chapter in *The Planner* starting on page 219 for numerous job suggestions. **NOTE:** A working status may affect your elder's Social Security benefits. Review all regulations before your elder takes any job.

PLAN THIRTEEN
Understand Medicaid eligibility guidelines.

State Medicaid spending policies protect the assets of one spouse, should the other move into a nursing facility. Without professional advice ahead of time, overspending can then leave the remaining spouse virtually penniless and family members may be penalized for implementing certain spending strategies. Seek valuable advice from an attorney specializing in elder law.

Low-Cost and Free Resources

The securities industry maintains a **central registration depository (CRD)** about stockbrokers and their firms. A full report, usually free, is available from your state securities agency.

If financial planners give investment advice, they must be registered with the **Securities and Exchange Commission.**

Family members may be eligible for **dependent care tax breaks** if their elderly relative resides in their home. Seek additional information from a tax adviser.

Elders in danger of having home utilities turned off because they haven't paid bills can call the electric **utility company** to work out a payment plan. The **telephone company** offers discounts and free services to customers with hearing and sight disabilities. Contact the special needs center of the telephone company.

During tax time, services to homebound elderly are available. Contact the local **Internal Revenue Service** office. The IRS also offers **Tele-Tax,** an automated information line that offers recorded tax information. **Taxpayer's rights advocates** can be found at the state board of equalization office.

Free medications. Some pharmaceutical companies distribute medications free of charge to low-income elders. Eligibility requirements vary. If your family member is eligible, the drug company sends the medications to the patient's physician for distribution.

If you believe that your elder may have forgotten about cash and valuables in bank accounts or a safe-deposit box, call the **state treasurer's office,** which keeps a list of unclaimed money and property.

If your elder is a war veteran, there is a wealth of services available through the local office of the **Veteran's Administration.**

Catholic Charities Centers provide nondenominational family and individual assistance with debt obligations. Loans and grants are available for qualified individuals. Look in the White Pages for the number of the local chapter.

If you and your elder have decided that you will handle bill paying, make it easy on yourself—bill paying via **Internet** and **telephone** is a practice more caregivers are adopting. Contact your elder's banking institution to get started.

Elders on limited incomes can obtain many services free of charge from volunteers working at many of the **senior centers.**

ORGANIZATIONS

Consumer Information Center
(To obtain hundreds of federal consumer publications)
Dept. WWW
Pueblo, CO 81009
(888) 878-3256
Website: *www.pueblo.gsa.gov*

Health Care Financing Administration
(Information about Medicare and Medicaid)
7500 Security Boulevard
Baltimore, MD 21244

(410) 786-3000
Website: *www.hcfa.gov*

Internal Revenue Service
(Tax counseling for the elderly)
(800) 829-1040

National Center for Home Equity Conversion (NCHEC)
(Consumer information on reverse mortgages)
360 N Robert, Suite 403
Saint Paul, MN 55101
(651) 222-6775, Fax: (651) 222-6797
Website: *www.reverse.org*

National Committee to Preserve Social Security and Medicare
10 G Street, NE, Suite 600
Washington, DC 20002-4215
(800) 966-1935, Fax: (202) 216-0451
Website: *www.ncpssm.org*

Pension and Welfare Benefits Administration (PWBA)
U.S. Department of Labor
200 Constitution Avenue, NW
Washington, DC 20210
(202) 219-8771 (searching and retrieving documents)
(202) 219-8776 (pension and health benefits questions)
Website: *www.dol.gov/dol/pwba/public/guide.htm*

Medicare Hotline
(800) 638-6833

Social Security Administration
Office of Public Inquiries
6401 Security Boulevard, Room 4-C-5 Annex
Baltimore, MD 21235-6401
(800) 772-1213, TTD: (800) 325-0778
Website: *www.ssa.gov*

Financial Adviser Referrals

American Institute of Certified Public Accountants (AICPA)
1211 Avenue of the Americas
New York, NY 10036
(888) 777-7077
Website: *www.aicpa.org*

Institute of Certified Financial Planners (ICFP)
3801 E. Florida Avenue, Suite 708
Denver, CO 80210-2544
(800) 322-4237, (303) 759-4900, Fax: (303) 759-0749
Website: *www.icfp.org*

International Association for Financial Planning (IAFP)
5775 Glenridge Drive, NE, Suite B-300
Atlanta, GA 30328-5364
(800) 945-4237, (404) 845-0011, Fax: (404) 845-3660
Website: *www.iafp.org*

Licensed Independent Network of CPA Financial Planners (LINC)
P.O. Box 1559
Columbia, TN 38402-1559
(800) 887-8358, Fax: (615) 242-4152
Website: *www.lincpfp.com*

National Association of Personal Financial Advisers (NAPFA)
3555 W. Dundee Road, Suite 200
Buffalo Grove, IL 60089
(888) 333-6659
Website: *www.napfa.org*

Society of Financial Service Professionals
270 Bryn Mawr Avenue
Bryn Mawr, PA 19010-2195
(888) 243-2258, (610) 526-2500, Fax: (610) 527-4010
Website: *www.financialpro.org*

Financial Adviser Background Checks and Complaints

Certified Financial Planner Board of Standards
1700 Broadway, Suite 2100
Denver, CO 80290-2101
(888) 237-6275, (303) 830-7500, Fax: (303) 860-7388
Website: *www.cfp-board.org*

National Association of Insurance Commissioners (NAIC)
120 West Twelfth Street, Suite 1100
Kansas City, MO 64105-1925
(816) 842-3600, Fax: (816) 471-7004
Website: *www.naic.org*

National Association of Securities Dealers Regulation (NASDR)
Call for district office location
(800) 289-9999
Website: *www.nasdr.com*

North American Securities Administrators Association (NASAA)
10 G Street, NE, Suite 710
Washington, DC 20002
(888) 846-2722, (202) 737-0900
Website: *www.nasaa.org*

Securities and Exchange Commission (SEC)
(Office of Investor Education and Assistance)
450 Fifth Street, NW
Washington, DC 20549-0213
(800) 732-0330, (202) 942-7040, Fax: (202) 942-9634
Website: *www.sec.gov*

Action Checklist

THE COST OF CARING	To Do By	Completed
Become familiar with eldercare related expenses		
elder's home	_____	❏
household items	_____	❏
basic living	_____	❏
home health care	_____	❏
Consider the cost of long-distance assistance		
travel	_____	❏
home	_____	❏
destination	_____	❏
Review your finances		
keep written record	_____	❏
locate important documents	_____	❏
Consider ability to contribute to expenses	_____	❏
Budget eldercare expenses		
short-term	_____	❏
long-term	_____	❏

Protect personal financial stability _____ ❏

Review elder's financial stability _____ ❏

Develop a family plan
    current expenses _____ ❏
    future expenses _____ ❏

Create eldercare account
    savings _____ ❏
    checking account _____ ❏

Record and file eldercare expenses receipts _____ ❏

Evaluate elder's financial needs every six months _____ ❏

Ask family to give time and resources _____ ❏

READY CASH

Complete Financial Fitness Worksheet _____ ❏

Help your elder reduce
    debts _____ ❏
    living expenses _____ ❏
    medical costs _____ ❏
    insurance costs _____ ❏
    travel expenses _____ ❏

Consider the services of a financial adviser
    get referrals from reliable resources _____ ❏
    ask specific questions _____ ❏
    do background checks _____ ❏

Set financial goals
    short-term _____ ❏
    long-term _____ ❏
    tax planning _____ ❏
    estate planning _____ ❏

Increase your elder's income via
    Social Security _____ ❏
    veterans' benefits _____ ❏

    pensions _____ ❏
    relief programs _____ ❏
    life insurance _____ ❏
    home ownership _____ ❏
    gifts and loans _____ ❏
    employment _____ ❏

Learn the state Medicaid spending policy _____ ❏

Budget for your elder's
    housing expenses _____ ❏
    living expenses _____ ❏
    medical expenses _____ ❏
    insurance _____ ❏
    service providers _____ ❏
    funeral expenses _____ ❏

Record the phone numbers of your elder's
    tax preparer _____ ❏
    accountant _____ ❏
    legal adviser _____ ❏
    bank _____ ❏
    financial adviser _____ ❏
    insurance agents _____ ❏

Keep phone numbers
    at home _____ ❏
    at work _____ ❏
    in wallet or purse _____ ❏

Distribute phone numbers to key family members _____ ❏

· 6 ·

LEGAL MATTERS

Estate Planning

There are many advantages to estate planning; yet very few people do it. Why? Several reasons: They may not even be aware of the option, and consequently, the benefits; they hold to a common misconception that estate planning is only a concern of the wealthy; they simply find it hard to make decisions now about what will occur after their death. Failing to engage in estate planning is an example of benign neglect; many people just assume their affairs are legally in order because they own everything jointly with their heirs. **This can be a potentially costly mistake.**

As a way to take action, ask yourself this important question: What might happen to *your* financial future if your elder lives longer than expected? In addition to planning for distribution of family assets in the event of death, a key element of estate planning also includes the preservation and distribution of wealth *before* death. In an age where many people are living one-third longer than their parents, it is wise to investigate your options now.

This section of *The Planner* simplifies the process of estate planning. You will gain a basic understanding of the legal terms and how proper planning provides for orderly distribution of assets while minimizing court delays, fees, and taxes. Gifts, title transfers, contracts, and trusts can be coordinated to maximize the financial benefits for those persons your relative wishes to provide for.

ESTATE PLANNING

- If someone doesn't have a will (is intestate), the state will divide his or her property with no regard for the family's special needs. The state will select heirs, leave unnecessarily large bequests to the tax collector, and will charge for services.

- Estate planning not only focuses on property distribution after death, but also on protecting hard-earned assets during an elder's lifetime.
- If people don't take steps to plan for incapacity, the state has the authority to set standards as to what the incompetent patient would want.

If your elderly family member is avoiding estate planning, perhaps taking the process step-by-step and locating elder law professionals will ease him or her into the process.

OBJECTIVES

After completing Estate Planning, you will be able to:

Gain basic knowledge of estate planning terms and legal forms.

Locate affordable elder law resources.

Maintain control of decisions in the event of your elder's incapacity.

Avoid the devastating consequences of inadequate legal documentation.

 PLAN ONE
Get to know the terms.

Estate planning is less intimidating and easier to grasp once you have an understanding of the terms:

A **will** instructs how an individual wants his or her estate to be distributed upon death. The document may include provisions for a trust, and usually names an executor.

A trustee and an executor are individuals designated by the creator of the will who oversee proper execution of the will. A trustee manages a trust, while an executor sees that specific provisions of the will are followed and pays estate taxes, debits, and expenses. The trustee and executor can be the same person.

A **trust** is a way to bequeath money or property that takes advantage of tax benefits and accomplishes the desires of the person setting up the trust. A trust controls the release of money before or after death. A **testamentary trust** is one that is created by, and does not take effect until, the death of the creator of the will.

A **living trust** transfers stocks, property, and other items from one living person to another, avoids probate, and also protects in the event of incapacity. A revocable living trust gives the creator of the trust the right to change the terms of the trust or even to end it.

A **letter of instruction** is prepared for the beneficiaries of a will or trust. The letter is meant to serve as a guide for closing out the affairs of an individual upon his or her death. Although this letter is not a legal document, the composition should be consistent with the individual's will. The letter of instruction should also include a list of the people to notify when death occurs and should cover the disposition of possessions and specify any particular wishes regarding the funeral.

A **durable power of attorney** gives a person the legal right to sign his or her name to business transacted in another person's name, and gives power over all assets. This documentation must be prepared while the individual is still competent, and can be terminated at any time upon the person's written request. **NOTE:** Banks and other financial institutions typically do not honor power of attorney forms other than their own. Check with each banking institution to obtain proper documents. Be aware that some states order safe-deposit boxes sealed upon the tenant's death and do not permit them to be opened until a state tax commission representative is present. Other states require a court order to open a box that was rented in the decedent's sole name.

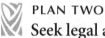

PLAN TWO
Seek legal advice.

Family members should not draft their own wills. Documents not prepared in accordance with the law might be contested in court, or heirs might end up paying more estate taxes than they should.

A simple will can cost as little as a few hundred dollars to prepare. Keep original copies of legal documents in a safe place with 24-hour-a-day access, leaving copies of the documents with the attorney. Remind your relative to keep the contents of legal documents up-to-date.

An estate planning attorney can be found through personal referrals, attorney referrals services, or by calling the local bar association. Check the attorney's qualifications and shop around to compare fees, services, and experience.

PLAN THREE
Implement gift-giving strategies.

Money and property are not the only assets your elder may have. There is usually a household containing furniture, photographs, books, letters, collectibles, jewels, and other items that can be distributed. Some elders prefer to dispose of personal possessions to loved ones while they are still alive, enjoying the giving process as they go. Others prefer to distribute personal possessions through a letter of instruction as part of their will.

PLAN FOUR
To gain better control, anticipate your elder's incapacity.

Few people plan for disability or incapacity during their lifetime. The result is often a loss of control over who will make the family's decisions, and how to make them. Proper eldercare planning includes documentation that allows financial and health care decisions to be made by family members, without court intervention or conservatorship proceedings.

A **durable power of attorney** is legal documentation transferring decision-making authority to a designated person and continues that authority in the event of incapacity. This document must be completed while your relative is still competent. Regular powers of attorney are not honored in these situations.

A **durable power of attorney for health care** gives another person legal authority to make medical decisions in the event of incapacity. Individuals must be of sound mind and able to give informed consent when composing this document. The durable power of attorney for health care specifies how life-support decisions are to be made, and under what conditions. It is not necessary to hire an attorney to complete this document; they are available, free of charge, at hospitals, doctor's offices, senior centers, and nursing homes. Each state has its own form; be sure you have the form where your elder resides. Have the completed forms reviewed for accuracy by the geriatric case manager employed by the hospital. Services are usually provided free of charge.

Legal guardianship and conservatorship are legal processes for assuming control over an already incapacitated individual's affairs. This is usually the last method considered. A court hearing is required.

A **directive to physician** instructs doctors to withhold medical treatment if it would not aid in recovery but only prolong illness or delay death. If the doctor disagrees ahead of time with any key terms, consider switching physicians. Include these instructions in the durable power of attorney for health care. Instruction also should be left by those who do not want their lives ended by the withdrawal of treatment, no matter how ill or long they are incapacitated.

A **living will** is a document that states the medical situations under which a patient would not want to be kept alive. Some doctors and hospitals may refuse to honor this document. State laws vary widely. **NOTE:** The medical system is set up to save lives and is reluctant to turn away a dying patient, no matter what the wishes of that individual. A living will holds many limitations and is not legally binding, unlike the durable power of attorney for health care.

PLAN FIVE
Discuss and distribute estate planning devices.

Forms, legal documents, and directives won't be useful unless other family members are made aware of their existence. Be sure that your elder has distributed and discussed the contents of important information with designated family members, doctors, friends, nursing home facility directors, and other key people.

Keep original documents in a safe-deposit box or other 24-hour accessible place. Give the attorney copies instead of originals. You and your elder may be consulting with different attorneys from time to time.

Durable power of attorney for health care agents should be prepared to present proof of this document at a moment's notice. If your relative enters the hospital or a nursing home facility, attach copies of any notarized forms and directives to his or her medical chart. Ask nursing home directors to agree, in writing, to comply with your elder's wishes. Update all documentation as needed.

Elder Advocacy

The United States Census Bureau estimates that within ten years the number of Americans over 85 will be more than triple what it is today. With this kind of growth in an aging population, government programs that serve the elderly are in serious financial jeopardy. Every year, policy makers cut the budgets and staffs of social service organizations, placing nearly the entire burden of eldercare on the backs of family, friends, and volunteers.

The current dearth of easily accessible eldercare programs makes the family caregiver's task a test of endurance. Family members are often overwhelmed by the red tape of their fact-finding mission. Our available time and stamina quickly start to dwindle. To make matters worse, most elderly Americans do not meet the rigid criteria to qualify for the government's free and low-cost services. Programs like Medicare don't pay for the basic day-to-day care and assistance that most elderly people require.

Family elder advocacy includes taking on a bigger role in the fight against Medicare fraud. Millions of dollars are lost to health care fraud every year by way of double billing, charging for services not provided, performing unnecessary services, and other Medicare abuses. To combat this loss, elders and Medicare beneficiaries are being asked to report to government regulators activities that they believe are fraudulent or abusive.

This section of *The Planner* encourages you and your elders to become active advocates for improvements in government-funded eldercare programs and services. Getting involved keeps eldercare programs thriving, today and tomorrow.

ELDER ADVOCACY

- Be aware that some policy makers want to turn back the clock, placing virtually the entire burden of eldercare on the backs of family, friends, and volunteers.
- There is a critical need for government programs that help family caregivers.
- Overt acts of discrimination are a daily occurrence for most older people.

One of the most effective ways to safeguard the well-being of the elderly is to protect the rights of senior citizens and join in the fight for responsible government policies.

OBJECTIVES

*After completing **Elder Advocacy**, you will be able to:*
Contact politicians who are establishing eldercare policies.
Stay involved and informed about policies affecting elderly Americans.
Recognize and report incidents of Medicare fraud and abuse.

PLAN ONE
Keep an alert and wary eye on politicians.

Monitor the activities of politicians who consider programs for elderly Americans an expense, not an investment:

- Stay informed
- Attend local government meetings
- Vote

PLAN TWO
Get involved.

Local, state, and federal eldercare programs exist as a result of various activities of advocacy groups. Become a member. Lobbyists will notify you when the time is right for sending letters to legislators. Letters and e-mails add up to action, and when election time rolls around, the politicians need the seniors' votes to win. Political action takes dedication and energy. Join others in making important changes in eldercare policies and services, locally and nationwide.

PLAN THREE
Fight for improved eldercare policies and programs.

Topics of elder advocacy that deserve attention are:

Health care	Long-term care
Home health care	Nursing home policies
Social Security	Medicare and Medicaid
Supplemental health insurance	Respite care
Senior community activity programs	Tax laws
Elder law	Nutrition programs
Transportation services	Employment and job training
Education	Senior centers funding
Pension entitlements	Subsidized housing
Retirement policies	Estate planning
Funeral arrangement policies	Disability policies

Contact the following advocates if you suspect that any elderly person's rights are being violated: Long-term care ombudsman, family service agency, hospital social services director, local agency on aging, and the local department of social services' adult protection services.

 PLAN FOUR
Report Medicare fraud and abuse.

It's only natural that when we hire someone to do a job for us, we discuss how much it will cost and ask for written estimates of the services to be provided. After the job is complete and the bill comes, we match it up to what we were told it would cost. If the invoice doesn't appear correct, or seems unreasonably high, we have the option of asking the service provider for an explanation.

Medicare service providers should not be exempt from these fair expectations. The Department of Health and Human Services is waging war against Medicare fraud and enlisting elders and family members to report billing errors, overcharges, and other evidence of possible wrongdoing.

Fraud and abuse threaten the financial soundness of the Medicare system. Here are some suggestions on becoming a Medicare "fraud-buster":

What is Medicare fraud?

Medicare fraud is defined as an incident or practice that intentionally deceives or misrepresents claims against the Medicare program. The violator may be a physician or other practitioner, a hospital or other institutional provider, a clinical laboratory, an employee of any provider, a billing service, or any person in a position to file a claim for Medicare benefits.

Fraud and abuse appear in many forms:
- Improper billing practices
- Overcharging for services and supplies
- Billing Medicare patients at a higher rate than non-Medicare patients
- Offering or accepting kickbacks, bribes, or rebates
- Fraudulent diagnoses
- Waiver of patient deductibles and co-payments
- Billing for services not furnished
- Falsifying certificates of medical necessity
- Using another person's Medicare card

Fraud Tips:

Be suspicious if health care providers tell your elder that:

- the test, equipment, or service is free, but they only need his or her Medicare number for their records.
- the more services they provide, the cheaper they are.

Be suspicious if health care providers:

- waive any fees.
- advertise "free" consultations to Medicare beneficiaries.
- bill Medicare for services not furnished.
- use high-pressure sales tactics, telemarketing, and door-to-door selling as marketing tools.
- use ambulance companies for trips that aren't an emergency.
- give the wrong diagnosis on the Medicare claim form.
- bill Medicare for telephone calls, conferences with the family, or scheduled, but not kept, appointments.
- bill Medicare for tests received as a hospital inpatient or within 72 hours of admission or discharge.

How to report Medicare fraud and abuse:

Most health care providers are honest, and the questionable charge may be the result of a clerical error. That's why many people call their provider first. However, if your elder isn't sure or doesn't feel comfortable talking with the health care provider, or the provider's answer is not satisfactory, you or your elder need not hesitate to report a questionable charge to the **Medicare Fraud Hot Line (1-800-447-8477).**

Your elder will need to answer three questions about each charge:

Did you receive the service or product for which Medicare was billed?

Did your doctor order the service or product for you?

To the best of your knowledge, is the item relevant to your diagnosis or treatment?

Before contacting the Medicare claims processing company, carefully review with your elder the particular scenario in question. Then, *write down* the following information:

1. Provider's name and identification number.
2. Item or service in question.
3. Date on which the item or service was provided.
4. Amount approved and paid by Medicare.
5. Date of the Explanation of Benefits (EOB).
6. Name and Medicare number of the person who supposedly received the item or service.
7. Reason Medicare should not have paid.

If your elder prefers to write a letter rather than call, he or she should clearly state at the beginning of the letter that he or she is filing a fraud complaint. This will help to ensure that the complaint is forwarded to the fraud unit.

Low-Cost and Free Resources

Legal advice is available for elders with limited incomes. Contact the local agency on aging, the local bar association, or the district attorney's office. Also, call a local law school to find out if community services are offered.

The **secretary of state's office** has a TDD (Telecommunications Device for the Deaf) for voter registration and election information. For persons with visual disabilities, audiotapes of the state and county candidates are available in the county clerk-recorder's office.

Free copies of the **durable power of attorney for health care** forms are available at your local agency on aging, doctor's office, senior center, nursing home, and at the hospital senior services department. Many hospitals provide free assistance in filling out these forms.

ORGANIZATIONS

American Bar Association
750 N. Lake Shore Drive
Chicago, IL 60611
Website: *www.abanet.org*

ABA Commission on Legal Problems of the Elderly
Website: *http://scratch.abanet.org/elderly/home.html*

Legal Services Corporation
(Legal help to low-income individuals in civil matters)
750 First Street, NE, 10th Floor
Washington, DC 20002-4250
(202) 336-8800
Website: *www.ltsi.net/lsc/help.html*

National Academy of Elder Law Attorneys, Inc.
1604 N. Country Club Road
Tucson, AZ 85716
(520) 881-4005, Fax: (520) 325-7925
Website: *www.naela.com*

National Guardianship Association
1604 N. Country Club Road
Tucson, AZ 85716
(520) 881-6561, Fax: (520) 325-7925
Website: *www.guardianship.org*

National Network of Estate Planning Attorneys
410 17th Street, Suite 1260
Denver, CO 80202
(800) 638-8681
Website: *www.netplanning.com*

National Senior Citizen Law Center
Washington, DC Office
1101 14th Street, NW, Suite 400
Washington, DC 20005
(202) 289-6976, Fax: (202) 289-7224

Los Angeles Office
3435 Wilshire Boulevard, Suite 2860
Los Angeles, CA 90010-1938
(213) 639-0930, Fax: (213) 639-0934
Website: *www.nsclc.org*

Senior Law Website
(Information about elder law and related subjects)
Website: *www.seniorlaw.com*

Elder Advocacy Groups

Association For Protection of the Elderly (APE)
528 A Columbia Avenue, Suite 127
Lexington, SC 29072
(800) 569-7345
Website: *www.apeape.org*

Boomer Agenda
1275 K Street NW, Suite 602
Washington, DC 20005
(202) 682-6899
Website: *www.boomeragenda.org*

Close-Up Foundation
44 Canal Center Plaza
Alexandria, VA 22314-1592
(800) 256-7387, (703) 706-3300
Website: *www.cpn.org/close_up*

Government Directory
(The single best source of Government information)
Website: *www.govstartpage.com*

Gray Panthers
733 15th Street, NW, Suite 437
Washington, DC 20005
(800) 280-5362, (202) 737-6637, Fax: (202) 737-1160
Website: *www.graypanthers.org*

Medicare Hot Line
(To report Medicare fraud and abuse)
(800) 447-8477

National Council of Senior Citizens
8403 Colesville Road, Suite 1200
Silver Spring, MD 20910-3314
(888) 373-6467, (301) 578-8800, Fax: (301) 578-8999
Website: *www.ncscinc.org*

Older Women's League
666 11th Street, NW, Suite 700
Washington, DC 20001
(800) 825-3695, (202) 783-6686, (202) 783-6689
Website: *http://pr.aoa.dhhs.gov/aoa/dir/207.html*

Federal Government Websites
White House: *www.whitehouse.gov*
United States House of Representatives: *http://house.gov*
United States Senate: *http://senate.gov*

Write your Senator or Representative
Address envelope to:
Senator (Name), United States Senate
Washington, DC 20510
Representative (Name), United States House of Representatives
Washington, DC 20515

Action Checklist

ESTATE PLANNING	To Do By	Completed
Set estate planning goals		
short-term	_____	❑
long-term	_____	❑
Locate elder law resources	_____	❑
Draw up		
will	_____	❑
trust	_____	❑
letter of instruction	_____	❑
durable power of attorney	_____	❑
durable power of attorney for health care	_____	❑
Duplicate, distribute, and review documents with *key family members*	_____	❑

Review assets _____ ❏

Store original documents _____ ❏

Make plans to review and update legal documents _____ ❏

Store durable power of attorney document in a safe,
   24-hour-accessible location _____ ❏

Obtain and record important legal telephone numbers _____ ❏

Distribute legal phone numbers to key people _____ ❏

Read up on estate planning _____ ❏

ELDER ADVOCACY

Research senior citizen advocacy groups _____ ❏

Know how to reach
   city hall _____ ❏
   village of _____ _____ ❏
   mayor's office _____ ❏
   city council members _____ ❏
   senator _____ ❏
   congressman _____ ❏
   governor's office _____ ❏

Vote in local and national elections _____ ❏

Stay informed
   community newspapers _____ ❏
   city newspapers _____ ❏
   political flyers _____ ❏
   Internet _____ ❏

Recognize Medicare fraud and abuse _____ ❏

· 7 ·

INSURANCE

Insurance Coverage for a Longer Life

In today's world, it seems almost inconceivable that a person would allow his or her entire personal wealth to be at risk. You certainly know better. You carry many different types of insurance: on your car, on your home and belongings, on your life. But do you really have any idea whether your elderly family member may have let a policy or two lapse over the years, or have neglected to upgrade his or her coverage commensurate with the current value of his or her assets?

Making sure your elder has adequate insurance can be a matter of economic survival for the entire family, and taking an in-depth look at your elder's existing insurance policies may reveal under- and over-insurance coverage. It also may disclose an absence of insurance coverage that should be in place. Your elder's insurance needs may have changed since the purchase of the original policy and now, rather than under emergency conditions, is the time to gather and review your elder's insurance documents.

This section of *The Planner* will help you update your elder's insurance coverage. Establishing a relationship with his or her insurance agent and asking for explanations on policy coverage and limitations will help eliminate potential insurance problems down the road.

INSURANCE COVERAGE FOR A LONGER LIFE

- People often purchase insurance as one service, without adequate information.
- Your elder's insurance needs may have changed since the purchase of the policy.
- The most important protection you can have against accidents is knowing how to avoid them.

If it has been more than one year since your elder's insurance policies have been reviewed, now would be a good time to check to see whether he or she has too much or too little protection.

OBJECTIVES

*After completing **Insurance Coverage for a Longer Life**, you will be able to:*
   Know if your elder's insurance coverage has been secured.
   Bring your elder's insurance coverage up-to-date.
   Examine an insurance company's financial stability.

 PLAN ONE
Scrutinize your elder's insurance policies for over- and under-coverage.

At some point in time, your elder may have purchased insurance coverage for home, auto, life insurance, disability, personal property, or business. Obtain copies of each policy and review the conditions under which they were purchased. Note possible family changes that may affect the beneficiary status.

The most important role of insurance is to protect the policyholder from catastrophe. Extended personal liability insurance (umbrella coverage) can be coordinated with your elder's home and auto insurance. The cost of insurance depends on numerous variables, including the rate of the deductible. Renewing present insurance policies for adequate coverage may be less expensive than purchasing additional insurance.

Insurance is big business. Television ads and direct mail offers with celebrity spokespeople can be misleading, since they are paid by the insurance company to endorse the product, and their image has nothing to do with the quality of the policies advertised.

Keep in mind that insurance agents are salespeople, and asking them to offer an opinion on one policy versus another is like asking a car salesman if it's better to buy the blue car or the red car. Do your homework and be informed so you will know what questions to ask when it's time to renew or buy. The Internet offers up-to-date news bulletins on this vast subject.

To find a licensed insurance agent, ask for a referral from someone you trust. The local agency on aging also can offer family members the names of insurance advisers who advocate the special insurance needs of elders. Policies should always be reviewed by a third party before signing.

Following are a few types of insurance to consider:

Home owner—If your elder's home and personal possessions were destroyed by fire or water damage, or if the home was burglarized, would your elder be able to replace many of his or her belongings with new items? Would he or she be able to rebuild? Could he or she afford to stay someplace else during reconstruction? Home owner policies cover these issues and more.

Valuables—Collectibles, paintings, antiques, jewelry, and furs, among other specialty items, should be insured individually since coverage under home owner and renter's insurance policies is limited.

Auto—The cost of owning a car goes well beyond the sticker price and includes all the expenses of keeping that car running year after year. Insurance premiums, a vital expense element, can account for more than one-fifth of ongoing car costs.

Life—Family members should carry life insurance if there are dependents who would suffer financially if they die. People also buy life insurance to pay for inheritance tax and probate costs, debts, mortgages, and funeral expenses.

Disability—Experts agree that anyone who has a full-time job outside the home should consider a disability policy. Proper coverage averages 60 percent of a person's salary for as long as the policyholder cannot work.

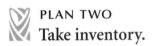

PLAN TWO
Take inventory.

Prepare inventory lists and photographs of your elder's household and business possessions to help establish the proper amount of coverage needed. Videotaped records work just as well. Keep photos and negatives separate. Store negatives in a safe-deposit box along with other important documentation. Itemize all valuables. The insurance company will require sales receipts and appraisals for all valuables. Keep receipts in a safe-deposit box.

If your family member has to file a loss claim, the insurance agent will need a written report of the items. Photographs and videos will be of great value in obtaining a fair settlement.

PLAN THREE
Go behind the scenes.

You can examine the financial stability of any insurance company. Insolvencies do happen as a result of bad investments, and some states don't guarantee funds when an insurer goes broke. Investors cannot count on warnings of impending insolvencies from regulators.

Insurance company ratings are conducted by A.M. Best Company, Moody's Investors Service, Standard & Poor's, and Duff & Phelps. If the insurance company is assessed by only one of these companies, that could indicate a problem. You will find these rate books at the public library, or you can obtain rating information on the Internet.

Another method is to contact the insurer's home office and request the most recent quarterly and annual report. Review the quality of the insurer's investments, which provide the income it needs to meet financial obligations to policyholders.

Beyond Medicare

Medicare, the government health insurance plan for older Americans, offers minimal coverage for health care costs. Existing gaps in this basic insurance program mean that your elder may be unprotected from today's soaring health care expenses. A chronic illness such as arthritis or diabetes can put the financial resources of the entire family at serious risk, since Medicare won't pay for the kind of day-to-day care these illnesses demand.

To help customers make informed health care insurance decisions, Congress imposed tougher standards on supplemental insurers (also known as Medigap insurers). Companies are required to sell standardized policies so that customers can easily compare competitive products. To ease comparison procedures, insurers must also provide potential buyers with detailed outlines of policy coverage.

This section of *The Planner* explains the interplay between Medicare and private supplementary insurance and suggests specific questions to ask when purchasing health and long-term care insurance. Additionally, states across the country have expanded counseling programs on Medicare and other health care issues. Encourage your elder to take advantage of this free advice to ensure a wise choice in his or her health insurance supplement.

BEYOND MEDICARE

- If your elder's medical bills aren't at least partially covered by an employer's insurance plan and he or she doesn't carry a "Medigap" policy, the wealth of the family is at serious risk.
- Medicare benefits exclude chronically ill elders who need some form of long-term, general nursing care as a result of strokes, Alzheimer's, and arthritis, for example.
- The key to buying supplemental health insurance is to review and compare policy differences. If what the insurance company offers sounds too good to be true, it probably is.

Since Medicare doesn't cover all of a patient's medical expenses, buying some form of health insurance supplement is essential.

PLAN ONE
Become familiar with Medicare options.

Today, Medicare beneficiaries are offered a range of choices in how they receive Medicare services. Depending on the particular plan package, the range of services covered or not may vary, with some of those costs being borne by the elders themselves. Each Medicare plan offers all covered Medicare services; but some dole them out more generously than others.

The Medicare menu includes:

Traditional Medicare—a federal insurance program that covers a portion of medical and hospital bills for those aged sixty-five and older, regardless of income, and those already receiving Social Security benefits. The program is actually two health plans in one. Part A (hospital) and Part B (medical). Part B isn't free and requires a monthly premium payment. At this printing, details were still being firmed up on a proposal that would expand the Medicare program and allow beneficiaries to purchase a limited prescription drug benefit. Even if your relative hasn't elected to begin receiving Social Security, he or she can still receive Medicare coverage. Apply for Medicare with the local Social Security office.

Medicaid—federal and state assistance that helps pay medical bills of low-income people of all ages.

Qualified Medicare Beneficiaries (QMB) and **Specified Low-income Medicare Beneficiaries (SLMB)**—part of the Medicaid program that pays Medicare premiums, deductibles, and co-payments for low-income enrollees. Any state, welfare, social service, or public health agency that handles Medicaid applications also accepts QMB and SLMB applications.

PLAN TWO
Explore the need for supplementary insurance coverage.

Most seniors back up their traditional Medicare with private "Medigap" policies, bridging the gap between what Medicare covers and what your elder must pay for.

Standardized Medigap supplemental insurance policies pay for a percentage of, if not all, hospital deductibles and doctor co-payments not covered by Medicare. These policies must conform to one of ten standard plans designed to provide a specific range of benefits. Insurance agents are prohibited by law from selling your elder more than one Medigap policy.

If your elders have plans to travel outside of their insurance area, especially overseas, they should seek information on optional benefits. Also, if you are concerned that your elder may forget to pay premiums, you should arrange for automated bill paying, and ask the insurance company to send *you* duplicates of the bills.

Sources for supplemental health insurance options include:

Medicare health maintenance organizations (HMOs), **Medicare preferred provider organizations** (PPOs), **provider-sponsored organizations** (PSOs), and **independent practice associations** (IPAs) with **point-of-service** options and **private fee-for-service** plans.

Medical savings accounts (MSAs)—Under this plan—which, at this time, is only being offered to 1 percent of Medicare beneficiaries on an experimental basis—a Medicare beneficiary would choose a private insurance policy with a very high deductible to cover catastrophic health care expenses. Medicare would pay the premium and make deposits into a savings account to fund payment of routine medical expenses.

Group coverage—insurance policies obtained through employment, club memberships, fraternal and religious groups, workers' unions, or the chamber of commerce.

Individual private coverage—Coinsurance companies offer various coverage and payment plans for the general public.

 PLAN THREE
Implement health insurance safeguards.

Knowing these basic insurance regulations keeps your elder's coverage in check:

- Buy only one supplemental policy and get rid of duplicates. *(It's the law.)*
- If your elder is eligible for Medicaid, don't buy additional policies.

- Review eligibility for continued medical insurance coverage for the spouse upon your elder's death.
- Waiting periods are not allowed when one Medigap policy is bought to replace another.
- Medicare-managed care plans cannot deny or delay enrollment because of preexisting health conditions.
- Know the rules regarding reinstating your elder's Medicare coverage *before* dropping it for another health care plan.

If your elder is considering a Medicare HMO, complete the HMO Questionnaire provided below. Make copies of the form for each interview, and encourage your elder to shop around and compare *before* signing up.

Be informed about HMO closures. Protections giving a senior guaranteed access to certain Medigap policies—regardless of preexisting medical conditions—apply only after the HMO terminates coverage, not if a person leaves voluntarily.

THE COMPLETE ELDERCARE PLANNER'S MEDICARE HMO QUESTIONNAIRE

Be well-informed. Have your elder get answers to these questions <u>before</u> signing up with an HMO provider.

Questions about the Doctor

If I'm unsatisfied, how easy is it to switch primary care physicians?

What if the plan doesn't include a specialist that I need?

Do doctors get a bonus if they make fewer referrals to specialists?

How many doctors leave the plan each year?

Questions about Prescriptions (very important)

Do you carry my current prescription?

Do you ever remove drugs from your list?

What recourse do I have if you remove my prescription from your preferred list?

Questions about Services

When I need to see the doctor, how long must I wait for an appointment?

How will I get prompt care in a medical emergency?

Who decides what is "medically necessary" in my case?

How do I appeal a medical decision?

What extras does the plan cover? (dental, chiropractic, mental health)

Are there special treatments and services for chronic ailments?

Which hospitals, nursing homes, and home health care agencies do you use?

What are the procedures for filing complaints or leaving this plan?

How do members get emergency care while traveling outside the HMO service area?

Questions about Costs

What are the monthly Part B premiums? What about copayments? Deductibles?

What is your policy on rate increases?

How long is the open-enrollment period before I am locked into this plan?

PLAN FOUR
Know the Medicaid spending policies.

State Medicaid spending policies protect the assets of one spouse should the other move into a nursing facility. Without professional advice ahead of time, overspending can then leave the remaining spouse virtually penniless and family members may be penalized for implementing certain spending strategies. Seek advice from an attorney specializing in elder law.

PLAN FIVE
Long-term care insurance—yes or no?

There is good reason why the government is giving us the hard sell on buying long-term care insurance for our elderly dependents and handing out tax incentives to do so; such policies help with the escalating costs of the kind of hands-on care commonly associated with assisting elderly people. Today, more than 75 percent of those who receive nursing home care become impoverished in just one year.

At the same time, we are aware of another kind of care called assisted living. This concept is a little like calling for room service from your hotel suite. Need someone to cook a meal, change the sheets, or help get you dressed? These seemingly simple, yet knotty problems are not only common, but also prohibitively expensive to remedy. Again, access to this level of quality care must be paid for privately—out-of-pocket, or through private insurance.

People often assume that if they do nothing, the government will pay for their long-term care, and that it's easy to get on Medicaid. In reality, by not thinking or worrying about it, and worse yet, by not planning for long-term care, your elder's access to quality care can be severely restricted.

Long-term care insurance—under the right circumstances—can be a pretty good deal, but it's not for everybody. If the need is already just around the corner, most likely the premiums are going to be prohibitively high; family members may not even qualify if they are in poor health or have an alcohol or drug addiction. But at the very least, it's worth your time to investigate whether long-term care insurance is the right choice for your elder, and for you.

What does long-term care insurance buy?

Long-term care can provide an aide who carries out the basic support tasks of daily living when a person is incapacitated due to an illness, injury, or cognitive impairment. More than nursing home care, long-term care covers help with activities such as eating, dressing, mobility, bathing, homemaker chores, supervision, and respite (time off for the family caregiver). Long-term care can be administered in the person's home, in an adult day care center, an assisted-living facility, or a nursing home.

Where to find long-term care insurance:

through your employer

association memberships

private insurance companies

senior citizen organizations

fraternal societies

continuing-care retirement community (CCRC), if your elder is a resident or on the waiting list

 PLAN SIX
Shop around for a quality long-term care policy.

In order to capture their share of the market, insurance companies are developing policies that cover long-term care such as domestic help and personal-care services so that elderly people can remain in their own homes. However, there may be a substantial gap between what consumers think they have bought and the level of help they actually receive.

Many policies do not provide *immediate* at-home assistance—they don't go into effect until sixty or ninety days have elapsed. Also, strict criteria must be met before a policy covers assistance to someone who is not completely disabled but simply needs help with eating, dressing, bathing, or domestic chores. The situation has to be far more serious than most people expect. [*CAVEAT:* Insurance coverage or benefits may be denied completely if the company can prove that untrue statements were made on the application.]

Follow these guidelines when shopping for a long-term care insurance policy:

The application process:

- The applicant—not the insurance agent—should fill out the medical history questions on the application.
- Make sure your elder answers all questions truthfully and completely. If an agent tells your elder not to list a health condition, find another agent.
- During the free-look period (thirty days after the policy is delivered), check the application to make sure that the agent answered the questions correctly and has not changed any answers. If you spot an error, notify the company immediately and insist that the company respond in writing.
- Submit a currently dated physician's statement along with the application. Request written proof of acknowledgment from the insurance company that they are in receipt of this information and have filed it with the insurance policy. Keep a copy of the physician's statement in your files.

The insurance carrier:

- Beware of agents who say they can get coverage in a very short period of time (24 to 48 hours).
- Beware of insurance companies that are willing to sell an insurance policy to anyone over the age of eighty-five.
- Check with your state insurance department to see if they have information on how the company in question pays claims or engages in "post-claims underwriting"—the practice of health insurance companies who check policyholder's medical history only after a claim is filed, instead of at the time of application.
- Look for an "A" or better rating in the *A.M. Best Company* (insurance reference guide) found at the public library.
- Know that insurance coverage is governed by laws of the state in which it's issued.
- If switching insurance companies, be sure your elder's coverage under the old policy stays in effect until the new coverage kicks in.
- Make sure the policy defines complaint-filing procedures.

The conditions of care:

- No prior hospital stay should be required.
- Medicare approval should not be required.
- Be wary of the limits on both the maximum daily benefits and the number of days (or visits) per year for which benefits are paid.
- Identify the waiting period before benefits begin.

The levels of care:

- Full coverage for Alzheimer's disease and other dementia.
- Coverage for respite care (time off for the family caregiver), adult day care, home health care benefits, and hospice.
- Coverage for all levels of care—skilled, intermediate, and custodial.
- Payment for any type of care in *any* licensed facility.
- Ability for the insured to use the benefits either for care within a nursing facility or at home.
- Payment of the same daily rate no matter where the care is given, although there may be reduced payments for adult day care.
- Coverage of care in assisted-living facilities and community senior centers.
- Benefits for personal grooming and homemaker services are included.
- Automatic increases in benefits, or the ability for the insurer to upgrade to higher benefits or less-restrictive coverage.
- No reduction in policy benefits.

Financing the policy:

- Age and current health are the key determinants of cost.
- You can save money on the policy by buying only three or four years of coverage.
- If you agree to pay for the first ninety or one hundred days of care, you can cut premium costs (much like raising the deductible on a car insurance policy).
- You can request a spousal and dependent discount when purchasing coverages for two lives or more.
- The policy should be guaranteed renewable.
- Premium levels are locked; they cannot be raised due to health or age.
- The policy should explain "class basis" as a condition of raising premiums.
- The policy has inflation protection.
- Premium adjustment will be done upon the death of the insured.
- The policy should waive the premium payments once you start using the benefits.
- The benefits received from the policy are income tax free (up to $190 a day in 1999) and do not affect seniors' Social Security benefits.
- The premiums may be tax-deductible on itemized returns, since they are considered a medical expense, although there are some restrictions.
- Ask about how the benefits are paid. Some companies demand that the insured submit nursing care receipts for reimbursement, others will pay providers directly, and others simply send a check for the promised monthly benefit.

PLAN SEVEN
Take action to file a complaint.

Do something immediately. Most health insurance claims, including Medicare, have a time limit on appeals. Most plans notify the insured, in writing, of any denial, reduction, or termination of services, and describe the appeal process available. You must receive notification within sixty days of your request of services. That doesn't mean you have to sit back and wait to receive this notice. Call periodically to inquire about the status of the case. If not satisfied with what you have been told, ask to speak to someone at the management level and demand more, or more specific, information. Keep a log of all such conversations including the names of everyone you speak with and the dates of the conversations.

Write to the insurer. Request reconsideration in writing. Include the company's letter of denial along with any facts that back up your argument. Keep copies of all correspondence. Again, keep calling to find out the status of the complaint.

Request a hearing. If you are notified of an adverse decision, request a hearing from the plan's review board. The letter informing you of its decision to deny services must include detailed instructions on starting this process. Identify your request as "expedited," to give notice that you want a response within seventy-two hours, and assert that a delay of up to 60 days could impact the patient's health.

Appeal to all possible channels. Send a copy of your letter and claim to the insurance company's sales director. If you have knowledge that other companies do cover the particular service in dispute, refer to that fact, and demand comparable coverage.

File a formal complaint. Each state has an insurance commission to oversee the industry and resolve disputes. Contact the Health Care Financing Administration (HCFA) and request a hearing from an independent review board by an administrative law judge. Refer to the list of organizations at the end of this chapter for additional support.

Take legal action. Retain an attorney to fight for your rights, or consider suing in small claims court, which does not require a lawyer.

Low-Cost and Free Resources

Your state's **department of insurance** can provide a wealth of information and/or assistance, including: the complaint history of any insurance company; answers to questions about a given policy; suggestions and alternatives for people who are having trouble getting insurance in the first place; or counseling programs. Look in the Blue Pages of the telephone directory under State Government.

To secure **Medicare** and **Medicaid,** visit or call the local Social Security office. Home visits from agency representatives are also available.

The local **department for the aging** assists elders with Medicare billing problems and insurance policy selections. They also provide lists of participating health care providers.

Health insurance programs are sprouting up citywide through **county bureau of health services.** County bureaus coordinate health activities through hospitals, public health departments, schools, and community centers. People can use these facilities if they have insurance, are on Medicare or Medicaid, or have no health insurance. For more information, contact the county office where your elder resides.

ORGANIZATIONS

Coalition for Quality Patient Care
1275 K Street, NW, Suite 602
Washington, DC 20005
(202) 789-3606
Website: *www.cqpc.org*

Department of Veterans Affairs
810 Vermont Avenue, NW
Washington, DC 20420
(800) 827-1000
Website: *www.va.gov*

Health Care Financing Administration
(Runs Medicare and Medicaid)
7500 Security Boulevard
Baltimore, MD 21244
(410) 786-3000
Website: *www.hcfa.gov*

Health Insurance Association of America (HIAA)
(Offers insurance guides for consumers)
555 13th Street, NW
Washington, DC 20004
(202) 824-1600
Website: *www.hiaa.org*

Insurance Information Institute
111 William Street
New York, NY 10038
(800) 331-9146, Fax: (212) 791-1807
Website: *www.iii.org*

Joint Commission on Accreditation of Health Care Organizations (JCAHO)
One Renaissance Blvd.
Oakbrook Terrace, IL 60181
(630) 792-5000, Fax: (630) 792-5005
Website: *www.jcaho.org*

Medicare Hotline
(Will also help you locate insurance review boards)
(800) 638-6833
Website: *www.medicare.gov*

Medicare Rights Center Hot Line
(888) 466-9050
Website: *www.medicarerights.org*

Mr. Long-Term Care
151-A Eastwood Drive
Clifton Park, NY 12065-4299
(518) 383-5989, Fax: (518) 371-1418
Website: *www.mrltc.com*
Martin K. Bayne, Director

National Association of Insurance Commissioners (NAIC)
(To locate your local state insurance commission)
120 West Twelfth Street, Suite 1100
Kansas City, MO 64105-1925
(816) 842-3600, Fax: (816) 471-7004
Website: *www.naic.org*

National Committee for Quality Assurance (NCQA)
2000 L Street, NW, Suite 500
Washington, DC 20036
(888) 275-7585, (202) 955-3500, Fax: (202) 955-3599
Website: *www.ncqa.org*

National Committee to Preserve Social Security and Medicare
10 G Street, NE, Suite 600
Washington, DC 20002-4215
(800) 966-1935, Fax: (202) 216-0451
Website: *www.ncpssm.org*

National Insurance Consumer Helpline
(800) 942-4242

Senior Benefit Centers of America, Inc.
(The watchdog of Medicare HMOs)
6853 SW 18th, Suite 110
Boca Raton, FL 33433
(toll-free) (877) 466-0200, (561) 361-0165, Fax: (561) 361-1049
Website: *www.seniorbenefitcenters.com*

Action Checklist

INSURANCE COVERAGE FOR A LONGER LIFE	To Do By	Completed
Review insurance policies for proper coverage		
home owner	_____	❏
auto	_____	❏
life	_____	❏
disability	_____	❏
business	_____	❏
valuables	_____	❏
Set insurance coverage goals		
short-term	_____	❏
long-term	_____	❏
Review life insurance company for stability	_____	❏
Locate a reputable, trusted insurance agent	_____	❏
Review policies with insurance adviser	_____	❏
Take inventory		
photographs	_____	❏
inventory lists	_____	❏
video	_____	❏
Keep inventory documents in a safe, 24-hour-accessible place	_____	❏
Know phone numbers of your elder's insurance agents	_____	❏
Keep copies of phone numbers		
at home	_____	❏
at work	_____	❏
in wallet or purse	_____	❏
Give insurance phone numbers to key family members	_____	❏

Keep proof of insurance
    in car   _____ ❏
    in wallet or purse   _____ ❏

BEYOND MEDICARE

Become familiar with Medicare
    Part A   _____ ❏
    Part B   _____ ❏

Compare Medicare plans
    Traditional Medicare   _____ ❏
    Medicaid   _____ ❏
    QMB plan   _____ ❏
    SLMB plan   _____ ❏

Explore Medicare supplementary insurance options
    Medicare HMO   _____ ❏
    PPO   _____ ❏
    PSO   _____ ❏
    IPA   _____ ❏
    MSA   _____ ❏
    Group coverage   _____ ❏
    Private company   _____ ❏

Review Medicare supplementary insurance options
    point-of-service   _____ ❏
    private fee-for-service   _____ ❏

Review health insurance safeguards   _____ ❏

Accompany your elder to ask HMO questions   _____ ❏

Research Medicaid spending policy   _____ ❏

Review for need of long-term care insurance   _____ ❏

Shop around for long-term care insurance   _____ ❏

File formal complaints   _____ ❏

Know the phone numbers of
    Social Security office   _____ ❏
    Supplementary insurance company   _____ ❏
    Medicare   _____ ❏
    Medicaid   _____ ❏

Keep health insurance phone numbers
    at home   _____ ❏
    at work   _____ ❏
    in wallet or purse   _____ ❏

Distribute health insurance phone numbers to
    key family members   _____ ❏

Make a copy of your elder's health insurance card   _____ ❏

Monitor your elder's health insurance claims
    for proper billing   _____ ❏

·8·

HOUSING

Home Suite Home

Contrary to popular belief, most elders aren't sick enough to require institutionalized care. Only 6 percent of people over the age of 65 require skilled nursing home care. The majority of the aging population live independently—in spite of their "aches and pains"—and supplement their needs by getting help from family, friends, volunteers, and assisted-living community programs.

Ongoing transitions in an aging person's lifestyle—retirement, chronic illness, repositioning of finances, and limited mobility—signal that it's time for the family to examine their elder's housing needs. This is indeed a time of great adjustment. Study after study indicates that most elders want to remain in their own homes and communities; but lack of proper planning often forces them out of their homes. Moving, and even remodeling, is a traumatic experience for anyone. You will be able to minimize negative reactions to changes in your elder's living environment by proceeding thoroughly and slowly, especially if your relative recently has experienced a major loss, or other serious stress.

It is outdated to assume that your only options are nursing home care or having your aging family member move in with you. Unless your elder requires round-the-clock supervision and skilled nursing care, there are other choices to consider.

Yet, family caregivers may be reluctant to consider the nursing home option when they should. The time may come when we do not have the skills and stamina to give our aging relative proper care. Yes, the decision to place an elder in a nursing facility is a difficult one, but sometimes it is the only alternative. It is not a question of whether institutionalized care is inherently good or bad. The decision for this option should be based on medical treatment, preference of the family caregiver, financial resources, and the availability of quality facilities. The nursing home decision is a very personal and difficult one to make.

Since conversations about housing can be quite emotional, review the Communicaring chapter in *The Planner* before you initiate any discussions. This is one topic that should be approached with kid gloves. Once you have the basis for effective communication techniques, this section of *The Planner* will guide you through the maze of investigating housing and care options while emphasizing the importance of making decisions that work to the benefit of the entire family.

HOME SUITE HOME

- Eighty-six percent of Americans who are sixty or older have no desire to change their housing, but a lack of planning may force them to do so.
- With adequate information and planning, aging people can control their housing destinies.
- Polls indicate 88 percent of elderly family members never discuss their housing needs with anyone.

Meeting your aging family member's lifestyle needs now, and in the future, requires planning and could prevent last minute, regrettable housing decisions down the road.

OBJECTIVES

After completing **Home Suite Home,** *you will be able to:*

Evaluate your elder's current and future lifestyle needs.

Recognize housing circumstances that may require immediate attention.

Locate alternate housing resources.

Find opportunities to get on waiting lists for housing options.

Minimize the trauma of moving.

Obtain a family consensus before your elder moves in.

 PLAN ONE
Be aware of circumstances that may lead to change.

There are many reasons why elders move or stay put. Consider the following issues as you begin to think about your elder's current and future living arrangements:

Finances

Home maintenance and housekeeping

Access to family and friends

Assistance with day-to-day tasks

Social interaction and companionship

Safety and security

Climate

Second-floor and basement access

Interior and exterior wheelchair access

Transportation

Health insurance coverage

Access to preferred doctor

Familiar surroundings and community ties

Place of worship

Family history and memories

Other residents

Illness and dementia

Employment

Pets

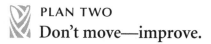

PLAN TWO
Don't move—improve.

Be prepared to make simple home modifications that can enhance your loved one's comfort, safety, and independence. Helping your elder to "age in place" is a win-win situation. Most elderly family members would prefer to remain in their own home if at all possible; accommodating their current and future lifestyle needs without a residential move lessens the caregiving demands on you.

No matter how familiar you think you are with your relative's home, you need to look at it anew, with a troubleshooting eye. To begin the process, take a walking tour of the home accompanied by your elder. Write down observations and ideas on a notepad. Your common goal is to customize his or her living environment to meet current and future lifestyle needs. If your elder uses a wheelchair and/or a motorized scooter, sit in the vehicle and take the tour from that perspective.

Plan to modify the home environment while creating a system of support, so that aging family members can remain as self-sufficient as possible. For any major home construction contemplated, first consider the applicable zoning laws and building codes. Financial assistance for home modifications may be available for eligible older people. Refer to the resources section at the end of this chapter for more information.

Elders will need help with . . .

interior and exterior repairs

home maintenance

housekeeping

heavy lifting

shopping and errands

transportation

cooking

personal grooming

health care

Expect to modify . . .

bathroom

kitchen

door widths, knobs and locks

lighting sources

light switches

shelf, sink, and counter heights

appliance control panels and dials

cabinet latches on doors and drawers

window openers

closet systems

carpeting

Expect to add . . .

first-floor bathroom, bedroom, washer and dryer

levers to replace knobs

handrails and grab bars

outdoor ramps

lifting platforms

Expect to buy . . .

glow-in-the-dark, large-dial clocks

talking clocks

smoke and carbon monoxide detectors

handheld or clip-on fans

nonskid rugs

adjustable furniture and bed

night-lights

illuminated light switches

programmable thermostats

room monitors

voice command systems

cordless telephones

telephone voice mail service

beepers

automatic turn off appliances

remote control devices

whistling teakettles

"reaching" devices

microwave and toaster oven

electric hand mixers

nonbreakable glasses and dishes

easy-grip kitchen utensils

bed tray

velcro clothes and accessories

nonskid slippers and socks

bath mats and suction cup accessory holders

shower and bath stool

raised toilet seats

grocery cart

health care aides

home hospital equipment

emergency paging systems and call buttons

medical alert bracelets or necklaces

Expect to obtain assisted-living services for . . .

homemaker chores

personal grooming

home health care

transportation

companionship and/or quality of life

Elders who have been diagnosed with Alzheimer's disease require a highly specialized home environment, since the disease leads to a loss of abilities to carry out daily life activities. Also, elders with Alzheimer's tend to wander off, a serious problem that presents unique challenges. Modifications and precautions that are appropriate in the earlier stages of the disease may not work for middle and later stages. Contact the local chapter of the Alzheimer's Association for a wealth of home modification suggestions, as well as emotional support.

 PLAN THREE
Learn about housing options.

Where an aging family member lives depends on many factors—health, money, safety, family and community support services, and preference. Here are some housing suggestions to serve as a guide in the decision-making process:

Shared housing is an arrangement when two or more related or unrelated people live together in the same house or apartment and share expenses. Tenants have private bedrooms, share the rest of the house, and may be able to arrange an exchange of services for rent.

ECHO housing (Elder Cottage Housing Opportunity) is the placement of a prebuilt, independently run cottage, on the private property of family or friends. Cottage units can be rented or purchased. Building codes and zoning laws regulate this option.

Retirement communities (homes, condos, apartments, retirement hotels, mobile homes, cooperative housing) provide age-segregated, independent living units and offer personal care services, social activities, and limited nursing supervision. Retirement communities vary significantly in costs and benefits offered and are not subject to any particular regulation.

Assisted-living facilities (residential care facilities, rest homes, homes for the aged, board and care facilities) provide some personal care and nursing supervision, medication monitoring, social opportunities, meals, and housekeeping. These facilities appeal to elders who can no longer live at home, yet do not need professional nursing care. Residents are physically and mentally able to handle their daily needs. Sliding-scale placement is available in most states. Facilities are generally licensed by the state department of social services.

Life-care retirement communities (continuing care retirement communities) offer eligible individuals the option to buy or lease an apartment unit and receive guaranteed care in a skilled nursing facility as part of the price of admission. When the leasing option is chosen, extended health care services may vary. Entrance fees and monthly charges typically accompany this option. Waiting lists are usually long. Life-care facilities are state licensed.

Group homes (congregate housing) are run by cities and profit and non-profit groups such as religious organizations. This option usually requires that the resident is self-sufficient. Services provided include meals, housekeeping, transportation, and social and recreational activities. Homes may or may not be regulated, depending on state laws. Financial assistance may be offered through the local public housing office.

Public housing is obtainable through the local housing authority. Homes and apartments are available throughout cities where landlords agree to accept prearranged, reduced rent. Waiting lists are long.

Adult foster care is a living arrangement in single-family residences in which unrelated elders live with a foster family that provides meals, housekeeping, and personal care.

Intermediate care facilities provide residences to elders who find it difficult to cope with the activities of daily living and need assistance managing medications. Elders in this setting may be in transition between hospital and home. Many nursing homes offer intermediate and skilled nursing care in one location.

Skilled nursing facilities (nursing home, convalescent hospital) provide continuous skilled nursing care for those requiring round-the-clock medical attention. Caregivers can take advantage of this housing option on a short-term basis if need be. Federal law prohibits nursing facilities from asking Medicare or Medicaid recipients for a deposit as a condition of admittance. Facilities are licensed by the state department of health services.

Elder housing options are listed in the Yellow Pages under Health Services, Homes-Residential Care, Hospitals, Nursing Homes, Rest Homes, and Retirement. Seek referrals from the hospital discharge planner or a geriatric social worker. Locate resources on the Internet, keyword search: senior housing, nursing homes, assisted living, retirement, life-care communities.

 PLAN FOUR
Proceed with caution when considering a retirement facility.

If your elder is considering moving into a senior living setting, including assisted-living facilities and continuing care retirement communities (CCRC), there is homework to do and many questions to ask before he or she signs on the bottom line. **But don't forget to keep your elder involved in every stage of the decision process.**

Getting started

- Location is an important consideration. Is the residence close enough for friends and family to visit on a regular basis?

- Inquire about the possibility of waiting lists.

- Visit all facilities under consideration, and stop by unannounced at several times of the day, during mealtimes, and at nighttime. If any facility restricts visiting hours, it may have something to hide.

- Do a thorough background check on financial stability, ownership, management, and staff qualifications.

- Use the services of an ombudsman (an advocate for residents) to inquire about any past resident or family complaints or even lawsuits. Ombudsman resources are listed at the end of this chapter.

- For each facility under consideration, verify that it has complied with all state licensing and accreditation requirements.

- Obtain a copy of the facility's last inspection report.

- Obtain audited financial statements from the facility director. Have these statements reviewed by an attorney or trusted financial adviser. If the director refuses to comply or does not have a financial statement, seek housing elsewhere.

- Get *written* copies of all oral agreements or promises; request a copy of the resident's bill of rights.

- Before signing any agreements, review contracts, printed matter, and resident rules and regulations with an attorney.

During your visit use *all* your senses. Ask yourself . . .

Is this a safe, comfortable, pleasant place?

Is the staff cheerful and friendly?

Are there odors I don't recognize or like?

Are the rooms well-kept and nicely furnished? Homey?

Is the overall facility clean? Organized? Secure? Bug-free?

Is the kitchen clean?

Is the refrigerator clean and stocked? Are dishes, pots, and pans clean?

Are smoke and carbon monoxide detectors and fire extinguishers visible?

Does every room, including each bathroom, have an emergency call system?

Are bathrooms and showers properly maintained and stocked?

Are all rooms, hallways, and elevators wheelchair accessible?

Are telephones within reach of wheelchair-bound residents?

Are there plenty of handrails and grab bars in every room and hallway?

Are floors slippery?

Are heating and cooling systems working? Adequate?

Are there accessible outdoor areas for residents to enjoy?

Are the buildings and grounds well kept?

Is the lawn mowed? Snow shoveled?

Are the sidewalks and curbs even and smooth?

Make sure things are in working order

- open doors, drawers, and windows
- turn on lights
- press emergency call buttons
- turn on televisions and radios
- see if the telephones work

Observe residents (and get personal comments from at least three residents and their families)

- Do they have bruises on their arms, legs, or faces?
- Are they dressed, or still in their nightgowns?
- Are they wandering or sitting aimlessly in halls?
- Do they seem comfortable, active?
- Are they making use of the outside areas?

Ask the admissions director . . .

Staff issues

What is the current occupancy rate and staff-to-resident ratio?

Do volunteers work here?

How do you screen your volunteers and staff?

What is the staff turnover rate?

Have your staff and volunteers undergone specialized training?

How are workers and volunteers supervised?

Health care issues

Will the family doctor be able to continue to care for the family member?

How many doctors and nurses are on your staff, or on call?

On what basis are they available?

Are residents required to carry health insurance?

Who monitors medications? What is the monitoring procedure?

Who evaluates a resident's illness?

Does the facility offer physical therapy?

How are medical emergencies handled?

How is the family kept informed? How often?

Quality of life issues

Do residents have their own newsletter?

Can residents choose their own menus?

Are intergenerational activities available on a regular basis?

What social, educational, and exercise programs are provided?

Is transportation for residents provided?

Are telephones readily available?

How are resident's religious and spiritual needs met?

Does the facility regularly celebrate holidays? Birthdays?

May residents furnish their rooms with their own furniture and furnishings?

Are linens and housekeeping services included?

How are personal laundry needs handled?

Are assistants available to help with getting dressed? Walking? Mealtime?

Can residents control their own heat or air-conditioning in their rooms?

Are televisions and radios permitted in the resident's room?

Is storage space available?

Does the facility offer on-site personal grooming services such as hairstyling?

Are postage stamps and incoming and outgoing mail services available?

Who is responsible for the resident's personal shopping?

Does each resident have an individual savings account for incidentals?

Are pets allowed?

Safety and complaint issues

What is the security system?

Are fire drills held regularly?

What are the smoking rules? Alcohol use rules?

How do you deal with problems between roommates?

How do you handle theft of personal possessions?

Is there a resident and family council that handles complaints?

Does the facility have resident and family support groups?

Financial and contractual issues

Is there an entry fee in addition to the regular monthly charges?

What are the total monthly costs?

What payment options are available?

What is and is not included in the monthly costs?

What is available for an extra charge?

What is the policy regarding rate increases?

What is the facility's history with regard to fee increases? When was the last one?

How much notice are residents given before an increase?

How are residents informed of rate increases?

Do residents have any protection if fees go beyond their budget?

What costs are covered by Medicare? Medicaid?

What costs are covered by the resident's health insurance?

Are refunds available? Under what conditions?

How long will the facility hold the room when a resident has to be hospitalized?

If a resident leaves for part of the year, is there a reduction in fees?

Is the resident guaranteed a room upon his or her return?

On what grounds can the contract be canceled?

Questions for the life-care retirement community director

What types of admission plans are available?

Are entry fees put into an escrow account?

Are entrance fees refundable? Under what circumstances?

Who decides when and to what facility a resident is transferred?

What fees do residents continue to pay if they are sent to nursing units?

If one spouse is sent to the nursing unit, does the remaining spouse have to move to a smaller unit? Is there a change in the fee structure?

What are the resident's rights under remarriage? Must the new spouse meet requirements and pay an entrance fee?

What is the plan to accommodate future high costs of health care services?

Are residents required to have long-term care insurance in place?

Does the facility have a cash reserve?

What are the future expansion and refurbishing building plans? How will this affect the residents' fees?

How are residents kept informed of the community's financial status?

On what grounds can the contract be canceled?

PLAN FIVE
Review the nursing home resident's bill of rights.

Under federal law, all nursing homes must have a written description of the rights of the residents. A copy of the nursing home's "Resident's Bill of Rights" statement must be made available to any resident (and family member) who requests it. The issues that should be covered in the bill of rights include the right to:

be informed of your rights

be informed, in writing, of the nursing home's policies

be informed of the nursing home's services and charges

be informed of charges not covered by Medicare or Medicaid

be informed about your medical condition unless restricted by doctor's written orders

participate in the planning of your care, including refusal of treatment

choose your own physician

manage your personal finances, or authorize someone else to manage them for you

privacy, dignity, and respect

wear your own clothing

use your own possessions while not infringing upon the rights and safety of others

be free from mental and physical abuse

be free from chemical and physical restraints unless authorized in writing by a physician

voice opinions and grievances without fear of coercion and retaliation from others

be discharged or transferred only for medical reasons

appeal a discharge or transfer

be accessible to visitors or to refuse visitors

immediate access by family members

receive visitors during at least eight hours of a given day

privacy and confidentiality for meetings or conversations with visitors

receive assistance from an advocate in asserting their rights and benefits

PLAN SIX
Know what's in store *before* you ask your elder to move in with you.

Sometimes well-meaning family members insist that their aging relatives move in with them without giving full consideration to all the potential consequences. The arrangement of sharing one's home with an aging family member is likely to stir ambivalent feelings among everyone involved. The possibility of caregiver frustration is great.

Besides the emotional considerations, be aware that moving an elder from one location to another will most likely affect his or her health insurance and medical care. Find out if this would happen in your case, and research options before you begin any conversations about moving in.

If you and your elder are thinking about combining households, discuss the following *before* the move:

Ask your elder

Do you want to move in?

Do you want to share a household with these family members?

How long are you prepared to live here?

Are there any relationship conflicts that need to be resolved before you move in?

Are you prepared to help with any costs?

How will this move affect your health insurance coverage and medical care?

Ask family household residents

Would anyone resent this living arrangement?

How do you feel about this relative?

How do you feel about spending time with this relative on a daily basis?

What adjustments would you have to make to your lifestyle?

Is it possible for you to treat the elder as a full member of the family, not to be ignored or isolated?

Ask yourself

Is this decision based on guilt or a sense of obligation?

How will this decision affect my marriage?

How will this decision affect my relationship with my children?

How will this decision affect my job, and other professional commitments and goals?

How will this decision affect my personal commitments?

How would I feel about spending time with my relative on a daily basis?

Is there a plan in place if I am unavailable to care for my elder?

Are there ways for my elder to contribute to the family and feel needed?

Is there a plan to preserve privacy and autonomy for everyone?

Have I anticipated how to deal with mood swings?

Is my family financially and emotionally stable enough to take this on?

Is there any other member of the family that currently requires a lot of attention and time? All things considered, are these plans realistic?

Discuss with the family members
- The plan for dealing with potential changes in family status—loss of income, divorce, death, marriages, births, pets, vacations.
- Family and friends' visitation rights.
- Elder's access to a full range of activities—inside and outside of the home—including places of worship, friends, relatives, shopping, entertainment.
- Sharing responsibilities.
- What are the costs and who pays?

 PLAN SEVEN
Consider the shared housing option.

Sharing a home with people outside of the immediate family is fast becoming a practical living arrangement, replacing the idea of living strictly with relatives.

Doubling up means cutting housing costs, sharing chores, and providing an opportunity for friendship, support, and love. This form of sharing has its problems; living close to others always does. Living alone creates isolation. As your elder ages, the ability to get along with others will become increasingly important.

There are plenty of people available to share a home: other elders, grandchildren, college students, nursing students, foreign exchange students, single parents with kids, friends, neighbors, coworkers, church members, and club associations.

 PLAN EIGHT
Plan for a smooth move.

Eight weeks before
- Shop for a moving company.
- Get three estimates and compare services.
- Ask about price breaks and low-season discounts.
- Ask how payments are made.
- What are the insurance claim procedures for damages?

One month before
- Request moving checklist from moving company.
- Review the moving agreement details.

- Start packing. Discard, distribute, and donate unwanted possessions.
- Photograph valuable possessions before having them moved.
- Fill out change of address cards. (Available at the post office.)
- Transfer prescriptions to the new pharmacy.
- Arrange disconnection and connection of utilities and telephone.
- Arrange the transportation of pets and plants.
- Reserve the elevator in high-rise buildings.

Final week
- Make arrangements for payment of movers.
- Arrange for packers to start boxing items to be moved.

Moving day
- Be home when movers arrive.
- Watch as belongings are inventoried, packed, and loaded on truck.
- Check the bill of lading.
- Review destination with movers.
- Give movers the telephone number of where you can be reached on other end.

Delivery day
- Be home when movers arrive.
- Be prepared to pay with cash or money order upon delivery.
- Keep moving-related receipts for tax purposes.

Low-Cost and Free Resources

Manufacturers of helpful products that provide solutions to living independently can be found in the Yellow Pages under the following headings: Home Health Care, Home Medical Equipment, Medical Supplies, Assisted Living Products, and Independent Living. Internet keyword search: **independent-living products.**

Universities with gerontology centers can provide information about housing options, home safety, and chore services.

Your area's **agency on aging** and the **state treasurer's office** can provide information on federal, state, city, and county programs aimed at setting up assisted-living programs for those who want to age in place and live independently.

Home modification financial assistance is sometimes made available to eligible older people. Sources include Farmers Home Administration for rural low-income elders; the community development department; welfare or energy department for funds to weatherize the homes of lower income persons; funds from Medicare and Medicaid are available for durable medical equipment with a doctor's prescription; local agency on aging for funds to modify and repair homes.

Hospital discharge planners can assist family with decisions about appropriate levels of care and housing.

The public library, bookstores, and bookstores on-line have many **books** available on retro-fitting your elder's home for a lifetime.

ORGANIZATIONS

Assistance in finding assisted-living products

National Rehabilitation Information Center (NARIC)
1010 Wayne Avenue, Suite 800
Silver Spring, MD 20910
(800) 346-2742, TDD: (301) 495-5626, Fax: (301) 562-2401
Website: *www.naric.com*

Christmas in April
A national volunteer organization that works in partnership with communities to rehabilitate housing, particularly for low-income elderly or disabled homeowners.
9335 Hazard Way, Suite 100
San Diego, CA 92123
(619) 505-6300, Fax: (619) 505-6400
Website: *www.christmasinapril.org*

National Council on Aging
409 Third Street, SW
Washington, DC 20024
(202) 479-1200, TDD: (202) 479-6674, Fax: (202) 479-0735
Website: *www.ncoa.org*

Assistance in finding housing options

American Association of Homes and Services for the Aging (AAHSA)
901 E Street, NW
Suite 500
Washington, DC 20004-2011
(202) 783-2242, Fax: (202) 783-2255
Website: *www.aahsa.org*

Assisted Living Federation of America
10300 Eaton Place, Suite 400
Fairfax, VA 22030
(703) 691-8100, Fax: (703) 691-8106
Website: *www.alfa.org*

BR Anchor Relocation Experts
2044 Montrose Lane
Wilmington, NC 28405-6208
(910) 256-9598, Fax: (910) 256-9579
Website: *www.branchor.com*

CareGuide
Website: *www.careguide.com*

National Accessible Apartment Clearinghouse
201 N. Union Street, Suite 200
Alexandria, VA 22314
(800) 421-1221, Fax: (703) 518-6141
Website: *http://knowledgeway.org/resources/2091.html*

National Association of Area Agencies on Aging
(To locate your local area agency on aging)
927 15th Street, NW, 6th Floor
Washington, DC 20005
(202) 296-8130, Fax: (202) 296-8134
Website: *www.n4a.org*

National Resource and Policy Center on Housing and Long Term Care
(Information about shared housing)
321 E. 25th Street
Baltimore, MD 21218
Website: *www.aoa.dhhs.gov/Housing/SharedHousing.html*

United States Department of Housing and Urban Development (HUD)
(Provides low-cost housing)
451 7th Street, SW
Washington, DC 20410
Website: *www.hud.gov*

Assistance with nursing homes and ombudsman services

Administration on Aging
(To obtain telephone number of state ombudsman)
330 Independence Avenue, SW

Washington, DC 20201
(202) 619-7501, TDD: (202) 401-7575, Fax: (202) 260-1012
Website: *www.aoa.dhhs.gov*

Health Care Financing Administration (HCFA)
7500 Security Boulevard
Baltimore, MD 21244
(410) 786-3000
Nursing home database: *www.medicare.gov/nursing/home.asp*

National Citizens' Coalition for Nursing Home Reform (NCCNHR)
1424 16th Street, NW, Suite 202
Washington, DC 20036-2211
(202) 332-2275, Fax: (202) 332-2949
Website: *www.nccnhr.org*

Assistance with life-care facilities

Continuing Care Accreditation Commission
901 E Street, NW, Suite 500
Washington, DC 20004
(202) 783-7286
Website: *www.ccaconline.org*
William Thomas, M.D., Director

The Eden Alternative
(Improving the quality of life for people who live in long-term care facilities)
742 Turnpike Road
Sherburne, NY 13460
(607) 674-5232, Fax: (607) 674-6723
Website: *www.edenalt.com*

Assistance with home-care services

National Association for Home Care (NAHC)
228 Seventh Street, SE
Washington, DC 20003
(202) 547-7424, Fax: (202) 547-3540
Website: *www.nahc.org*

Action Checklist

HOME SUITE HOME	To Do By	Completed
List circumstances for possible change in housing	_____	❏
Set housing goals		
short-term	_____	❏
long-term	_____	❏
Determine modifications		
short-term	_____	❏
long-term	_____	❏
Check laws and codes for home modifications	_____	❏
Research loans and funds for home modification plans	_____	❏
Determine assisted-living systems		
homemaker	_____	❏
personal grooming	_____	❏
home health care	_____	❏
quality of life	_____	❏
Review housing options		
ECHO housing	_____	❏
Retirement residence	_____	❏
Life-Care or CCRC	_____	❏
Group home	_____	❏
Public housing	_____	❏
Intermediate care	_____	❏
Skilled nursing facility	_____	❏
Family member's home	_____	❏
Shared housing	_____	❏
Create facility questions and checklists	_____	❏
Secure contracts and documents	_____	❏
Review contracts and documents with attorney	_____	❏
Research a possible change in your elder's health insurance	_____	❏
Obtain family consensus before asking your elder to move in	_____	❏
Develop moving strategy	_____	❏

· 9 ·

SAFE AND SECURE

Minimize Distress over Distance

We are a society on the move, and a growing number of family members assist their elderly relatives from far away. Elders and family members go their separate ways to pursue professional and personal interests and opportunities and to improve the quality of their lives. More than half the adult children of aged parents live at least one hundred miles away.

At the same time, this separation is creating a disturbing mixture of anxiety and fear on both sides. Family members don't really know what's going on in their elder's lives on a day-to-day basis and are increasingly concerned that they won't be able to respond immediately to an eldercare emergency. Elders fear that something may happen to them and no one would know. How, then, do we help our elders balance their desire to remain at home—measurably independent—while ensuring their safety and security?

The answer requires family members to take the necessary precautions in making their elder's home a safe place, learning to recognize and avoid popular money scams and creating family and community systems of support. The action plans listed in this section of *The Planner* will specifically guide you in ensuring your elder's well-being.

However, no matter how much you plan for safety, feelings of anxiety may remain. When these emotions surface, you can sometimes find reassurance simply by picking up the telephone and calling far-away relatives just to hear their voices.

MINIMIZE DISTRESS OVER DISTANCE

- Crime statistics report that elder abuse is up a dramatic 50 percent. The most likely victims are women over 75 years of age.

- Scam artists play on aging people's fears about maintaining a comfortable lifestyle on a fixed income. The telephone is the most popular vehicle for committing fraud.

Use basic prevention strategies to help your aging family member avoid becoming a crime or accident statistic.

OBJECTIVES

After completing **Minimize Distress over Distance,** *you will be able to:*

Recognize existing or potential hazards in your relative's home.

Initiate safety and security precautions.

Create check-in systems.

Detect signs of elder abuse and neglect.

Identify potential and existing scams, frauds, and con artists.

 PLAN ONE
Home safety is no accident.

Creating a safe and accessible living space for our aging family members will help them maintain their independence. Be aware, however, that too much rearranging can confuse a person who relies on a series of routines and memory.

Following are things you can review to make your relative's home as safe and secure as possible:

Throughout the home

- Electric cords are properly plugged in and safely tucked away
- Extension cords aren't overloaded
- Smoke and carbon monoxide detectors are present and have fresh batteries
- Electrical outlets aren't warm to the touch
- The home is well-lit—inside and outside
- Night-lights are present in hallways, stairwells, bedrooms, and bathrooms
- Electric heaters are placed away from curtains, rugs, and furnishings
- Electric appliances are a safe distance from water
- Fireplace chimneys are clear of accumulation and checked yearly
- Light switches are present at the top and bottom of stairs
- Light switches are located near room entrances

- Stairwells are well-lit
- Stairways are free of objects
- Stair handrails are present and sturdy
- Stairs are marked for visibility with contrasting tape
- Steps are even and uniform in size and height
- Floors aren't slippery or highly polished
- Carpeting, linoleum, and plastic stair treads are secure
- Carpets do not have holes or snags
- Carpet edges are securely fastened
- Water temperature is reduced to prevent scalding
- Water faucets are clearly marked hot and cold
- House smoking rules are established
- Rope ladders are available on upper levels
- Furnace is checked yearly
- Room furniture patterns permit easy access to doors and windows
- Rooms are free of floor clutter
- Stairs and pathways are free of objects
- Drawers, doors, and windows open and shut easily
- Flashlights are available in every room
- Glow tape is stuck on key items to identify them in the dark
- Cleaners and poisons are clearly marked
- Step stools are sturdy
- Window and door locks are secure and operating
- Medications are properly stored and usage instructions are written down
- A first aid kit is available and contains up-to-date supplies

In the kitchen
- Dishes and food are stored on lower shelves
- Towels and curtains are kept away from the stove
- Lighting is sufficient over stove, sink, and countertops
- Radio and electric appliances are a safe distance from the sink
- "Off" indicators on stove and appliances are clearly marked with brightly colored tape
- A telephone is in the kitchen
- Emergency telephone numbers are displayed near the telephone and on the refrigerator

- A fire extinguisher is in easy reach and in working order
- Whistling teakettles and food timers are in use
- Food is properly stored in the freezer
- No expired food is in the refrigerator or cupboards
- Plastic, easy-open containers and dishes replace glassware
- Heavy pots or pans are replaced with lighter ones
- Handles on pots and pans are sturdy and stay cool during use
- Pot holder mitts are available and used
- Refrigerator and stove are in good working order
- Sturdy step stools are available
- Pet dishes are tucked away from the walking path

In the bedroom
- Lamps and light switches are within reach of bed
- The electric blanket is in good working order
- The telephone is accessible from the bed
- An emergency telephone list is near the telephone
- A flashlight and whistle are near the bed
- Medications are stored away from the nightstand
- The bed is an appropriate height

In the bathroom
- Nonskid decals and rubber mats are available for the tub and shower
- Floor rugs are secure and won't skid
- Grab bars and handrails are next to the toilet, and in the tub and shower
- Handrails are secure
- Shower and tub stools are present
- There is telephone access in the bathroom

Home exterior
- Tools and yard equipment are safely and securely stored
- Solvents, paints, and sprays are clearly marked
- Goggles are worn when using power equipment
- Stair rails are secure
- Walking paths are clear and safe, with no holes in concrete
- Leaves and snow are cleared away
- There is telephone access while outside

- Stairs are replaced with ramps if necessary
- Porch lights are in working order

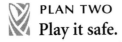
PLAN TWO
Play it safe.

The following safety precautions save lives:

Basic safety tips
- Make sure hands and feet are dry when using tools and appliances.
- Wear short sleeves when cooking.
- Plan two ways to get out of the house during an emergency.
- Know how to change fuses and circuit breakers.
- Keep a spare set of house keys, car keys, and eyeglasses.
- Read directions before installing and operating appliances and equipment.
- Display emergency phone numbers near telephones and on the refrigerator.
- Display a list of medications near the telephone and on the refrigerator.
- Take drugs responsibly.
- Purchase long-handled grippers, sponges, and dusters for easy reach.
- Buy a cordless telephone for easy use.
- Wear nonskid slippers and socks, and low-heeled shoes.
- Beware of robes and pajamas that are too long.
- Never store items on stairs.
- Get assistance when changing lightbulbs.

Guarding against burglary and other potential harm
- Never keep large amounts of cash in the house.
- Make sure the telephone answering machine message doesn't indicate that no one is home or that the owner is on vacation.
- Be discreet about letting others know you live alone.
- Never open the door for strangers.
- Never let strangers use the telephone.
- Never let service people in the house if you didn't request the service.
- Ask for proper identification from delivery and service people.
- Install peepholes and deadbolts.
- Befriend helpful, watchful neighbors.
- Participate in family, neighbor, and volunteer check-in systems.

- Draw blinds and drapes at night.
- Lock windows, doors, garages, gates, and car doors.
- Don't leave notes on the door when going out.
- Leave the lights, radio, or television on when going out.
- Don't put keys in the mailbox or under the doormat.
- Report all crimes and suspicious activities.
- Travel in pairs.
- Carry home owner or renter's insurance.
- Engrave valuables with your Social Security number.
- Keep a written inventory, videos, or photographs of possessions.
- Keep original documents and photocopies separate.
- Store important documents in a safe, fireproof place.
- Store valuables in a safe or in a bank safe-deposit box.
- Inquire about the bank's policy on insuring your safe-deposit box.

When going away on an extended trip
- Use light timing devices inside and outside the home.
- Notify neighbors and police of your absence.
- Suspend newspapers, and have the post office hold your mail.
- Arrange for the lawn to be mowed or snow shoveled.
- Leave the radio or television on.
- Make sure major appliances are turned off except refrigerator.
- Lock and secure all doors and windows.
- Store ladders inside.
- Disconnect the automatic garage door opener.
- Put valuables in locked storage.
- Leave phone numbers where you can be reached with family and friends.

While walking outdoors
- Walk purposefully and confidently, and keep alert to your surroundings.
- Wear shoes that promote balance and easy walking.
- Don't overload yourself with packages.
- Resist wearing a purse with a shoulder strap.
- Don't drape your purse strapped across your torso. Carry it like a football, close to the body.
- Walk in well-lit areas.
- Have keys ready in your hand when approaching doors or your car.
- Put a wide rubber band around wallets and change purses.

- Don't walk, jog, or bike with headphones.
- Carry a whistle or a loud alarm.
- If you're in danger, yell "Fire!" or "Police!"
- Get the license plate number of all suspicious cars and file a report.
- Avoid public transportation in very early or late hours.

While driving

- Check the front, back, and rear of car before entering.
- Keep doors locked and windows up.
- Stow your purse on the floor behind the driver's seat. Put all packages in the trunk.
- Keep a disposable camera in the glove compartment to document damage.
- If you are being followed, drive to a police station, fire station, or hospital emergency room entrance. Honk the car horn to summon help.
- Keep car in gear at stop signs and traffic lights.
- Travel well-lit streets.
- Keep emergency items in trunk—hat, gloves, long underwear, shovel, rags, water, throw rug, battery charger, spare tire, flashlight, umbrella, maps.
- Never pick up hitchhikers.
- If your car breaks down, pull off to the side, raise the hood, and turn on flashers. Then get back in the car and wait for help.

Safe banking and shopping

- Have monthly checks deposited directly into your account.
- Don't display large sums of cash.
- Avoid carrying cash.
- Don't retrieve cash from outdoor cash machines.
- Never leave your purse unattended.

For safety devices and services, see the Yellow Pages and the Internet, search under these key-words:

paging and signaling equipment	burglar alarm systems
radio communication equipment	security
safety equipment	locks and locksmiths
fire extinguishers	fire protection and alarm systems
smoke detection equipment	protection devices
flameproofing	medical alarms

PLAN THREE
Create check-in systems.

Any safety check should include an assessment of your elder's mental health. Depression and anxiety, for instances often increase the risk of accidents.

Whether your elder lives independently at home or in a group or nursing home setting, create ongoing check-in systems with family members, neighbors, community members, church groups, schools, volunteers, and professional care providers. Be sure all designated persons have keys to your elder's home.

If your relative becomes defensive about the amount of attention he or she is receiving, offer the following reasons for your actions

- To ensure safety and security
- To detect elder abuse and neglect
- To uncover hidden problems
- To avoid a crisis
- To protect his or her rights
- To offer peace of mind knowing someone is there

Check-in systems include:

Telephone reassurance programs. A telephone network that calls each day to check on a person's well-being. Failure to answer brings a second call within minutes. No answer results in a call to a designated person who goes to the individual's home.

Phone Alert League (PAL). A community program offering service to anyone living alone. If the person does not call PAL between a specific time frame, PAL will call and send someone to the person's residence.

Carrier Alert. Elders can register to participate in this program with the post office. A sticker is placed inside the mailbox to alert the mail carrier in the event of accumulating mail. The post office then calls the phone number on the sticker or the emergency number listed at the post office.

Emergency response device. Permits an individual to call for assistance. A variety of products are on the market. Get references from the hospital discharge planner.

In person check-in. Ask a neighbor or friend to check on your elder on a regular basis. Pay them for their time. If they don't accept money, buy them small gifts to show your appreciation.

Vial of Life program. Available through the county sheriff's office. Vital emergency data regarding an individual's health care is stored in a vial in the refrigerator. A sticker on the door alerts emergency personnel that the information is there.

Friendly visitors programs. Provide regular visitors to homes and nursing home facilities. Universities and church groups often participate.

Senior escort programs. The elderly receive transportation and companionship to community programs and doctor appointments. Contact the agency on aging, the local senior center, and a family service agency.

Ombudsman. Resolves complaints and investigates allegations of patient abuse. Listed in the telephone book White Pages under long-term care ombudsman.

PLAN FOUR
Get the facts about elder abuse and neglect.

The aging of our society as a whole presents many challenges. A substantial number of elderly people are cared for by adult children, spouses, friends, and volunteers. Elder abuse and neglect is not a new problem and can happen anywhere—in the home, residential facilities, and hospitals. Abusers can include family members, professional caregivers, volunteers, employees, and strangers.

Abuse and neglect may be due to the caregiver's lack of knowledge or capacity to care for the aging person. Abuse and neglect also can be a symptom of a stressed family or a long-standing difficult parent/child relationship.

Unintentional failure to fulfill a caregiving obligation, name-calling, ignoring, threatening, isolating, exploiting funds, physical abuse, denying access to food and water, medication mismanagement, failure to provide health care, violation of rights (such as opening mail), denial of freedom of speech, or the freedom to worship are all forms of abuse and neglect. Caregivers should be on the constant lookout for signs of elder abuse and neglect and report their concerns immediately.

PLAN FIVE
Outsmart the con artists.

Most elderly people have been raised to be polite and nice, and wouldn't think of hanging up on anyone who calls them on the telephone. Legitimate telemarketers and con artists are all the same to them—voices on the other end of the line requesting attention. Bad guys and good guys get equal treatment.

Research suggests that elders are more likely to be victims of financial exploitation than other kinds of neglect and abuse. In a Cornell University study, sociologists found property abuse to be almost twice as prevalent as psychological abuse, and five times more common than physical abuse. The number of cases of elders finding themselves penniless after unwittingly giving access to their bank accounts or turning over title to property is increasing at an alarming rate.

It all comes down to a matter of trust, and that is what makes it so hard to control. Con artists are slick and know how to catch people off guard. Unfortunately, an elderly person may easily become vulnerable to manipulation by strangers out of loneliness, fear, greed, and just plain gullibility.

Intelligent, well-read, and accomplished elders have succumbed to sympathetic-sounding salesmen who con them into paying for products and services that never arrive. And, fearing that exposure of the incident might bring their competence into question and threaten their independence, many elders want to forget the money and keep the incident a secret. Not only is there material loss in many cases, but among older people there is a concurrent loss of control and self-respect.

The FBI estimates that nearly 10 percent of this country's 140,000 telemarketing firms are fraudulent. Phone solicitations and offers through the mail make it very difficult for anyone to determine the difference between a con and the real thing. And there is a myriad of scams out there.

Popular cons include:

- Home medical equipment sold over the telephone
- Free cars (if victim sends a $500 check for "taxes")
- Arthritis and Alzheimer's remedies
- Instant weight-loss schemes
- Sexual stimulants
- Baldness remedies
- Nutritional cure-alls
- Wrinkle removers
- Unsolicited home repair
- Home testing services, such as radon-testing schemes
- Lottery and sweepstakes swindles (victims send in money for a "processing fee")
- Donations to phony charities
- Funeral home investments
- Mail-order life insurance policies

Has the con artist already struck? Con artists know that isolated elders are easy targets. The key word to remember here is *isolated*. Here are signs that a relative may have fallen victim to a con artist:

- Elder is suddenly having trouble paying bills
- Elder is making payments via a wire service or private courier service
- Elder is writing checks to unfamiliar out-of-state and foreign companies
- Elder is accumulating cheap items (jewelry, watches, plastic cameras, small appliances) that may have been awarded as prizes
- Elder is receiving more frequent calls

Proactive thinking on your part will help outsmart the con artists. Start up a conversation (review the Communicaring chapter for tips on opening lines), and discuss this subject with your elder. Let him or her know that such fraud is common, you may even discover that he or she has *already* been the victim of a scam. Next, discuss the danger signs. Here is a list of things to watch for:

- Door-to-door salespeople
- Unexpected visits from people with official-sounding titles
- Unsolicited phone calls from people asking questions about money, family, burglar alarms, credit cards, or checking accounts
- Unsolicited money offers, and directions to transfer money from people who identify themselves as friends of the family, bank officials, insurance agents, law enforcement officers, telephone company representatives, and city inspectors
- Unsolicited offers for home repairs and "free home tests"
- Advertisements that make use of the words: "act now," "best," "must," and "opportunity of a lifetime," mailings using scare tactics, and pictures showing fistfuls of dollars and money trees
- "Urgent," official-looking government-type documents that come in the mail
- Investment offers that promise or guarantee a return on investment
- Investments located in faraway places—Alaskan oil, for example
- Post-it notes with "personal messages" attached to newspaper articles arriving in unmarked envelopes, making it look as though someone you know is recommending the product or service
- Mobile health labs offering the elderly "free" health-screening services not covered by Medicare
- Crooks wearing uniform jackets formerly worn by police officers and security guards
- Early morning (1 a.m.–4 a.m.) phone calls
- Urgent telephone messages that a relative is sick or has been arrested, with directions to call a phone number with an 809 prefix. (The (809) area code is in the Caribbean, and is not bound by United States 900-number regulations. This call can cost you over $100.)

These strategies will help your elderly loved ones ward off predators:

- Hang up *immediately* on all unsolicited sales calls and calls from strangers.
- Return all suspicious-looking mail to postal inspectors so they can track down offenders.
- Show family members all official-looking mail.
- Don't pay for or accept unsolicited C.O.D. packages.
- Do not endorse "gift" checks, coupons, sweepstakes entries, rebates sent by mail. You may be signing an agreement, or appointing some unknown person or company to provide unwanted services.
- Never donate cash to a charity. Write a check and get a receipt.
- Never send cash through the mail.
- Check with a trusted family member or financial adviser before making *any* investments.
- Don't believe anyone who tells you you've won a prize.
- Never spend money to claim a prize.
- Keep Social Security numbers, credit card numbers, and bank account numbers confidential.
- If calling a telephone number with a (900) area code, be fully aware of the costs involved. Read the fine print, and beware of bogus products sold through these numbers.
- Know that con artists create an aura of legitimacy by paying "satisfied customers" to lie about the company.
- Get Caller ID or a phone-answering service installed on your telephone. If you don't recognize the telephone number or the voice, don't answer the telephone or return the call.

Visitors and Salespeople

- Never open the door to strangers, not even if they identify themselves as city inspectors, telephone repair workers, or utility company employees, unless *you* requested the visit. Call the police.
- When homecare workers are present, put away valuables, cash, jewelry, watches, and credit cards.
- Have family members meet all new "friends."
- Never give money to strangers for any reason.
- Don't discuss personal finances with anyone outside the immediate family.

Products and Services

- Never authorize home services without upfront, signed estimates.
- Get all warranties and guarantees in writing. Check for the length of time covered, what coverage includes and excludes, and the replacement parts policy on any major purchase, new or used.
- Don't sign *any* contract without first having a family member review it.
- Have a trusted adviser review all estimates, warranties, guarantees, and contracts before authorizing work or making purchases.
- Make sure service providers are licensed and bonded. Avoid wandering "fix-it" types.
- Buy art, antiques, jewelry, and collectibles only from reputable dealers who provide insurance to cover the purchase price of the item if its value is misrepresented. Ask other collectors and museum curators for referrals.
- Don't buy goods offered from the back of trucks and cars. Most likely, you're buying stolen property.
- Ask for and check references and credentials of all service providers.
- Avoid deals you don't understand.
- Never take at face value advice from someone who is trying to sell you something.
- Ask your physician about the reputation of any "free" mobile health labs in question.
- Call the Better Business Bureau, chamber of commerce, state office on consumer affairs, state's attorney's office, or state's security office to check on the reliability of any business or charity. Inquire about license requirements and any disciplinary history.
- Report *all* suspicious transactions.

The Internet

The **Internet** is an unlimited resource for products and services; but Internet fraud and intentionally planted viruses are running rampant. With an estimated 13 million Americans over the age of 50 logging on the Internet, scam artists are sure to be lurking there. Here are some suggestions on avoiding cyberspace frauds:

- Locate the telephone number and address of the business on the website, so you can be sure you know where the company is located. Cyberspace businesses operate in every part of the world.
- Call and ask to speak to someone directly. If you cannot locate a telephone or address, or reach a live person on the other end of the phone, do not buy from this seller.
- Get the offer in writing. A legitimate business will be glad to provide in writing: what is being sold, the number of units sold, the total price, shipping instructions and costs, the delivery date, the return and cancellation policy, and the terms of any guarantee. Print out the information so that you have documentation.

- Do a background check through the local consumer protection agency for business licenses and registrations.
- Never give your bank account numbers, credit card numbers, or other personal information to anyone you don't know or haven't checked out.
- Don't provide information that isn't necessary to make a purchase, such as a Social Security number.
- Be wary of time limits for special offers and high-pressure sales tactics.
- Understand that items purchased through on-line auctioneers may have no or limited warranties or guarantees. Proceed with caution.
- Flashy, expensively produced websites are no guarantee of a legitimate Internet business.
- Delete and report all unsolicited e-mails (known as "spamming") to your Internet Service Provider (ISP).
- Chat rooms are hunting grounds for scam and spamming victims.
- Beware of pictures, music, and other e-mail attachments from unreliable and unknown sources. Delete, rather than download.

If money or property titles have already changed hands, call the

- company and demand return of money
- police department
- United States Attorney's Office
- FBI
- Federal Trade Commission
- Better Business Bureau
- chamber of commerce
- state securities office
- district attorney's office

Low-Cost and Free Resources

Telecommunication Device for the Deaf (TDD) and **Braille TDD's** are available for telephone customers with hearing and sight disabilities. Contact the special needs center of the telephone company.

To participate in a **self-defense class,** find listings in the Yellow Pages under Martial Arts Instruction or call your agency on aging to find classes especially for seniors.

A free **home safety guide** is available at a nearby American Automobile Association Motor Club office.

If you suspect elder abuse and neglect, call the department of social services' **adult protection services.** Contact the **state long-term care ombudsman** for abuse and neglect in residential and nursing home care facilities. In an emergency, call 911.

Have the **gas** and **electric companies** do a home survey on appliance safety and make energy-saving suggestions. Most major utility companies have a toll-free action line for questions. Get the telephone number for your particular state from the utility company.

The **police** or **sheriff's department** will pay a home visit to show how security can be improved.

Ask a **fire department inspector** to visit the home to check on fire hazards.

For evaluation of how your elder's home can be adapted for safer, easier living, contact the **visiting nurses association.**

Some communities have **neighborhood watch** programs. Call the police department to find out more.

To learn **CPR** (cardiopulmonary resuscitation), contact the American Heart Association, American Red Cross, or the fire station to find out where courses are given. Check the Yellow Pages under First Aid Instruction.

If you have questions about air quality, or solid or hazardous waste, contact the **state department of environmental protection.**

Conduct an **Internet keyword search** for resources and information on these topics: elder abuse, fraud, home safety, con artists, scams.

ORGANIZATIONS

The Better Business Bureau
(To locate local offices in United States & Canada)
Website: *www.bbb.org*

Direct Marketing Association
(To be removed from unsolicited mailing lists)
Attention: Mail Preference Service
P.O. Box 9008
Farmingdale, NY 11735
Website: *www.the-dma.org*

Direct Marketing Association
(To be removed from unsolicited telemarketer lists)
Attention: Telephone Preference Service

P.O. Box 9014
Farmingdale, NY 11735
Website: *www.the-dma.org*

National Center on Elder Abuse
1225 I Street, NW, Suite 725
Washington, DC 20005
(202) 898-2586, Fax: (202) 898-2583
Website: *www.gwjapan.com/NCEA*

National Consumers League
1701 K Street, NW, Suite 1201
Washington, DC 20006
(To report a fraud) (800) 876-7060
(202) 835-3323, Fax: (202) 835-0747
Website: *www.natlconsumersleague.org*

National Fraud Information Center (NFIC)
P.O. Box 65868
Washington, DC 20035
(800) 876-7060
Website: *www.fraud.org/welmes.htm*

National Safety Council
1121 Spring Lake Drive
Itasca, IL 60143-3201
(800) 621-7619, (630) 285-1121, Fax: (630) 285-1315
Website: *www.nsc.org*

United States Consumer Product Safety Commission
4330 East-West Highway
Bethesda, MD 20814
Consumer Hotline: (800) 638-2772
Consumer Hotline for TTY: (800) 638-8270
Website: *www.cpsc.gov*

Action Checklist

MINIMIZE DISTRESS OVER DISTANCE	To Do By	Completed
Set safe and secure goals		
short-term	_____	❏
long-term	_____	❏
Review home hazards		
throughout home	_____	❏
kitchen	_____	❏
bedroom	_____	❏
bathroom	_____	❏
exterior	_____	❏
garage	_____	❏
Have elder's home surveyed by		
police department	_____	❏
fire official	_____	❏
electric company	_____	❏
gas company	_____	❏
Implement safety precautions		
at home	_____	❏
on an extended trip	_____	❏
walking	_____	❏
driving	_____	❏
banking	_____	❏
shopping	_____	❏
Create check-in systems		
telephone	_____	❏
Carrier Alert	_____	❏
beepers	_____	❏
visitors	_____	❏
Lifeline	_____	❏
Vial of Life	_____	❏
escorts	_____	❏
ombudsman	_____	❏
Check for abuse and neglect	_____	❏
Plan to ward off con artists	_____	❏

*Make sure an elder with hearing/sight disabilities
has access to a telephone*   _____ ❏

Know the telephone numbers of
    police department   _____ ❏
    fire department   _____ ❏
    electric company   _____ ❏
    water company   _____ ❏
    gas company   _____ ❏
    plumber   _____ ❏
    electrician   _____ ❏

· 10 ·

TRANSPORTATION

Steer Clear

Losing driving privileges in today's mobile society is a serious emotional loss—for anyone. When elders are no longer in the driver's seat, they have even fewer social contacts and become increasingly dependent on others.

There is little doubt that we have to get *high-risk* elderly drivers off the road; but before you bring up the subject with elderly family members, beware. While it may seem obvious to you that they pose a real danger to themselves and others, you should expect to encounter extreme resistance to your suggestion of giving up the old family car.

A safe, competent driver must possess specific skills at any age: the coordination to find and apply the brake pedal quickly; the ability to see clearly night and day and to distinguish between light and dark areas, such as silhouettes of people crossing streets at dusk; the ability to interpret road signs and directions; the ability to hear well enough to react to audible warnings of impending danger; the clearheadedness to locate a particular destination and map out a travel route both going and returning; the decision-making ability and self-control to manage the use of drugs and alcohol. *Ability*—not age—determines whether or not your elder should give up the car keys.

This section of *The Planner* offers specific suggestions for getting impaired elders off the road. At the same time, recognize that your communication approach is an essential part of the process. Your goal is gently to remind your elder that you are concerned for his or her safety in these particularly dangerous times. This may be all that is needed to help him or her decide to stop driving.

STEER CLEAR

- Countless drivers insist on getting behind the wheel while medicated.
- By age 85 and older, drivers have more serious injury and fatal accidents per mile driven than teen drivers.
- Even if a person has 20/20 daytime vision, nighttime vision will have weakened considerably by the age of 40.
- Seventy-six percent of side-impact crashes involve drivers over 50.

If someone you love is a hazardous driver, be prepared to take certain steps to get him or her off the road and eliminate a potentially serious danger.

OBJECTIVES

After completing Steer Clear, you will be able to:

Prepare yourself for confrontational driving-related conversations.

Encourage elderly drivers to monitor their own ability to drive.

Suggest transportation options.

Minimize the potential for your elder to become isolated and inactive.

 PLAN ONE
Use negotiating skills to get an impaired elderly driver off the road.

There are no national standards or systems to identify older drivers who have critical impairments. Ideally, your elderly family member will decide for himself or herself not to drive anymore. Frustrated relatives, in the meantime, may resort to underhanded tactics like hiding the car keys and disabling the car. These drastic measures sacrifice trust, honesty, and maturity in your relationship with your elder.

If you have evidence that your elder is unable to drive safely (has a bad driving record, perpetually gets lost, drives while medicated), and he or she refuses to compromise, a family intervention to take away the car keys may be the only recourse. Bring in a "heavy" to do the job—for example, a doctor who may be willing to discuss medical issues with your elder and write a "prescription" to stop driving. You might ask a member of the clergy or a policeman to stop by for a visit to reinforce the message. [NOTE: Do not expect much help from your elder's friends. They may be struggling with the same issue.]

The topic of giving up the car typically evokes a resistant response, forfeiting one's driver's license is among one of the most serious losses of independence anyone must consider. If you are just now beginning to question your elder's ability to drive safely, and you want to talk about it with him or her, *how* you approach this delicate subject will affect what happens next. For starters, take the time to review the Communicaring chapter of this book.

Our first instinct when a loved one is doing something that we know is potentially harmful is to tell him or her what to do. Unfortunately, adult relationships become strained or even severed that way. For best results, resist the urge to *command* an elder to stop driving, and instead, *negotiate* him or her off the road by asking questions. While this approach might take a little longer, it will get your elder thinking about the subject (even if he or she doesn't let on), help make him or her aware of potential dangers, and encourage him or her to self-evaluate driving skills. Conversation starters might include some of these examples:

Sometimes when I drive at night, it's hard to see. Does this happen to you, too?

Do other drivers make you nervous? I know I get jumpy when everybody goes too fast.

Maintaining a car these days sure is expensive. How do you do it?

Isn't parking getting more difficult and expensive these days?

This is one issue that will not be resolved quickly. Be understanding as to how difficult this transition is for your elder, and allow enough time between conversations for him or her to adjust to a new lifestyle. Spread out the discussions over time—several weeks, or perhaps a month or two. Remember that keeping the conversation in the form of questions creates a more trusting communication environment and better results. If the conversation seems to be going well, here are some inquiries to add when the time is right:

I just read about the 55 ALIVE program offered by AARP. What do you know about it?

What did the doctor say about your medications and driving?

How do you get around when your car is in the shop?

Have passengers refused to drive with you? What did you do then?

Would you like to know more about the senior discount taxi program?

Did you know that the train lets you off a block away from the event?

How about letting Mr. Jones drive for once?

What activities are you afraid of missing? Can anyone from this group pick you up?

When was your last eye exam? How did it go?

How much are you paying for car insurance these days?

What about garaging the car, and parking lot rates—pretty steep, huh?

What would you do if a carjacker approached your car?

Ultimately, you must decide what's best for you and your family. If you don't feel safe while riding as a passenger in your elder's car, you have the right to decline his or her offer to drive. Suggest, then, that your elder ride with you, or take two cars.

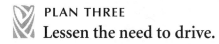

PLAN TWO
If all else fails, bring in the law.

If you have clear evidence that your relative is a danger to himself or herself and other drivers, there are legal steps you can take to alert authorities:

- Report impaired drivers to the department of motor vehicles. You may have to make a court appearance or you may be able to relate your concerns over the phone. Find out whether you can maintain your confidentiality, and what consequences you face should you file a report.
- Ask the department of motor vehicles to send your elder a notice to retake the driving exam. You will need to make this request in writing along with your elder's name, address, date of birth, driver's license number, and vehicle license plate number.
- If your elder insists on driving while heavily medicated, ask the prescribing physician to send a letter of request to the department of motor vehicles to put a stop to his or her driving—temporarily or permanently.
- Ask the doctor to write a "no driving" prescription.

PLAN THREE
Lessen the need to drive.

Door-to-door service is only a phone call away. These suggestions cut down on the need for your elder to get in the car:

- Ask and arrange for home deliveries.
- Shop over the Internet, even groceries and drugstore items are available on-line.
- Try TV and radio home shopping.
- Use mail-order catalogues (they gift wrap and send to receiver directly).
- Direct deposit, automated bill paying, and money transfers lessen the need for trips to the bank.
- Inquire about home visits from health care and personal care service providers, government services, and clergy.

PLAN FOUR
Supply transportation alternatives.

No conversation about giving up driving is complete without the ability to make suggestions on other ways to get around. Be prepared to offer these suggestions:

- Locate drivers and private transportation providers, including family, friends, neighbors, church members, volunteers, students, and youth groups. Professional drivers can also be hired if finances allow.
- Ask about transportation services supplied by health care organizations, shopping malls, community transfer services, and government agencies.
- Create a taxi fund. Encourage family members to contribute. Take advantage of senior citizen taxi discount coupons available in many communities.
- Carpool to regularly scheduled activities and shopping excursions.
- Supply your relative with public transportation maps and schedules. Senior citizen discounts are usually available.
- Obtain handicapped transportation information by contacting specialized transport companies with door-to-door services.

PLAN FIVE
Prevent isolation.

Try your best to keep your elderly family member connected with others:

- Invite your elder to regularly scheduled family activities such as birthday parties, weekend entertainment, meals, and holiday celebrations.
- Arrange to have regular home visitors such as other family members, friends, children, pets, clergy, and volunteers.
- Suggest that your relative get involved in clubs and activities where participants carpool.
- Senior centers are a source of numerous activities and often provide transportation.

Low-Cost and Free Resources

Independent transportation services for seniors are becoming more abundant. Door-to-door services take people to doctor appointments, grocery stores, dialysis centers, beauty shops, and anywhere else elders want to go. Negotiate rates if your elder will be a frequent customer. Look in the phone book under transportation.

Contact the local **AAA motor club** and request information on older drivers, driving assessment programs, and traffic safety.

Medical centers usually provide transportation to and from health care facilities. Call your local **agency on aging** or the **hospital discharge planner** director for details.

Some **shopping malls** provide transit services. Call them directly. Many **senior centers** throughout the country provide transportation to social activities. Call the individual centers for more information.

Senior citizen taxi coupons are available in most communities. Call your local agency on aging.

ORGANIZATIONS

AAA Foundation for Traffic Safety
1440 New York Avenue, NW, Suite 201
Washington, DC 20005
(202) 638-5944, Fax: (202) 638-5943
Website: *www.aaafts.org*

Community Transportation Association of America
1341 G Street, NW, Suite 600
Washington, DC 20005
(202) 628-1480, Fax: (202) 737-9197
Website: *www.ctaa.org*

Insurance Institute for Highway Safety
1005 N. Glebe Road, Suite 800
Arlington, VA 22201
(703) 247-1500, Fax: (703) 247-1588
Website: *www.hwysafety.org*

National Highway Traffic Safety Administration
400 7th Street, SW
Washington, DC 20590
Auto Safety Hotline: (888) 327-4236
Website: *www.nhtsa.dot.gov*

Action Checklist

STEER CLEAR	To Do By	Completed
Set transportation goals		
short-term	_____	❏
long-term	_____	❏
Monitor your elder's ability to drive	_____	❏
Look for evidence of auto accidents on your elder's car	_____	❏
Read intervention and communication suggestions before opening up the dialogue (review the Communicaring chapter)	_____	❏
If all else fails, bring in the law	_____	❏
Lessen the need for your elder to drive	_____	❏
Create ways for your elder to be socially active	_____	❏
Know phone numbers of		
auto insurance	_____	❏
auto club	_____	❏
motor vehicle department	_____	❏
Obtain copy of your elder's		
auto insurance card	_____	❏
auto club card	_____	❏

· 11 ·

HEALTH AND WELLNESS

Taking Charge: Healthy Living Tips

Many of us know that proper diet and exercise help us take charge of our physical and mental well-being. We are even encouraged to ask questions of our health care professionals if we don't fully understand their recommendations. Elders, on the other hand, tend to live by a different set of attitudes and roles when it comes to their own health care. For the most part, they were taught never to question their doctor's authority and may consequently believe that their health is solely in someone else's hands.

If elderly family members are going to get in the practice of caring for their own health, they will most likely have to learn many new behaviors. The deep-rooted habits of not challenging authority and not asking questions aren't easy to change, and the idea of taking charge of one's own health may seem foreign to your elder at first. Preaching the benefits of self-health care probably will not get you very far. Preaching about *anything* never does. Wellness advocates don't preach—they demonstrate. Eat right. Stay active. At best, we can be a source of information and influence on our elderly loved ones.

Keep in mind that elderly people will grasp this concept of self-health care only if they want to. Plenty of health care information is already available to them, but it is solely their decision to act upon it and make changes for the better. At the least, you can use this section of *The Planner* to help your elder make informed decisions about his or her own health care providers and quality of care. An educated consumer can make a big difference in weighing health management and treatment options.

TAKING CHARGE: HEALTHY LIVING TIPS

- "Older means weaker" is a myth. Many types of strength remain constant throughout life. In general, muscle strength begins to decline only after age seventy.
- Thousands of premature deaths could be prevented if family members would learn more about their family medical history.
- Even non-life-threatening diseases can mean the difference between living at home and living in a nursing home.
- Health is a means, not an end. Elders must assume a greater responsibility for their own health.

We are all paying for improper self-health care—financially and emotionally. Health care is one of the most complex issues this country faces.

OBJECTIVES

After completing Taking Charge: Healthy Living Tips, you will be able to:

Encourage your elder to live a more healthy lifestyle.

Acquaint yourself with health care professionals and the services they provide.

Combat your elder's inattention or over-attention to his or her health.

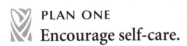

PLAN ONE
Encourage self-care.

Aging is inevitable; disease and disability are not. Many health problems are preventable. Before making any changes in diet and exercise, elders are advised to see their doctors. The suggestions below are meant to serve as springboards for self-health care conversations with your elder.

Exercise. It is never too late to start. One half hour of brisk walking three or four times a week has been shown to increase health substantially. Even ten- and twenty-minute chunks of time spent being active add up to improved health. More vigorous exercise improves mood states and self-esteem. Physical frailty can often be reversed by exercise. To stay active, feet must be comfortable. See a good podiatrist to help remedy corns, bunions, and calluses. Good shoes, with proper support, are essential. Senior exercise program information is available at the agency on aging and senior centers.

Activities include . . .

golf	biking
swimming	bowling
jogging	gardening
walking	dancing
hiking	tennis
climbing stairs	badminton
shuffleboard	croquet
billiards	lifting weights
racquetball	aerobics
softball	aqua aerobics
lawn bowling	yoga
horseshoes	stretch classes

Eat right. Ask the doctor about healthy weight averages. Women who gain just twenty pounds double their risk of heart diseases. Include five servings or more of fruits and vegetables in the daily diet. Limit the amount of salt, sugar, and high-fat food intake. Take advantage of community home and group meal programs such as meals on wheels, nutrition sites, and food banks. Contact the agency on aging and the local senior center to sign up for meal programs.

Poor eating habits may stem from limited finances (look into food stamps), depression, poor mental health, difficulty with grocery shopping and cooking, improper dental care, diminishing taste buds, and foods that cause stomach upsets. Simple dehydration (loss of the body's water supply) can bring on mental confusion, disorientation, and other problems.

Don't smoke. Experts say health benefits can be realized regardless of what age you quit smoking. Hospitals have support groups to help smokers kick the habit.

Limit alcohol intake. Drinking alcohol reduces life expectancy, causes nutritional deficiencies, contributes to physical disorders, and increases the risk of accidents. Seek help from Alcoholics Anonymous and Al-Anon if drinking is a problem.

Review medications. Over-the-counter and prescription drugs can be unknowingly abused both by an elder and the doctor who prescribes the drugs. See *Managing Medications* in the Emergency Preparedness chapter of *The Planner*, starting on page 85.

Breathe. Use breathing as a technique for relaxation and to keep the oxygen flowing. Take long, deep breaths on a regular basis.

Read labels. Find out what's in the food you eat by making it a habit to read labels. Use topical body lotions with caution. Understand labels on cosmetics, soaps, hair products, lotions, and deodorants. Buy small portions of a new product and conduct patch skin tests. The terms "natural" and "fragrance-free" can be misleading. Do not share cosmetics, hairbrushes, combs, toothbrushes, lotions, body sponges, face sponges, and undergarments with anyone.

Stay safe. Physical changes in hearing, vision, and the sense of smell affect comfort and safety. Get yearly eye and ear exams. Lack of smell may be a result of malnutrition or depression. Consult with medical professionals. Review the Safe and Secure chapter in *The Planner* starting on page 174.

Drive safely. Be realistic about the ability to maneuver an automobile on today's crowded, fast-paced streets. Nervousness and slower reaction times contribute to deadly accidents. Wear seat belts. See the Transportation chapter of *The Planner* starting on page 192.

Get a good night's sleep. Exercise, diet, and mental fitness contribute to rest and rejuvenation.

Maintain loving relationships. Companionship makes life more enjoyable and helps counteract depression. Spending time and talking about problems with those you love help to overcome periods of depression, loneliness, and also health problems. Family gatherings, social activities, church groups, volunteering, and sharing meals provide opportunities for togetherness. See the Quality of Life chapter of *The Planner* starting on page 219.

Be informed. Examine the family's medical history at least as far back as grandparents to discern patterns of disease inheritance. Investigate medical documents. Stay informed about the latest medical discoveries and care options.

Practice preventive medicine. Get regular medical, dental, ear, and eye checkups. Manage blood pressure.

Use medical services wisely. Find the right health care professional to be sure to get proper care. Ask for referrals from trusted sources.

 PLAN TWO
Get to know the health care professionals.

All doctors are not the same. This list can help you sort out the differences between and similarities among various fields:

General Practitioner (G.P.) and **Medical Doctor** (M.D.) are both physicians who treat diseases and injuries, do checkups, prescribe medicine, and perform minor surgery. They make referrals to specialists.

Board-Certified Specialist. M.D. followed by, for instance, F.A.C.G. (Fellow of the American College of Gastroenterology), F.A.C.S. (Fellow of the American College of Surgeons), etc. If your elder is having an operation, check credentials. A board-certified M.D. has to pass a rigorous exam to qualify.

Internist. M.D. specializing in the diagnosis of diseases of adults and its treatment.

Doctor of Osteopathy. (D.O.) M.D. specializing in the medication and surgery of bones, muscles, and joints. Most osteopaths are family practitioners.

Any of the above doctors may refer patients to these specialists
- **Cardiologist**—heart and coronary artery specialist
- **Dermatologist**—skin specialist
- **Endocrinologist**—specialist in gland and hormone disorders
- **Gastroenterologist**—stomach and digestive tract specialist
- **Gynecologist**—specialist in the female reproductive system
- **Hematologist**—blood specialist
- **Nephrologist**—specialist in the function and diseases of the kidney
- **Neurologist**—brain and nervous system specialist
- **Oncologist**—cancer and tumor specialist
- **Ophthalmologist**—eye specialist who also performs eye surgery
- **Orthopedist**—specialist in bone, muscle, and joint disorders
- **Otolaryngologist**—an ear, nose, and throat specialist
- **Proctologist**—specialist in disorders of the anus, rectum, and colon
- **Pulmonary specialist**—specialist in disorders of the lung and chest
- **Radiologist**—X ray specialist
- **Rehabilitation specialist**—specialist in correcting stroke and injury disabilities
- **Rheumatologist**—specialist in rheumatism and arthritis
- **Surgeon**—specialist in treating diseases, injuries, and deformities by operating on the body
- **Urologist**—specialist in urinary systems in both sexes and in the male reproductive system

Mental Health
- **Clinical Psychologist**—not an M.D., may have obtained an academic Ph.D.; specializes in family and one-on-one patient counseling.
- **M.F.C.C./L.C.S.W.** (Marriage, Family, Child Counselor and Licensed Clinical Social Worker)—trained to diagnose and treat emotional disorders.

Psychiatrist—M.D. or D.O. trained in the diagnosis and treatment of patients for physical and emotional behavior disorders.

Psychoanalyst—may or may not be M.D.; specializes in treatment of patients for emotional disorders.

Eye and Ear

Optometrist—not an M.D.; prescribes and adjusts glasses and contact lenses.

Optician—not an M.D.; fills prescriptions for glasses and contact lenses.

Audiologist—not an M.D.; tests patients for hearing loss.

Dental

Dentist—D.D.S. (doctor of dental surgery) treats tooth decay and gum diseases, provides dentures, can detect mouth cancer, diabetes, and eating disorders.

Dental hygienist—not an M.D.; cleans and polishes teeth, teaches dental hygiene, and takes X rays.

Endodontist—specialist in root canal.

Oral surgeon—performs difficult tooth removals and jaw surgery.

Orthodontist—straightens teeth.

Periodontist—specialist in gum diseases.

Feet

Podiatrist—D.P.M. (doctor of podiatric medicine) diagnoses and treats injuries and diseases of the foot.

Additional health care providers, many of whom are covered by insurance

Acupuncturist—not an M.D.; administers treatment by way of insertion and manipulation of needles into the skin. May be an Oriental Medical Doctor O.M.D.

Chiropractor—not an M.D.; physically manipulates and adjusts the spinal column, joints, and soft tissues.

Licensed practical nurse—(L.P.N.) assists physicians and registered nurses.

Massage therapist—uses pressure, friction, and strain upon the muscles and joints of the body for therapeutic or physical responses.

Naturopath—practices treatment of disease through manipulation of diet.

Nurse-practitioner—(N.P.) registered nurse additionally trained to conduct physical exams, counsel, and treat patients.

Occupational therapist—(O.T.) provides individualized programs of mental and/or physical activity.

Pharmacist—dispenses prescription medicines, knowledgeable about the chemical composition and correct use of medicines.

Physician's assistant—(P.A.) takes medical histories, conducts physical exams, performs routine diagnostic procedures, and gives treatment plans.

Physical therapist—(P.T.) restores mobility and strength to body parts affected by illness, disease, or injury.

Registered dietitian—(R.D.) specializes in dietary counseling.

Registered Nurse—(R.N.) staff member of health facility or private patient.

Speech or language therapist—evaluates and treats speech impairments.

PLAN THREE
Gently ease into action if your elder resists seeing a doctor.

Older generations seek medical assistance differently from younger generations. Preventive health care is not typically a part of an elderly person's thinking, nor a part of Medicare, which is geared toward critical acute care.

A visit to the doctor can be a traumatic experience. Review the Communicaring chapter of *The Planner* starting on page 47 for suggestions on talking about this sensitive subject. Compassion combined with "soft sell" communication techniques will be more effective in uncovering your loved one's underlying fears about the health care environment:

- Ask your relative if he or she likes the doctor. If not, ask if switching to a different doctor would make a difference.
- Suggest a less-threatening health care environment such as a health fair or drug store, where your elder's cholesterol and blood pressure can be tested.

PLAN FOUR
Recognize that frequent panic attacks may be calls for attention.

On the opposite end of the spectrum, your aging family member may request too much assistance on a regular basis, making it very difficult for family caregivers to determine when help is *really* needed. Become an investigator. Enlist the help of health care professionals and inform them of your relative's frequent patterns of requests.

Partnership for Quality Health Care

In the past, patients believed that their well-being was solely in the hands of their doctor. Today, the best decisions that are made about health care services, products, and methods of treatment are cooperative efforts between informed patients and their doctors. Even though this kind of doctor-patient relationship is healthy, most elders still feel reluctant to initiate conversations about diagnosis or treatment.

In recent years, consumer groups fought and won the right for patients to expand their knowledge and options for health care. These changes have brought a balance to the relationship between doctors and patients, and enhanced treatment outcomes. Encourage aging family members to become active participants in their own health care process, especially since compliance with the doctor's orders are a critical part of their medical treatment.

The more accurately your elder can describe symptoms and prioritize health concerns, the better the doctor can diagnose and treat his or her problem. Then again, clear communication demands a willingness to ask questions. Health care settings, with all the high-tech trimmings, can be intimidating. But you can improve the quality of your elder's health care by putting into practice the action plans suggested in this section—writing down questions, noting important changes in physical conditions, tracking the family's medical history, taking notes during appointments, keeping medical records, and seeking second opinions.

Everyone copes differently with illness. Some patients want all the information they can get in order to take action, while others just want to be told what to do. The responsibility for becoming an active partner in their own health care rests squarely on the shoulders of our elders.

PARTNERSHIP FOR QUALITY HEALTH CARE

- On the average, physicians interrupt patients within seventeen seconds of the office visit and generally allow only eighteen seconds for patients to ask questions.
- Surveys reveal that the elderly are rarely told of the side effects of medications.
- Physicians can also empower patients to become active participants in their own health care.

The way a doctor speaks and works with patients, and their family members, is critical to the quality of medical care. Some 70 percent of correct diagnoses depends solely on what a patient tells his or her doctor.

OBJECTIVES

After completing Partnership for Quality Health Care, *you will be able to:*

Gain a better understanding of your elder's attitude toward medical care.

Be a more-informed consumer of medical services.

Enhance the quality of your elder's medical care.

Advocate your elder's rights as a patient.

PLAN ONE
Be aware of your elder's attitudes regarding medical attention.

Following are some health care attitudes to watch out for. Your elder may:

- fear the truth, and postpone doctor visits for fear of what the doctor may say.
- not understand medical jargon and decline to ask the doctor questions.
- be misinformed and prejudiced about aging, and believe that the problem cannot be cured.
- maintain a death-wish attitude, and not be open-minded to any treatment.
- feel responsible for being ill and angry with himself or herself about being unhealthy.
- distrust health care providers and disbelieve what they say.
- have privacy issues that trigger a loss of dignity when anyone examines his or her body.
- be in awe of the doctor, he or she may hesitate to take up too much of the doctor's time and may be afraid of making the doctor mad.
- succumb to a false sense of security when the "experts" take over.
- rely on health care providers for feedback on how his or her own body is functioning.
- believe that a good patient is someone who doesn't ask questions or challenge the doctor's opinion.

PLAN TWO
Know your elder's rights as a medical consumer.

Patients are entitled to:

- privacy in treatment
- be treated with dignity and respect
- free initial consultation interviews
- informed, certified, properly trained practitioners
- practitioners who meet timely scheduled appointments
- be fully informed of medical conditions
- ask questions and participate in planning medical treatment
- refuse treatment and understand consequences of such refusal
- second or third opinions (costs of which may or may not be covered by insurance or Medicare)

- prompt, clear explanations of test results
- 24-hour-accessible medical services
- refuse to participate in experimental research

 PLAN THREE
Become a smart health care consumer.

Patients are better off when they come prepared for medical treatments; they are diagnosed more accurately, respond better to treatment, and recover more quickly At the same time, hurried doctors are a fact of life. Here are a few suggestions to discuss with your elder to help him or her get the most out of each doctor visit:

Before the doctor appointment

- **Describe the pain.** Write down the answers to these questions: What is hurting me? What does the pain feel like—piercing, aching, shooting, burning, throbbing? Does the pain change when I lie down or stand up? Do pain-killing medications work permanently, temporarily, or not at all? What makes the pain worse—walking, coughing, lifting, lying down, standing? How often am I in pain—all the time, part of the time, daytime and/or nighttime?

- **Put *everything* in writing.** Bring notes from home and take notes during the medical appointment. Bring a list of questions, health concerns, and symptoms. Jot down any situations that are causing you emotional stress.

- **Bring a medical history and list of prescription, over-the-counter, and alternative medications to *every* appointment.** (See Plan Four)

- Attend *all* appointments with a family member. No matter how routine the doctor visit, make arrangements for someone to be present to translate information, ask questions, take notes, provide comfort, and act as an advocate. Companions also help a person recall what the doctor said.

During the doctor visit

- **Prioritize health concerns.** Start with the most important problem. Also, let the doctor know about any stressful situations you may be experiencing at this time. When the doctor talks, write down explanations and instructions or use a small cassette recorder to tape the appointment and transcribe your notes later.

- **Ask questions.** There is no such thing as a silly question.

- **Understand the answers.** Ask the doctor to define medical jargon and repeat or rephrase complex terminology. Refer to medical diagrams and put information and instructions in writing. Keep asking questions until you fully understand what is being said. At the end of the appointment, ask the doctor to summarize the visit to be certain you did not miss any important points.

- **Retain copies of your medical tests** and ask someone to help you read them.

After the doctor visit

- **Get second opinions.** If you are unsure of what to do or you don't agree with the method of treatment suggested, get a second, or even a third, opinion.

- **Manage prescriptions.** See *Managing Medications* in the Emergency Preparedness chapter of *The Planner* starting on page 82.

- **Stay informed.** Read, watch medical programs when televised, attend classes and health fairs. The Internet is an unlimited resource for news articles and research on current developments in all areas of medicine and medical practice. *But, a word to the wise: according to the Journal of the American Medical Association, everything that you find on the Internet may not be complete or 100% accurate.* Focus on websites from acknowledged experts in health, such as the American Medical Association, American Heart Association, American Cancer Society, American Diabetes Association, and so forth.

- **Quality care is a two-way street.** Have the courtesy to call and cancel if you cannot make any doctor's appointments.

Shop around. Choose medical providers based on a satisfying relationship and the quality of care provided. Find a doctor who:

- seeks the patient's opinion
- explains how health can be improved with lifestyle changes
- conducts thorough medical examinations
- explains possible side effects of medication
- takes a thorough medical history
- does not keep patients waiting
- encourages questions about health conditions or treatment
- does not rush through visits
- cares about his or her patients' emotional well-being
- makes the patient feel at ease

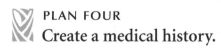

PLAN FOUR
Create a medical history.

Encourage your elder to become an active participant in his or her own health care by creating a *written* medical history and by bringing such documentation to *every* appointment. The more accurately your elder can describe symptoms, use of medications, and prioritize health concerns, the better the doctor can diagnose and treat the problem.

Thorough family medical histories permit better health care. Obtain a copy of your elder's medical history for yourself and distribute copies to other family members. Update this important information as needed, and include the following information in the medical history:

MEDICAL HISTORY

Patient's full name/maiden name _____

Date of birth _____

Birthplace _____

Blood type _____

Allergies _____

Previous attending physicians _____

Current attending physicians _____

Pregnancies and miscarriages _____

Immunizations _____

Causes and dates of past physical illness(es) _____

Causes and dates of existing health problems _____

Causes and dates of accidents _____

Operations and dates performed _____

Reasons and dates of hospitalizations _____

Reasons and dates of doctor's office visits _____

Negative reactions to medical treatments _____

Copies of lab test results _____

Current use of eyeglasses, hearing aids, walking devices, wheelchairs, and others

_____

Current use of bathroom accessories such as grab bars and raised toilet seats _____

Recent changes in bodily functions _____

Existing mental health problems _____

Personal stress and family problems _____

Mother's and father's dates and causes of death _____

Grandparents' cause of death _____

MEDICATIONS USAGE

Current use of prescription medications:

    drug name and purpose _____

    quantity _____

    timing and manner of administering doses _____

    side effects (if any) _____

Current use of over-the-counter drugs and alternative remedies:

    vitamins _____

    supplements _____

    herbs _____

    topical ointments _____

History of drug side effects

_____

_____

Keeping total control of family medical records may be impossible but there are steps to take to ensure accuracy and privacy:

- Never sign a blanket authorization that does not specify a limited use.
- Ask the doctor who will have access to the records, and for what purpose.

• Review the records for accuracy, especially if they are to be sent to a health insurance carrier, long-term care insurance provider, and/or life insurance company.

PLAN FIVE
Get involved by asking questions.

Your elder should have answers to the following questions *before* leaving the doctor's office:

The problem

What is the exact diagnosis?

What is this illness called?

What caused this illness?

Will this illness go away, get worse, or recur?

Are there any likely medical complications?

Will the pain go away?

What lifestyle changes can I expect?

May I review my medical chart?

The tests

Why are these tests necessary?

What will they tell us that we don't already know?

How reliable are these tests?

Will the tests indicate the exact diagnosis?

Will the tests let me know what to expect in the future?

Will the results significantly alter any treatment plans?

What are the risks involved?

Will my medications affect test results?

What happens if I refuse or postpone this test?

What are the chances of inaccurate test results?

What is the test procedure?

How will the test feel?

How am I supposed to prepare for this test?

Will I need help getting home afterward?

When will the test results be ready?

Can the test results be sent directly to me?

Do I phone you for the test results?

The treatment

What is your experience in treating similar cases?

How will you treat this illness? Why?

What are the risks associated with this treatment?

What are alternate ways to treat this illness?

What are the risks associated with those treatments?

What is the time frame for the treatment?

Is a hospital stay necessary?

How long will I be sick?

How long before I see some improvement?

Will I recuperate fully?

The medications

If medications are prescribed, see *Managing Medications* in the Emergency Preparedness chapter of *The Planner* starting on page 85.

The surgery

If surgery is recommended, see *If Your Elder is Hospitalized* in the Emergency Preparedness chapter of *The Planner* starting on page 91.

The costs

Do you accept Medicare assignments?

What is covered by Medicare?

What is covered by supplemental health insurance?

What costs are not covered by insurance?

How much can I expect to pay in the long run for treatment?

What are the costs of tests involved? Does insurance cover costs?

 PLAN SIX
Prevent unnecessary doctor's visits.

Before making a trip to the doctor's office, remind your relative to:

- Check and confirm the appointment time, date, and location.
- Verify that lab results are back from the lab, and have been analyzed.
- Confirm that the specialist has received the necessary charts from the referring physician.

PLAN SEVEN
Encourage second opinions when faced with a major medical decision.

Getting a second or even a third opinion does not necessarily mean you mistrust the first physician's judgment. You might take this course of action simply to confirm an initial diagnosis. For referrals for obtaining second opinions, ask the existing health care provider to recommend a doctor from a different practice or hospital. Or call the county medical association, a medical school, the health care insurance company, or Medicare for referrals.

Obtain a second opinion when
- treatment will irrevocably change the patient's lifestyle
- a surgical procedure is recommended
- radiation or chemotherapy is the suggested treatment
- the doctor orders a series of tests
- the patient is unsatisfied with explanations regarding treatments
- the patient feels uncomfortable with the doctor

 PLAN EIGHT
Check up on the doctor.

Patients owe it to themselves to get the best of care, and when it comes to any kind of important decision or medical procedure, it is essential that you have an experienced doctor. Never hesitate to ask about experience and credentials.

Thanks to consumer advocacy groups and new state laws, it is possible not only to investigate the certification and qualifications of medical personnel, but to discover any malpractice suits, misconduct charges, Medicare fraud, and disciplinary actions taken against medical providers and facilities by the state, peers, or patients. To obtain such information, call the state medical licensing board or the attorney general's office. Several states now require hospitals to provide data on procedures such as death rates and treatment complications.

Patients can ask medical providers directly
Have you ever been sued? For what?
What percentage of your patients die in the operating room?
Do you carry malpractice insurance?

To date, physicians are not required by law to reveal they have tested positive for the HIV virus. The Centers for Disease Control have documented only a handful of cases in which health care professionals with HIV have transmitted it to patients. However, if this is a concern,

Ask the doctor

Do you have HIV/AIDS?

Do any members of your staff have HIV/AIDS?

Do any of the hospital surgery staff members have HIV/AIDS?

When was your last HIV/AIDS test?

Are you willing to put this information in writing?

Low-Cost and Free Resources

Registered complaints and disciplinary histories of any doctor are available by calling your **state medical licensing board.** Ask directory assistance for the phone number.

Local chapters of **specialized illness organizations** such as the Alzheimer's Association, American Cancer Society, American Diabetes Association, Arthritis Foundation, Parkinson's Disease Foundation, American Lung Association, and the American Heart Association can be found in the White Pages of the telephone book or on the Internet.

If a **dietitian** is not part of your elder's health care team, a hospital dietitian, a home economist, or a home economics teacher may be able to provide consultation about proper eating habits.

A parish nurse is a professional nurse who is called and committed to the healing ministry of the church. The parish nurse helps to meet the emotional, physical, and spiritual needs of the members, including the elderly. Search the Internet for a program nearest to your elder. Keyword search: **parish nurse.**

Neighborhood emergency care clinics, hospital emergency rooms, and your neighborhood **pharmacist** can answer general health care questions if your elder's attending physician isn't immediately available.

Hospitals and adult education centers offer basic **nursing care programs** to family caregivers who are providing home health care services for their relatives.

ORGANIZATIONS

American Board of Medical Specialties
(To find out if the doctor is board certified)
(800) 776-2378

American Dietetic Association
(Nutrition information for older Americans)
216 W. Jackson Boulevard
Chicago, IL 60606-6995
(312) 899-0040
Website: *www.eatright.org*

American Health Assistance Foundation (AHAF)
(Alzheimer's Family Relief Program)
15825 Shady Grove Road, Suite 140
Rockville, MD 20850
(800) 437-2423, (301) 948-3244, Fax: (301) 258-9454
Website: *www.ahaf.org*

American Health Care Association (AHCA)
1201 L Street, NW
Washington, DC 20005
(202) 842-4444, Fax: (202) 842-3860
Website: *www.ahca.org*

American Heart Association
National Center
7272 Greenville Avenue
Dallas, TX 75231
(800) 242-8721
Website: *www.americanheart.org*

American Medical Association
(On-line doctor finder and health information)
Website: *www.ama-assn.org*

Families USA Foundation
(Health care policies and resources)
1334 G Street, NW
Washington, DC 20005
(202) 628-3030, Fax: (202) 347-2417
Website: *www.familiesusa.org*

Federation of State Medical Boards
(To find your state medical board)
Federation Place
400 Fuller Wiser Road, Suite 300
Euless, TX 76039-3855
(817) 868-4000, Fax: (817) 868-4099
Website: *www.fsmb.org*

National Association for Continence (NAFC)
P.O. Box 8310
Spartanburg, SC 29305-8310
(800) 252-3337, Fax: (864) 579-7902
Website: *www.nafc.org*

National Health Information Center
P.O. Box 1133
Washington, DC 20013-1133
(800) 336-4797, Fax: (301) 984-4256
Website: *http://nhic-nt.health.org*

National Institute on Aging (NIA)
(Booklets available on health-related subjects, and informacion en espanol)
Public Information Office
Building 31, Room 5C27
31 Center Drive, MSC 2292
Bethesda, Maryland 20892
(301) 496-1752
Website: *www.nih.gov/nia*

Visiting Nurse Associations of America
11 Beacon Street, Suite 910
Boston, MA 02108
(617) 523-4042, Fax: (617) 227-4843
Website: *www.vnaa.org*

Action Checklist

TAKING CHARGE: HEALTHY LIVING TIPS	To Do By	Completed
Set health care goals		
short-term	_____	❏
long-term	_____	❏
Access health care professionals	_____	❏
Have a plan if your elder refuses to see a doctor	_____	❏
Discuss your elder's health attitude with		
family	_____	❏
doctor	_____	❏

Obtain phone numbers (day and evening) of
  doctor _____ ❏
  dentist _____ ❏
  pharmacist _____ ❏
  hospital _____ ❏
  medical center _____ ❏

Keep important phone numbers
  at home _____ ❏
  at work _____ ❏
  in wallet or purse _____ ❏

Distribute phone numbers to key family members _____ ❏

PARTNERSHIP FOR QUALITY HEALTH CARE

Be aware of your elder's health attitudes _____ ❏

Review patient's rights _____ ❏

Set doctor visit goals with elder _____ ❏

Plan for someone to accompany your elder to all medical appointments _____ ❏

Create a medical history chart _____ ❏

Research your family medical history _____ ❏

Distribute copies of medical history to key family members _____ ❏

Prepare for doctor's appointments
  list of symptoms _____ ❏
  medical history _____ ❏
  drug usage chart _____ ❏
  list of questions, medical problems, and stressful
    events _____ ❏
  notepad or tape recorder _____ ❏

Verify appointments in advance _____ ❏

Get a second opinion if needed _____ ❏

Check up on medical staff and facility _____ ❏

Switch doctors if unsatisfied _____ ❏

· 12 ·

QUALITY OF LIFE

What's Age For, Anyway?

Age isn't a measuring stick for one's abilities; consequently, there's great diversity among what elders are still able to accomplish. For example, there are seventy-year-old people who need a cane to walk, and others who run marathons. Everybody ages differently. In addition to genetics, the process of aging is largely determined by an accumulation of life experiences and belief systems. Some elders welcome new challenges, while others shy away from trying anything different. Some are quite social and eager to reach out to help those in need, while others isolate themselves from the rest of the world.

People who are misinformed about aging diminish their chances of finding contentment in later years. There are many examples of people who continuously enriched their lives as they aged. Benjamin Franklin helped to write the United States Constitution at 81. Albert Schweitzer was running a hospital in Africa at 89. Coco Chanel was at the helm of her design firm at 85. Giuseppe Verdi wrote the opera *Falstaff* in his late seventies. Golda Meir worked up to twenty hours a day in her late seventies. Helena Rubinstein led her company until age 94. Winston Churchill wrote *A History of the English-Speaking Peoples* at 82. Pablo Picasso painted into his nineties.

The plans in this section will give you a wealth of ideas for keeping your loved one in touch with the things he or she loves to do, and awakening in them new possibilities and adventures. The benefits of participating in simple activities, such as reading a book to a child, may be just what your elder needs to feel good about himself or herself.

WHAT'S AGE FOR, ANYWAY?

- Elders are as misinformed and prejudiced about aging as any other age group.
- Elders can live enriched, active lives in spite of their aches and pains.
- The fear of dying is trumped by the fear of living too long and becoming useless.
- Older people don't want to be a burden; they may think about suicide as a way to make things easier on everyone else.

Many family caregivers have mistaken ideas about late-life depression, the chief cause of suicide among the elderly.

OBJECTIVES

*After completing **What's Age For, Anyway?**, you will be able to:*

Offer ideas for life-enriching activities.

Create special moments of togetherness.

Become aware of any serious expressions of depression and suicide.

 PLAN ONE
Add life to years, not years to life.

Telltale signs that your aging family member's mental and physical abilities are on the decline include an increased lack of interest in people and activities. Sometimes your elder's medications are at the root of the problem. (Review the *Managing Medications* section starting on page 85.) Emotional issues, however, may require specialized professional counseling. The more self-centered an elder becomes, the more problems develop; and a dependent lifestyle can add to the already time-taxed family caregiver's degree of responsibilities.

Issues stifling your elder may include:
- Fear of not being needed or useful
- Fear of inability to care for self
- Fear of isolation
- Fears of disability and dependency
- Fear of losing mental agility
- Fear of living too long
- Fear of death

Aging is a normal, lifelong process that includes an accumulation of experience, wisdom, and judgment. Given the right perspective, elders have the opportunity to live with more purpose than in their youth. If your relative is stuck in a rut, perhaps asking the following questions will rekindle his or her zest for living a meaningful life:

What interests you?

Where can you get information on things that interest you?

What is important for you to do right now?

Which friendships would you like to create or maintain?

Is there anything you would like to learn?

Where can you get instructions on what you want to learn?

Would you like to teach or volunteer?

Would you like to pursue any unfulfilled dreams?

Who is alone and lonely that you can visit?

Have you restored any strained relationships?

Have you contacted everyone you want to see or talk with?

Would it be helpful for you to talk with a professional counselor?

 PLAN TWO
Suggest ways for your elder to stay in touch.

Lucky are elders who have time on their hands. Perhaps any one of these activities will cultivate a new interest and encourage new possibilities to learn and connect:

drawing and painting	fitness and mall-walking
e-mail and Internet	handicrafts and sewing
pottery	journal writing
creative writing	storytelling
teaching	playing a musical instrument
inventing	singing and dancing
acting and modeling	caring for animals
letter writing	telephoning shut-ins
cooking and baking	reading
baby-sitting	volunteering
taking a class	employment (give your elder
learning a foreign language	a research project)
traveling	games and puzzles
collecting stamps and coins	photography
gardening and caring for	religious activities
gardening and caring for	cultural pursuits
houseplants	

PLAN THREE
Focus on quality travel services.

Travel outfitters and places of interest that cater to the special needs of elders can be found in the Yellow Pages and on the Internet. Try looking under these headings:

amusement	auto club
bed and breakfast	boats and boat charters
campgrounds	chamber of commerce
cruises	guest ranch
historic places	hostels (elderhostels)
motels	resorts
retreat facilities	river trips
sightseeing tours	ski resorts
tours and tour operators	travel agencies

 PLAN FOUR
Encourage loved ones to learn something new.

The learning process never ends, and learning centers come in all shapes and sizes and prices:

community colleges	universities
adult education classes	senior centers
public libraries	seminars
lectures	elderhostels
clubs	semester at sea

 PLAN FIVE
Ask elders to share their specials talents and skills.

Research indicates that it is the desire to feel useful—not income—that is the number-one reason older people seek work during retirement. Employment opportunities for elders are plentiful. The law recognizes claims of job discrimination on the basis of age. One's employment status, does, however, affect an individual's Social Security entitlements, so before starting any job, your elder should seek advice from the local Social Security office.

Employment opportunities are listed in the classified section of the newspaper and at employment agencies.

Employment options (the complete list is endless)

security guard	salesperson
consultant	bookkeeper
telephone surveyor	maid or butler or valet
house sitter and pet sitter	tutor
baby-sitter	day care worker
companion	food service worker
gardener	restaurant host
proofreader and editor	actor or model
doorman	concierge
cashier	parking lot attendant
receptionist	handyman
housekeeper	tour guide
office worker	mail room worker
chauffeur	temp work

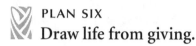

PLAN SIX
Draw life from giving.

Elders have much to offer, and are usually willing to share their know-how and experience when invited to do so. Volunteering and teaching provide your aging family members ways of making new friends, staying connected to others, and becoming a positive influence in someone else's life.

Sample volunteer opportunities:

youth groups	men's and women's organizations
child day care	adult day care centers
special interest groups	museum/park/zoo docents
religious groups	community outreach programs
schools/libraries	Senior Olympics
senior centers	reading to the blind
theater groups	animal shelters
hospitals	nursing homes
family service agency	senior advocacy groups
tutor	literacy corps
court watcher	tour leader
hot line operator	consultant

PLAN SEVEN
Facilitate your elder's spiritual needs.

Maintaining spiritual and religious connections as we age provides an unfailing source of support. Spiritual quests often provide meaning and direction; clergy can be an invaluable resource, offering your aging family member emotional support and spiritual guidance.

Your relative also might want to get involved in the many activities and services most congregations have to offer, including:

counseling	volunteering
education	bible study groups
retreats	choir
socializing	prayer groups

PLAN EIGHT
Take talks of suicide seriously.

Studies reveal that most elderly people who attempt suicide fully intend to die. Failure to complete the act is usually a result of poor planning, not an attempt "to get attention." Elderly males are the highest risk group.

Mental illness, loneliness, poverty, grief, pain, and severe depression are some of the reasons why older adults consider this violent act. You might hear them say, "I'd be better off dead," or, "My family would be better off without me," and, "I won't be around much longer." Look for these clues:

no appetite

change in sleep habits

discontinuing medical treatment

direct or indirect mention of suicide

increased drinking

driving under the influence of drugs and/or alcohol

less interest in family, socializing, churchgoing, and personal interests

mismanaging medications

neglect in personal appearance and hygiene

lethargy, no joy in life

If you suspect that your elder is contemplating such action and repeats messages of despair and hopelessness follow these guidelines:

- Contact family members, the local hospital, or a law enforcement agency and tell them of your concerns.
- Ask your elder directly if he or she is intending to commit suicide. You won't be putting the idea in your elder's head. If he or she doesn't have these intentions, the response will be a firm "No!" Anything short of that should be considered a dangerous clue.
- Don't act shocked or disapproving if the answer is yes, for that may break the bond of trust between you.
- Don't lecture—your elder needs love and support, not an argument. Offer reassurance that his or her feelings are temporary, and that depression can be treated by a mental health professional.
- Volunteer to take him or her to see an expert immediately. If you have serious concerns, take him or her to the hospital emergency room right now. Seek professional help immediately! Take every threat seriously.
- Do *not* promise to keep this conversation a secret, and tell your elder you intend to talk with professionals and family members.
- Lock up guns, razors, knives, pills, alcohol, and scissors.
- Make a plan for medication management.

Aging with a Disability

The Americans with Disabilities Act has dramatically changed the lives of elders and others who live with disability and chronic illness, facilitating everything from employment opportunities to access to public programs and telecommunication relay services. Anyone with a disability can pursue an active lifestyle if he or she chooses to do so. Advancements in medicine and technology have played a major role in helping people accept and manage their physical impairments.

Understanding what our elder is experiencing in the throes of a disability or chronic illness will help us cope with our own personal struggles, as we assist him or her in daily life. Caring for an elderly person who has a disability is a difficult job—one that requires an iron will, emotional and physical strength, and the patience of a saint. At the same time, care *receivers* often endure great emotional turmoil because the idea that they are a burden on someone else is devastating.

Managing the caregiving process under these highly demanding and interactive circumstances also requires constant changes in your elder's living environment. This section of *The Planner* will guide you in minimizing the psychological and physical risks that play an important role in your elder's ability to master his or her own basic daily tasks. Ultimately, people who are disabled and in control of their immediate surroundings tend to lead productive, independent, and satisfying lives.

AGING WITH A DISABILITY

- Arthritis is the most common chronic condition that older people manage on a daily basis.
- The Americans with Disabilities Act gives every disabled person the right to a productive, independent, and satisfying life.

Most of the problems that family members encounter with their relative's disabilities can be eased by some attitude adjustment.

OBJECTIVES

*After completing **Aging With A Disability**, you will be able to:*

Separate facts from myth about your elder's disability.

Help your loved one maintain independence and a quality lifestyle.

Gain a healthy perspective on what life with a disability is like.

 PLAN ONE
Dispel false assumptions about living with a physical disability.

The key issue when dealing with an elder's physical disability is not the person's age, but the duration of the disability. Age does not define the treatment of the disability—rather, we look to the nature and severity of the disability.

Living with a disability doesn't necessarily mean living with sickness. The family's attitude toward their elder's disability will greatly influence the choices of treatment as well as their relative's quality of life.

If your aging family member is living with a disability, be careful not to mischaracterize your elder as sick or unmotivated. Your elder—anyone, for that matter—is the best expert on his or her own body; it is to your advantage to remain flexible and let your relative advise you as to what he or she needs.

One myth about people in wheelchairs is that they are necessarily weak or feeble. To the contrary, it takes enormous energy to sit in one position for several hours, let alone all day. Also, it takes great physical strength to move a wheelchair. Individuals in manual chairs, therefore, may reject electrically driven chairs, seeing them as signs of failure, weakness, or giving in.

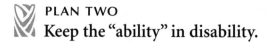

PLAN TWO
Keep the "ability" in disability.

Separate your elder's medical problems from psychological problems—they entail entirely different considerations:

- Maintain access to knowledgeable health care professionals as well as educational and vocational resources.
- Find out what is correctable, treatable, and curable.
- Find a health care provider who is willing to entertain new ideas.
- Eliminate architectural barriers in your elder's living quarters, and rearrange his or her environment to meet both physical and psychological needs. Independent living enhances your elder's ability to stay in control of his or her own life and minimizes eldercare responsibilities for the rest of the family.
- Allow your elder's feelings of sadness, anger, and resentment to surface. Stifling negative emotions may wear away at your elder's immune system.
- Acknowledge your elder's feats of accomplishment, however small. Achievements give meaning to the lives of those with disabilities.
- Find elderly role models that are successfully engaged in life in spite of pain or disability.

PLAN THREE
Adjust your attitude to get through tough times.

There will be times when caring for your family member will be overwhelming and extremely frustrating. Make sure you ask for and accept plenty of help from others. Then take a moment to look at life from your elder's perspective.

Elders with a disability:
- have psychological hurdles on top of physical disabilities
- live with silent messages that they don't belong
- must find ways to feel productive while accepting assistance from other people
- live with the physical reminders of a disability (canes, wheelchairs, walkers)
- may be living in constant pain
- use more energy and take more time to do the same basic tasks as you
- often experience feelings of loss and isolation
- fear abandonment

- worry increasingly about paying for medical bills
- live in fear of losing even more control

Family Power

Taking on the role of family caregiver is certain to alter your life, and there is yet another dimension to eldercare that is often not openly discussed—the issue of family preservation. With a developing trend of "returning to the nest," family members are reconnecting with each other emotionally, physically, and spiritually. This is becoming evident in the rise in family church attendance, children being raised by their grandparents, the frequency of family reunions, and an increasing interest in the subject of genealogy. In this fast-paced world, getting together and staying together through thick and thin isn't easy; but worth every effort.

What you may soon come to realize in the caregiving process is that our elders are, first and foremost, our teachers. We must create the situations and environments that encourage them to hand down their stories, traditions, know-how, and legends—the elements of what makes the family unit strong—and, in turn, protect those who live within its influence.

Acknowledging each other's accomplishments, big and small, staying in touch, learning to forgive—these are the steps to strengthening and preserving family bonds and culture. You will reap the benefits of this effort many times over, and the memory of *feeling* familial will remain with you for the rest of your life.

The safekeeping of family treasures, values, stories, and traditions requires the family's willingness to make the effort. This section of *The Planner* offers simple suggestions on how to learn from your elder about your family's past in order for you to carry on the spirit of the family for generations to come.

FAMILY POWER

- The family is still the strongest element in our society, and cross-generational socializing is vital to all generations.
- It is up to the family unit to maintain its own quality of life, since there is no inherent social system to guarantee it.
- Making the commitment to move from "me" to "we" improves family effectiveness.

Making a family work well takes cooperation, maturity, and an acknowledgment of values, tradition, and culture.

PLAN ONE
Make time to make memories.

When we wake up to the fact that our elders have more yesterdays than tomorrows, we can maximize the quality of time we have left to share together. Here are a few activities that help bring you together:

Stay in touch. There are an almost unlimited number of ways of communicating in this computer age: e-mail, voice e-mail, e-greeting cards, and Internet visual dialoguing. At the same time, the old-fashioned methods work just fine: telephoning, letter writing, exchanging recent photographs, taking family videos, sending postcards, visiting each other, cooking and eating meals together, shopping together, creating and attending family parties and reunions, recording stories, singing songs on tape, and vacationing together.

Acknowledge each other. Congratulate each other, compliment each other, send birthday and anniversary cards, share events and milestones, send report cards, send copies of awards and newspaper clippings, invite family to plays and performances. Celebrate all family achievements, big and small.

Let others feel special. Ask and give small favors. Ask for advice. Ask your elders to teach you to knit, play bridge, or draw a picture for a greeting card cover. Say please and thank you, often.

Fulfill commitments. Let family members know they can rely on you to do those things you say you will do.

Be forgiving. Allow for weaknesses, failures, mistakes, and illnesses. Stick up for each other in private and public.

Know your family history. Explore family traditions and cultural ties and teach them to the next generation. Share memories, search for family roots, and create a family tree. Document family stories on video and cassette. Keep family possessions in the family.

Say, "I love you," before it's too late.

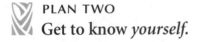

PLAN TWO
Get to know *yourself.*

The methods of searching for your roots (genealogy) and the places you will look for clues will be as diverse as your family. Start by conducting interviews with the eldest members of the family. Create a list of questions to ask ahead of time. Write down the answers and use a tape recorder as a backup. Don't interrupt your elders when they're talking or they may lose their train of thought. There are many books at the library on this subject.

Show elders old photographs. Ask them to tell you the names of the people in the picture, how they are related to the family, the date of the photo, where it was taken, and what they were doing at the time the picture was taken. Write down what they tell you.

If your elder has possession of antiques, collectibles, or heirlooms, ask him or her about the circumstances of how or when the items were acquired. Very often, photos and possessions will trigger memories that can reveal a generous amount of fascinating family history.

Explore attics. Look for some of these objects to verify names, dates, and places of special family events: newspaper clippings, documents, letters, report cards, invitations, passports, autograph books, costumes, musical instruments, dolls, collections, toys, hats, diplomas, notebooks, diaries, yearbooks, scrapbooks, baby books, programs from plays or concerts, trophies, paintings and artwork, maps, award certificates, photographs, and obituaries.

Search for family records such as birth and death certificates, marriage licenses, divorce decrees, citizenship papers, wills, deeds, and medical histories. Visit or write the state archives and public records office for birth and death certificates. A death certificate will tell you when and where the person was born. The birth record will name the parents. Documents can be obtained from the county clerk's office, state vital statistics bureaus, or state health departments.

PLAN THREE
Gather the clan.

Follow these suggestions to stay connected:

Take photographs. Make it a habit to take along a camera or video camera to capture family members and events on film. Record the dates, places, and people on the backs of photos. Ask other family members to exchange photos and add them to your photo album. Transfer home movies, photos, and slides to video and make duplicates for everyone to see.

Draw a family tree. Create a chart that shows how family members are related. There are software programs that can help. Local, regional, state, and private libraries offer valuable family data such as obituaries, maps, local history books, private letters, and legal papers.

Organize a family reunion. Hold a family meeting and decide on the event format (one day, weekend, picnic, formal, informal). Delegate reunion responsibilities: event coordinator, secretary to handle correspondence, and a treasurer to collect funds and pay bills. The library and the Internet have many books and websites on the topic of how to organize a family reunion.

Share stories and write them down. The simple process of storytelling places enormous value on your elder's life and culture. Draw up a list of specific questions or check out the many wonderful heirloom and memories books that are available at the bookstore. Here are a few questions to get you started. Write down your elder's answers:

What was the most memorable day of your life?
What was your wedding day like?
How did you and (mom or dad) meet?
What was your grade school like?
What were your grandparents like?
How did grandma and grandpa meet?
Who in the family emigrated to this country?
Where did they come from?

Give gifts of memories. Write down and preserve favorite family recipes, knit sweaters, crochet blankets, frame family works of art and needlepoint. Make sachets with flower petals from wedding bouquets. Reset jewelry into a contemporary setting to pass down to the next generation.

Preserve family traditions. Practice and respect them, so that they will live on.

PLAN FOUR
Invest in the future.

Elders and youth are a magical combination. In addition to carrying values, traditions, and wisdom, elders help our children channel their energy and enthusiasm toward more reflective and sensitive words and deeds. When elders are given an opportunity to do their "job," our youth will more likely grow into adulthood thinking about what they can give back to others. We need to create environments that allow this important interchange to take place.

Bringing generations together can benefit everyone's health and well-being. Intergenerational programs at community centers, senior centers, churches and temples, and child day care centers combat isolation, increase physical and mental stimulation, and, most important, provide elders with a sense of purpose. Check out the resources at the end of this chapter on how seniors can participate in these types of rewarding activities.

PLAN FIVE
Help your elder be a grand grandparent.

When grandparents and their grandchildren live a long distance from each other, and frequent get-togethers aren't possible, they can stay in touch with each other in a variety of ways. Here are some suggestions:

Visit on video. Document stories, act out nursery rhymes, sing and dance, give a guided tour of your home or neighborhood, play a musical instrument, ask questions about school projects. Give each other opportunities to remember voices and faces.

Exchange photo albums. Include pictures of family, friends, family pets, and places you've lived and visited. Label each picture with a short description.

Write letters, and encourage responses. Children love getting mail addressed to them. Put fun things inside the envelope like stamps, stickers, comic strips, drawings, photos, animal pictures, candy, and packets of bubble bath.

Record bedtime stories on cassette. Send the book and the tape along so the child can "be with you" at bedtime.

Initiate telephone and e-mail visits. Make it a point to help grandparents know what's going on in their grandchildren's lives. Discuss school projects, recitals, sports, friends, and hobbies. Use the phone more than e-mail—grandchildren need to hear their grandparents' voices.

An increasing number of elders are finding themselves in the unplanned role of parent to their grandchildren. Alcohol abuse, drug addiction, and illness on the part of the parents sometimes create these unanticipated unions. Across the country, support groups for grand-parents raising grandchildren are surfacing and helping elders cope with the special challenges they face. Review the resources listed at the end of this chapter.

PLAN SIX
Encourage your elder to give back to the family.

There is little question that our elders are happier when they feel needed and respected within the family. Get them involved and active with the following activities:

minor home repairs	chores
baby-sitting	house-sitting
office work	advice
gardening	light cooking and baking
storytelling	documenting family traditions and history
sewing	small errands
clipping news articles	organizing your photos in an album

PLAN SEVEN
Pets can play an important role.

Elders often transfer much of their love and attention to their pets as a way of dealing with natural losses in their lives; pets can fill emotional voids. Though you may not share your family member's enthusiasm for his or her pet, it's important to recognize the depth of your elder's emotional attachment to the animal.

Pets provide companionship and make our elders feel needed. Playing with pets and caring for them takes their mind off worries and health issues. Larger animals, like dogs, may make them feel more secure. Watching fish in an aquarium or stroking a cat or dog helps reduce stress and lower blood pressure and can help minimize depression. Birds make music, and some can even be trained to talk. The goal is to have close and continuing contact. Animals make no distinction between the sick and the healthy or the young and the old, and their love is unconditional.

Low-Cost and Free Resources

Sources for volunteer opportunities: Yellow Pages—see social services organizations, classified section of community newspapers, public library, local agency on aging, chamber of commerce. Search the Internet at keyword search: senior volunteer.

Type in these keywords on the **Internet** for information on aging with a disability: disability, travel disability, independent living, assistive technology.

State bureau of tourism, state historical society, state parks, and **chamber of commerce** offices supply travelers free information and maps.

Computer software programs are available for those who are interested in creating a family tree or conducting an Internet search (keywords: genealogy, ancestry, family tree) to connect with a multitude of resources.

Pet adoptions are usually free to senior citizens. Contact the humane society.

For a wealth of information on **activities for seniors,** conduct an Internet search, at keywords: older workers, seniors, senior travel, grandparent, intergenerational programs.

You may also wish to contact your local **agency on aging** to learn if there are special grandparents support groups which meet regularly in the community. These support groups bring together custodial grandparents for mutual support and information sharing.

ORGANIZATIONS

Quality Living

ABLEDATA
(An assistive technology information exchange, serving the nation's disability, rehabilitation, and senior communities)
8401 Colesville Road, Suite 200
Silver Spring, MD 20910
(800) 227-0216, (301) 608-8998, TTY (301) 608-8912, Fax: (301) 608-8958
Website: *www.abledata.com*

Brookdale Center on Aging of Hunter College
425 E. 25th Street
New York, NY 10010
(212) 481-4426, Fax: (212) 481-5069
Website: *www.brookdale.org*

Equal Employment Opportunity Commission
1801 L Street, NW
Washington, DC 20507
(800) 669-4000, (202) 663-4900, TDD (800) 669-6820
Website: *www.eeoc.gov*

Interactive Aging Network
Website: *www.ianet.org*

Leadership Council of Aging Organizations
Website: *www.lcao.org*

National Aging Information Center
Administration on Aging
330 Independence Avenue, SW, Room 4656
Washington, DC 20201
(202) 619-7501, Fax: (202) 401-7620
Website: *www.aoa.dhhs.gov/naic*

National Library Service for the Blind and Physically Handicapped Hot Line
(800) 424-9100

National Mental Health Association
1021 Prince Street
Alexandria, VA 22314-2971
(800) 969-6642, TTY: (800) 433-5959, Fax: (703) 684-5968
Website: *www.nmha.org*

Minority Aging

Administración del Envejeciente
(Hispanic Aging Resources)
Administration on Aging
330 Independence Avenue, SW
Washington, DC 20201
(202) 619-7501, Fax: (202) 260-1012
Website: *www.aoa.dhhs.gov/espanol*

National Caucus and Center on the Black Aged
1424 K Street, NW, Suite 500
Washington, DC 20005
(202) 637-8400, Fax: (202) 347-0895
Website: *www.ncba-blackaged.org*

National Indian Council on Aging
10501 Montgomery Boulevard, NE, Suite 210
Albuquerque, NM 87111-3846
(508) 292-2001
Website: *www.nicoa.org*

National Pacific/Asian Resource Center on Aging (NAPCA)
Melbourne Tower, 1511 Third Street, Suite 914
Seattle, WA 98101-1626

(206) 624-1221
Website: *www.napca.org*

Inter-generational activities

Administration on Aging
Intergenerational Programs
Website: *www.aoa.dhhs.gov/aoa/webres/intergen.htm*

Generations United
440 First Street, NW, Suite 480
Washington, DC 20001-2085
(202) 662-4283, Fax: (202) 638-7555
Website: *www.gu.org*

Genealogy

National Archives and Records Administration
700 Pennsylvania Avenue, NW
Washington, DC 20408-0001
Website: *www.nara.gov*

Grandparenting

AARP Grandparent Information Center
601 E Street, NW
Washington, DC 20049
Website: www.aarp.org

GrandsPlace
154 Cottage Road
Enfield, CT 06082
(860) 763-5789
Website: *www.grandsplace.com*

Volunteer Opportunities

Administration on Aging
Volunteer Programs
Website: *www.aoa.dhhs.gov/aoa/eldractn/voluntr.html*

Corporation for National Service
1201 New York Avenue, NW
Washington, DC 20525
(202) 606-5000
Website: *www.cns.gov*

Action Checklist

WHAT'S AGE FOR, ANYWAY?	To Do By	Completed
Ask life-enriching questions	_____	❑
Encourage an active, interdependent lifestyle	_____	❑
Facilitate spiritual quests	_____	❑
Watch for depression	_____	❑
Be sure your relative has access to a telephone	_____	❑
Be sure your elder has information on		
special interests	_____	❑
travel	_____	❑
education	_____	❑
employment	_____	❑
volunteering	_____	❑
Locate		
community centers	_____	❑
senior centers	_____	❑
religious congregations	_____	❑
support groups	_____	❑
volunteer services	_____	❑

AGING WITH A DISABILITY		
Review facts and myths of disabilities	_____	❑
Help your elder maintain an independent lifestyle		
medical goals	_____	❑
psychological goals	_____	❑
access to professionals	_____	❑
environmental barriers removed	_____	❑
transferring issues	_____	❑

transportation issues   _____ ❏
other role models   _____ ❏

Review attitudes about disability   _____ ❏

Stay informed of research and treatments   _____ ❏

FAMILY POWER

Create goals to make memories   _____ ❏

Research family history   _____ ❏

Document family events
photo album   _____ ❏
scrap book   _____ ❏
family tree   _____ ❏
audio and video library   _____ ❏

Encourage intergenerational activities   _____ ❏

Redefine the role of grandparent   _____ ❏

Facilitate your elder's giving back to the family   _____ ❏

Recognize the importance of your relative's pet   _____ ❏

Read up on
genealogy   _____ ❏
family reunions   _____ ❏
grandparenting   _____ ❏

· 13 ·

DEATH AND DYING

Saying Good-bye

Something wonderful happens when elders begin the process of letting go. Not letting go of life, or hope, not resignation and despair. But the normal part of the dying process when they let go of their love for and attachment to people and objects that hold memories. They must, for they would otherwise be unable to accept their impending death.

We are never quite prepared when our elders decide to let go; we are not finished with them, yet they may be finished with life. And, as we seek to understand the dying process, we experience the pain, the sorrow, the anger, the fear, and the sense of being adrift in the world. Robert Hellenga wrote in his book, *The Sixteen Pleasures,* "Death was a lens that would reveal things as they really were: what was important would assume its true importance, what was unimportant would recede into the shadows." And, it is also true of this profound caregiving experience, we family members are given the greatest gift of all—the privilege of being with a loved one who is walking toward death's door.

Intellectually, we know that the caregiving experience ends with the death of our elder. Emotionally, however, we have no way of preparing or predicting how we will accept and deal with our loss when the time comes. For some caregivers, the death of their aging family member may seem like a blessing, especially if their loved one suffered from the effects of ill health. Others may find the death especially traumatic. This section of *The Planner* offers insight on the dying process, including compassionate and sensitive things to do and say that help us to convey our final farewells, and allow our loved ones to die a dignified, peaceful death.

SAYING GOOD-BYE

- Baby boomers are less likely to discuss death with their aging parents than they are to discuss safe sex and drugs with their teenagers, reports a National Hospice Foundation survey. It's time we started talking.
- Medical schools are now teaching students how to deal with dying patients.
- For many, the hardest part of dying is the uncertainty that our lives were worthwhile, or that our responsibilities to others have ended.

In many ways, our elders may be way ahead of us in their attitudes toward death.

OBJECTIVES

*After completing **Saying Good-bye**, you will be able to:*

Create moments of quality time with your elder.

Offer comfort, with dignity, to the dying.

Identify sources of bereavement support.

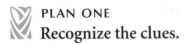

PLAN ONE

Recognize the clues.

As in life, nothing about death is written in stone; it is as unique as the individual who is experiencing it. The dying process can take place over a long or short period of time, or death can strike in an instant. Death is the last great unknown, coming in its own way, with no apparent timetable or predictability.

Each person approaches death in his or her own way, bringing to this very last of experiences his or her own particular formula. Whether in sickness or health, our elders give us signals that they are beginning a separation process from the existence they have known, and they do it in a way that is meaningful to *them.*

There are no concrete rules; some of the clues, all of the clues, or none of the clues may be present as our elders begin their separation process. Accepting our elders' impending death and coming face-to-face with the fact that they will be taken away from us, makes us more aware of the scarcity of our remaining time together and prepares us to help them make the transition from life to death. In turn, as we work our way through this incredible journey, we are rewarded with many gifts, including time to resolve old conflicts, and getting to know each other in another way.

Letting go

It is natural for elderly people to want to give away household objects, photographs, jewelry, cards and letters, collectibles, and anything that holds memories; they are letting go, lifting relationship boundaries, and creating space to travel on a journey where we cannot follow them. We have to be mature to understand this letting go process. When our elders tell us, "I just don't care about these things any more," or, "I have no use for these," their words may jolt us, and we may try to talk them out of it by saying, "*Why* are you doing this?" or "Do we have to do this *now*?" Coming to grips with the fact that our elders are preparing to die is frightening.

At the same time, their letting go can be a turning point in our own lives. Facing our own fears about mortality and our elder's impending death allows us to be receptive to the gifts of life they still have to give us today. The letting go process is not necessarily a signal that death is right around the corner; there still may be plenty of time left to spend with your elder. What we have been given is a window of opportunity to say what is important, and to convey our feelings.

One way to spend quality time together is to help your elder to reminisce—recalling warm times, old friends, special days and events, moments of insight, and the relationships that have made life worthwhile. Next visit, take along a tape recorder or notepad (or a video camera if you don't feel it would be too intrusive). As you sift through photographs and objects together, ask questions such as, how old were you when this photo was taken? who are these people? or who gave this item to you? Here's your chance to learn more, not only about your elder, but also your entire family, and even yourself. This may also be the ideal time to fill in those heirloom books of remembrances that can be purchased at most bookstores and specialty shops. If you wait any longer, your elder may feel uncomfortable answering reflective questions, or worse, by then it may be too late.

Not everything your elder recalls will be pleasant, for the letting go process can also surface unexpressed guilt, frustration, anger, and sadness. There may be broken relationships that he or she now wants to mend. If this is the case, ask if writing a letter (mailing it or not), making a telephone call, scheduling a visit, or keeping a journal will liberate him or her from their unfinished emotional business. Be prepared—anything can happen when you help a person reminisce.

Attaining goals

During this time, your elder also may speak of attaining an important goal or expressing a strong desire to reach a particularly important date or event, such as attending a grandchild's graduation or wedding, reaching their hundredth birthday, or completing a major task. As long as our elders have something to look forward to or something to live for, once the goal is reached, they may decide that they are done with life. The question then becomes, what can we do to help them reach their goal?

Withdrawing

Finally, people turn inward and become reflective on a lifetime of achievements—big and small. Your elder may stop watching television or reading newspapers, or experience a greatly reduced need to interact with people, even loved ones. Some elders may even leave town to die (which was the case with my own father). Two-way conversations become a one-way commentary as they complain about their failing bodily functions and loss of memory, or become impatient, short-tempered, and unapproachable. All these may be signs of shutting down.

Our elders may sleep more, and spend entire days in bed. This may look like napping but there's important work going on of which we "outsiders" are not to know. They may stop eating and tell you nothing tastes good. They may prefer liquids to solids. It's okay for our elders not to eat. Food keeps us alive, but a different and spiritual kind of energy is sustaining them now.

They may be aware that they are pulling away, or they may not—it doesn't much matter. This is a journey that they are going on alone. Do not take it personally. Their withdrawal is not a rejection. If we are not picked as part of their "inner circle," it does not mean that we are unloved or unimportant; it means our roles with our loved ones are completed. A dying person's wishes must be respected.

Most elderly people do not fear death so much as the whole process of dying. Nobody wants to be kept suspended indefinitely in a vegetative state by technology. There are steps to avoid it. No one can possibly prepare you for the responsibility of being asked to deal with highly complex medical information and life-ending decisions. You will do the best you can. If you haven't done so already, this is an appropriate time to talk about funerals, nutritional and respiratory life-support systems, a durable power of attorney for health care, and physician directives. You will want to be well-informed before you initiate these conversations, so reviewing the *Managing Death's Details* section of this chapter, and the Legal Matters chapter of *The Planner* would be helpful at this time.

PLAN TWO
Offer final gifts.

Spending time with a dying loved one is quite a unique experience. Time and sleep become unimportant, and a zombie-like numbness may overcome us. One moment we are at peace with the situation, the next we feel as though something we just said or did was not the right thing to do, or worse yet, someone else tells us so. It is normal to feel totally helpless, for we have no control over what is happening, and we can't "solve" this "problem." We may ask ourselves over and over what we can do or say to someone who is dying.

Saying good-bye is a very important part of the dying process, for this is the last time that we can say words to each other and *mean* them. However, those who are dying may have difficulty talking about death, even if they would like to. If in life a person did not talk candidly about his or her feelings, the likelihood of opening up on a deathbed isn't great; but the unmistakable message from a dying person is, "Don't abandon me." When there is no cure, the best medicine is the gift of presence, comfort, and dignity, administered in regular doses by loved ones.

This is a good time to call upon the assistance of a member of the clergy, a social worker, or the hospice nurse. They have a lot of experience dealing with a death event and know how to interact with the dying, as well as with you. The actual process of dying can take a long time or come quickly. We just never know.

What you can do

You can sit together. Watch television together. Read stories and poetry or psalms from the Bible. You can discuss families or work or historical events. You can talk about flowers. You can talk about illness, and yes, you can talk about death. Sometimes, acknowledging your elder's dying comes as a relief to them. Questions like, "You don't feel well, do you?" or, "You feel like you're dying, don't you?" Give your elder permission to stop putting on a show of being strong, when he or she is not, and allow him or her the opportunity to let go and say, "Yes, I am dying." We can't say good-bye unless we admit the end is near. Let your elder know that you will be with him or her to the end.

Sometimes being together with our elders gives them a chance to say thanks for all that we have done or to reassure us that whatever happens, they will be all right. They may also want to give us further instructions on what they want for us after they're gone. Being together gives them the chance to say goodbye to us. These are reasons enough to try to get together one more time before they die.

Saying good-bye is our final gift of love to our elders, for it helps them validate their own lives. You might tell them what being their son or daughter (or other) has meant to you, or it may be as simple as saying, "Thank you for taking good care of me," or, "I love you."

And, it is okay to cry—when you cry, you give permission for the dying to cry, too. Tears can break through many layers of isolation.

Cling to small joys

Though the dying are dying, they are still able to enjoy certain moments of pure pleasure—and never were they more entitled to them. They may want real butter, not margarine; they may want to go to the park; they may want to have this light off and that light on, a window open, another blanket. By being allowed their choices, however small, they can still count themselves among the living. The dying person has the same physical needs as any other person—to be kept clean, comfortable, and free from pain. By asking your elder, "Is there anything I can do to make you feel comfortable?" you are making the best use of your time.

No words at all

A warm, supportive atmosphere conveys comfort and care: music, candles, soft light, holding hands, hugs, smiles, touching, and sitting in the room are gifts enough. Be aware that some people do not want to be hugged—just touch or hold their hand. If your elder is in a hospital setting, make arrangements to stay overnight.

Even if your elder is incapacitated, or in a comatose state, speak as though he or she can hear you (chances are, he or she *can*). When you speak to others, speak as though your loved one is present in the room; do not refer to him or her as if he or she were already dead. If there is a need to discuss funeral plans, leave the room.

Permission to let go

When a loved one is clinging to life and trying to stay alive beyond what seems medically possible, a family member can assist the dying by offering the ultimate, unselfish parting gift: words that give the elder permission to let go. Our elders may try to hold on to be sure those who are left behind will be taken care of. We can release them from this concern by giving them reassurance. We might say, "Don't worry about Mom, we promise to watch over her," or, "I will be fine, Mom, and well taken care of." You can also say, "Dad, if you don't want to be here anymore, you can go now. It's okay."

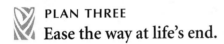 **PLAN THREE**
Ease the way at life's end.

The best medicine we can give ourselves is a plan for dying. Unfortunately, most elderly never discuss death with their doctor or their family, leaving both to make painful decisions about the end of their life. Most hospitals have **professional counselors** who provide advice and moral support for family members of terminally ill patients. If your elder has already empowered you legally to be the decision maker regarding the manner and degree of medical care to be administered in the final stages, now is the time to make the patient's wishes clear to the medical staff.

For patients who are receiving institutionalized medical care, the **Federal Patient Self-Determination Act** requires that all hospitals give registering patients information regarding their right to accept or decline any kind of medical treatment, including life support. A patient can also elect to wear an **armband** which directs staff not to resuscitate if he or she so wishes.

Manage pain

People need not die in pain. Family members are encouraged to become advocates for their loved ones who may be suffering in silence. **Hospice** is a philosophy of care that is based on the belief that every person with a life-limiting illness, no matter what age, is entitled to be as free of pain and symptoms as possible. Hospice seeks neither to hasten nor postpone death. Care and concern for the entire family is what makes this kind of care different from traditional health care.

Hospice services are available when specific criteria are met: the patient's doctor and the hospice medical directors agree that the patient has a life-limiting illness; the patient and family agree with the hospice philosophy; the patient and family are seeking supportive services rather than curative medical treatment. While hospice care is most often provided at home, gradually more hospitals, nursing homes, and residential facilities are offering this option. Private insurance companies and Medicare/Medicaid may cover the costs of services if hospice is available in the community.

Pain management is a family affair. Those of us who have spent long periods of time with people in pain know that patients rarely speak up for themselves. First, ask your loved one if he or she is in pain. If the answer is "yes," ask the doctor for more painkilling medicine. If your elder is not under hospice care, and the doctor will not prescribe larger doses of painkillers for fear of disciplinary action, call your state medical board and report the incident. Also, ask if hospice is an option. Do not give up the fight.

 PLAN FOUR
Help those who are left behind.

After a loved one's death, there are many tasks and responsibilities to handle that will keep us busy and distract us from our grief. But, as those activities wind down, and we attempt to go back to our daily routines, we slowly realize that life will never be the same. Grieving is completely necessary and natural, for it is the time we need to adjust to the world without the person we loved.

Bereavement experts tell us that the stages of accepting the death of a loved one include shock and denial, bargaining for time, anger, depression, and, finally, acceptance. They conclude that these stages of completion do not necessarily follow any special order. The grieving process, and its duration, vary greatly among individuals.

The following are just *some* of the feelings and manifestations people experience during the grieving stages:

- Tears and expressions of deep feelings
- Diminished appetite or loss of weight
- Periods of helplessness and despair
- Vivid dreams of the recently deceased
- Guilt and regret
- Anger directed at, variously, the person who died, God, the family doctor, or other family members

Watch for excessive behavior patterns:

- Poor self-care, not exercising, not eating right
- Isolating oneself from contact with others
- Speaking of the dead in the present tense in ways that are not healthy
- Severe depression, nonstop crying, thoughts of suicide
- Abuse of alcohol or drugs

Make use of bereavement support resources:

Your network of friends and family is an important source of strength during times of grief. Since each individual handles loss differently, you might also want to consider resources of support that lie outside the family, such as clergy, a bereavement support group, a family therapist, or individual bereavement counseling.

Managing Death's Details

Death is never an easy thing to confront, and consequently, *planning* proactively for one's own passing is almost unheard of. Many of the tasks and decisions that are carried out when death does occur are drenched in pain and grief, but many related responsibilities could have realistically been handled in advance, when heads were clear and hearts unburdened.

This section of *The Planner* helps family members focus on the business-related aspects and consequences of the death process. By knowing up front what is entailed in "managing a death," you may even be inspired to talk with your elders *now,* providing them an opportunity to be involved in the planning of their own passing.

Before opening up a dialogue about this most sensitive of all topics, you may find the recommendations in the Communicaring chapter of *The Planner* starting on page 47 to be very helpful. To the extent that you are able to make any headway at all or, if you are one of the lucky few whose elders have already completed their own planning, consider yourself ahead of the game.

But even if you have been left in the position of starting from scratch when the time comes, you are in good hands. From making funeral arrangements, to writing the obituary, to dividing up the estate, this chapter provides you with a comprehensive yet concise guide, enabling you to get through the entire process and, one hopes, offering you some relief and peace during these emotionally trying times.

MANAGING DEATH'S DETAILS

- By the age of fifteen, media experts say, the average American has seen tens of thousands of television murders and has been exposed to war, famine, and holocaust in the daily news. At the same time, ironically, in our real lives, we have probably been isolated from the actuality of death. Consequently, a habit of denial has been bred in our culture.
- Planning ahead to avoid making decisions at the last minute could reduce the price of a funeral by at least one-third.
- Families are most vulnerable in the case of a sudden death, and most mourners don't realize that it is possible to shop around for funeral merchandise and services, even in their hour of need.

There's money to be saved, and peace of mind to be gained, by being well-informed and unintimidated when facing the business side of death.

OBJECTIVES

*After completing **Managing Death's Details**, you will be able to:*

Encourage relatives to plan ahead for their own funerals.

Choose from a variety of funeral arrangement options.

Handle the deceased's financial affairs.

Locate missing documents for the collection of rights and benefits after death.

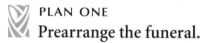

PLAN ONE
Prearrange the funeral.

A funeral is an important event; it helps give meaning to a person's life and enables family and friends to gather together to express feelings of sadness, grief, joy, and loss. Funerals also provide an emotional vehicle to help us make a transition from life as we knew it, with our loved ones in it, to a new and different lifestyle after they are gone.

Planning one's own funeral takes the guesswork out of what survivors may think we want and helps to ease the financial burdens of related expenses. Ultimately, it offers peace of mind in the realization that our final wishes will be fulfilled. Ideally, your elder will want to spare the rest of the family from having to pay and arrange for the funeral, and will make plans to cover the details ahead of time. If your elder is open to talking about funeral planning, it behooves you to become familiar with the many options that are available today. When discussions lead to decisions, take notes, make arrangements, and incorporate the funeral as part of the letter of instruction in your elder's will. See the Legal Matters chapter of *The Planner* starting on page 125.

If you never did any funeral planning and now find yourself thrust in the position of making all the arrangements, the plans in this section will guide you through the entire post-death process.

In the event of a loved one's death, you will first have to decide what to do with the deceased's remains. The options are:

- **Ground burial**—The deceased is placed in a casket and set in a grave. Burial occurs after a ceremony or service, or without any service. **Burial at sea** also is an option.
- **Entombment**—The deceased is placed in a casket and laid to rest above ground in a tomb, mausoleum, or crypt.
- **Cremation**—The deceased is taken to a crematorium where a heating process reduces the remains to ashes and bone particles. The cremated remains are placed in a container that can be buried or stored in a vault, retained in a decorative memorial urn, or scattered on private property or in cemetery scattering gardens.
- **Whole body donation**—The deceased may have made arrangements ahead of time to donate his or her body to a medical school for research. Donation of the body can occur after a funeral service. The cremation option remains available after the school has completed its use of the body.
- **Simple disposition**—The deceased is taken directly to a cemetery or crematory. A memorial service may take place afterward.

Funeral directors serve the family as a consultant during these difficult times. Keep in mind that you are always free to choose where you purchase merchandise such as caskets and urns. You can expect them to assist you with the following details:

- Advice on funeral planning, memorial services, and a final resting place
- Purchasing caskets, urns, guest sign-in books, acknowledgment cards, and related merchandise
- Open-casket preparation, in terms of grooming and clothing
- Arranging services with clergy
- Arranging transportation for the deceased and family
- Shipping the remains to other locations
- Completing the death certificate and delivering it to the attending physician
- Obtaining burial permits
- Coordinating organ donations
- Writing the death notice, and coordinating with newspapers
- Complying with local, state, and federal laws and regulations

In the event of death you will need to secure the following vital statistics for making funeral arrangements and settling financial affairs:

- Full legal name and maiden name
- Current residence
- Last residence
- Date of birth
- Birthplace
- Citizenship
- Social Security number
- Military record, if any
- Marital status
- Spouse's name (maiden name)
- Heirs
- Father's name
- Father's birthplace
- Mother's maiden name
- Mother's birthplace
- Marriage date
- Divorce date
- Employment record, if any

Today, funerals are increasingly seen as a celebration of the deceased's life, and just about "anything goes." It is best to choose only what you want and a style that suits *you*, and only what you are willing to pay for. Here are some options and details to consider:

- Funeral home, chapel, church, synagogue, military site, and home visitations
- Style of casket
- Open viewing or private family viewing
- Open or closed casket
- Deceased's hair, clothes, jewelry, glasses
- Coffin enclosures
- Pallbearers
- Flowers
- Charitable donations
- Conductor of services
- Speakers
- Music, hymns, soloists, choir, instrumental only, accompaniment
- Eulogy and scripture readings
- Video tribute

- Cremation services
- Clergy
- Religious services
- Ethnic customs
- Grave-side services
- Military honors services
- Burial site
- Memorial marker and inscription
- Limousines and coaches
- Motor escort
- Guest book
- Family acknowledgment cards
- Coffee and light refreshments
- Special requests

 PLAN TWO
Become cost-conscious.

Some people prefer the cost-effectiveness and ecological soundness of a cremation, while others prefer an elaborate, personalized ceremony. Getting what you want isn't the problem; paying for it is. From preparation of the deceased and professional fees for making arrangements to motor vehicles, custom caskets, and funeral home use, it all adds up, and quickly.

Use these buying tips:

- Get a *written* itemized list up front of charges for services, facilities, and equipment. (It's the law.) Watch for hidden charges such as food service, and use of common areas like restrooms and parking lots.
- Take your time. Shop around for funeral homes, caskets, and other merchandise. Prices vary, and funeral homes may display only mid-range to expensive caskets.
- It is illegal for a funeral home to charge a *handling fee* if you wish to use a family-built casket or purchase one elsewhere; however, the casket must meet the standards of the cemetery selected.
- In the event of cremation, the law does not require the purchase of a casket before cremation.
- If the funeral director tells you "the state requires . . ." request written proof of the law.

Sources of income for paying for a funeral include:

Social Security benefits
Veterans Administration benefits
Prepayment plans
Life insurance policies
Burial trusts
Savings accounts

In the event that a loved one died while traveling investigate whether or not he or she purchased trip insurance offered by most airlines, cruise lines, and travel outfitters. This kind of insurance covers the costs of transporting the body back home, emergency travel expenses of family members, and medical care your elder may have received while traveling. When family members plan a trip in the future, ask them to purchase trip insurance for this purpose.

Planning ahead does not mean you have to pay ahead. Some funeral directors will simply keep a person's wishes on file. If you choose to enter into a pre-paid funeral arrangement, talk with an attorney *before* you sign a contract. Prepayment plans should be guaranteed, provide for inflation, transfer to another location, and trigger little or no penalty for cancellation. Be well-informed.

PLAN THREE
Notify others of the death.

Family, friends (including people from the old neighborhood and childhood friends), coworkers, even merchants with whom the deceased had frequent contact—all will want to know about a loved one's death. Be prepared to make many telephone calls. These calls are very emotionally draining, so as you call people, ask them if there is anyone else that needs to be contacted and, when appropriate, ask them to make some of these calls on your behalf.

If your elder is in the funeral-planning mode, ask for a list of people to notify upon his or her death. Get names and telephone numbers, and information on how your elder knows them. A simple way to accomplish this time-consuming task is to photocopy your elder's personal address book and put a star next to the names to call.

Make copies of this notification list and distribute to key family members. Include a copy of the list in the letters of instruction as part of your elder's will. Ask your elder to keep the list as current as possible.

You may also choose to submit a **death notice** and an **obituary** to local and national newspapers, as well as to alumni, club, and job-related newsletters. A death notice typically offers the following information: the deceased's full name, any nickname, maiden name, cause of death, age, names of survivors, donation requests, and visitation information. Submit a photo, if you like. An obituary can be as creative as you like. Submit a photo and include information such as educational background, degrees earned, religious affiliations, civic accomplishments, offices held, employment, club or union memberships, military record, hobbies and interests, special achievements, awards, and even amusing or interesting anecdotes or quotes for which the decedent had been responsible. If you are writing the obituary after your elder's death, ask his or her close friends, coworkers, and relatives to supply you with biographical details.

PLAN FOUR
Settle financial affairs.

After the funeral, you will have to face the very stressful task of handling the deceased's finances such as paying final bills, taxes, and debts. In order to do this, you will need to apply for survivor's benefits from the following sources of the deceased's income and savings. You will need a certified copy of the death certificate, insurance policy numbers, and proof that you are the beneficiary to file claims:

cash-on-hand

checking accounts

savings accounts

employer paychecks

company pensions

life insurance policies

individual or group health insurance

accident insurance

disability income insurance

long-term care insurance

private, association, and fraternal insurance

annuities

retirement accounts

tax refunds

trusts

money owed

security deposits

Social Security benefits

Veterans Administration benefits

Railroad retirement benefits
Teacher's retirement benefits
civil service benefits
union benefits

There may also be funds available from less-obvious sources. For example, various travel clubs, airline frequent-flier miles, and credit card companies may include certain entitlements upon death among their benefits. Therefore, be alert for any membership handbooks and manuals of the deceased's that you come across—and read the fine print.

To collect funds, legal heirs and beneficiaries must contact each source directly. Most likely a certified copy of the death certificate will be required for each resource. As a prompter to locate funds, companies, institutions, individuals, and agencies that may owe the deceased money, use the **Documents Locator** in this book as a guide.

Family members will need to obtain the following documentation to close out the deceased's personal and business affairs:

- Will
- Trusts
- Letters of instruction
- Life insurance policies
- Social Security benefits and death benefits
- Certified death certificates
- Social Security number
- Citizenship papers
- Birth certificate
- Adoption papers, if any
- Company pension records
- Bank records
- Bank power of attorney
- Power of attorney
- Safety deposit-box records
- Marriage license
- Divorce decree
- Military records
- Property deeds and titles
- Mortgage and loan documents
- Credit card statements and applications

- Property rental contracts
- Income tax records and returns
- Personal and business contracts
- Vehicle titles
- Stocks and bonds certificates
- Home inventory list
- List of assets and liabilities
- Receipts for valuables and collectibles
- Proof of debts paid
- Proof of money owed to or by the deceased

Transfers of property ownership upon death can be effected in many different ways besides the decedent's last will and testament. Some occur by operation of law (joint ownership of, for example, bank and investment accounts), by beneficiary designations in trusts, contracts, and life insurance policies. As to all other property owned solely by the deceased, in most cases his or her estate must undergo—whether or not a valid will was left—**probate** (the process of identifying and paying heirs, creditors, and determining taxes). This legal process usually takes a minimum of six months, and often much longer. If there is a will, the estate should have appointed an executor to carry out the decedent's instructions and property transfers.

When a person dies without a will (the legal term is "intestate"), family members can designate an individual to act as the administrator of the estate or the court will appoint one.

Before banks and other financial institutions can legally permit withdrawals or transfers of assets of the decedent, either **letters of office**—which can only be issued by the probate court—or an affidavit of some sort, must be obtained and presented. Powers of attorney, if created by the decedent during his or her lifetime, may also come into play.

As you can see, there are many legal requirements and pitfalls involved in all these matters. The laws governing death-related proceedings vary from state to state. By all means, you should contact an attorney at the earliest stages to get transactions started.

Once you have legally secured access to your decedent's funds, you can then continue paying his or her bills such as the mortgage, loans, taxes, lawyer and accountant fees, liability insurance, and utility bills out of the estate until assets are sold. *Family members are under no obligation to pay the bills of the deceased out of their own pocket unless the bills are also in their name.* Maintain detailed notes and files on financial transactions and decisions. You may be questioned later on and the notes can be used to back you up.

Purchase at least ten certified copies of the **death certificate** for filing claims, transferring titles and securities, and collecting benefits. The family doctor, hospital, funeral consultant, or nursing home director can obtain copies for you.

PLAN FIVE
Find missing documents and assets.

If you and your relative did not complete **The Documents Locator** section of *The Planner,* and you have limited knowledge of the existence of important documents that may reveal money that is owed, there are steps you can take to retrieve the information. Avoid unsolicited "finders" who charge you for information that leads to settlements. Instead:

- Review your elder's **personal address book** for names and telephone numbers of important people and places.
- Locate your elder's checkbook and savings book for **account numbers** and names of banking institutions. Read the checkbook entries to find out where your elder has been spending money and to define sources of deposits.
- Review your elder's **bill-paying history** to uncover payment plans and refund sources.
- Call each of your elder's **credit card companies** to find out if your elder took out an insurance policy. Cancel all credit cards.
- Search through your elder's **storage areas** at home and at work to find papers and documents.
- Review the contents of your elder's **home safe** and **bank safety-deposit box.** If your elder did not provide you with a key or entry privileges to the safety deposit-box, the bank, by law, may not allow access to the box. If that is the case, ask the bank what they require for you to gain access.
- Contact your elder's **employers,** past and present, regarding company pensions, life insurance policies, retirement savings, and union memberships.
- If you believe that your elder had a **will** and you have searched unsuccessfully among the decedent's personal effects, check the local probate court to see if a will has been filed. You can also advertise in the classified section of the local newspaper and local bar association publication to inquire about the existence of the will. If several months pass and no will is found, it is safe to assume that your elder died without one.
- You can apply for certified copies of **marriage licenses** and **divorce decrees** at the office of the county clerk where the license and divorce were issued.
- Copies of **death certificates** of relatives are available at the county's administrative offices, usually the county clerk or recorder's office.
- If your relative was a veteran, you will need a certificate of honorable discharge to collect benefits. Contact the local **Veterans Administration** office to get the process started.

- Search the state's **unclaimed property division** usually located within the department of revenue or treasury.

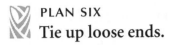

PLAN SIX
Tie up loose ends.

When the funeral services are over, and the legal distribution of property and assets is in progress, the fact of your family member's death slowly starts to sink in. This stage of death management is by far the most emotionally challenging. You will most likely experience intense feelings of helplessness and sadness, and your best defense is to postpone *any* decisions.

Deal with your grief before dealing with the estate. Take as much time as you need to make decisions regarding your relative's personal belongings. Come to a consensus with other family members on what to keep, what to give away, what to sell, what to auction off, and what to donate.

When you are ready, take on these tasks:

- Notify the post office of the death and provide a forward mailing address.
- Cancel credit cards, newspaper, and magazine subscriptions.
- Cancel club and union memberships.
- Cancel insurance when properties are sold or transferred.
- Cancel utility services, telephone, and cable television.
- If your elder rented an apartment or home, clean up and ask for the security deposit back plus any interest due.
- File a final tax return; store past tax records.
- Transfer vehicle titles.
- Lock up any additional property, such as vehicles or second homes, to protect against accidents and claims against the estate until such property is sold.
- Send acknowledgment cards to those who sent flowers and donations. You are not obligated to send cards to everyone who sent sympathy cards or attended funeral services unless you want to.

Low-Cost and Free Resources

People who wish to make an **organ donation** must make such arrangements in advance. Contact organ banks, a hospital, a medical school, the department of motor vehicles, and the local agency on aging for further information.

To keep the cost of a funeral down, you can buy a casket or urn directly from a manufacturer. Look in the Yellow Pages and on the **Internet** under casket companies.

ORGANIZATIONS

Funeral Information

Elderweb
Website: *www.elderweb.com/funeral.htm*

Federal Trade Commission
(Regulates the funeral industry)
Consumer Response Center 240
Washington, DC 20580
(877) 382-4357 (toll-free)
Website: *www.ftc.gov*

Funeral and Memorial Societies of America (FAMSA)
(To file a complaint)
P.O. Box 10
Hinesburg, VT 05461
(802) 482-3437
Website: *www.funerals.org/famsa*

National Funeral Directors Association
400 C Street, NE
Washington, DC 20002
(202) 547-0441, Fax: (202) 547-0726
Website: *www.nfda.org*

End-of-Life Issues and Grief Support

Americans for Better Care of the Dying (ABCD)
2175 K Street, NW, Suite 820
Washington, DC 20037
(202) 530-9864, Fax: (202) 467-2271
Website: *www.abcd-caring.com*

Choice In Dying
(State-specific living wills and advance directives)
1035 30th Street, NW
Washington, DC 20007
(202) 338-9790, Fax: (202) 338-0242
Website: *www.choices.org*

Growth House, Inc.
San Francisco
(415) 255-9045
Website: *www.growthhouse.org*

Hospice Association of America
228 Seventh Street, SE
Washington, DC 20003
(202) 546-4759, Fax: (202) 547-9559
Website: *www.nahc.org/HAA/home.html*

National Hospice Organization
1700 Diagonal Road, Suite 300
Alexandria, VA 22314
(703) 243-5900, Fax: (703) 525-5762
Website: *www.nho.org*

To Locate Missing Documents

Pension Benefit Guaranty Corporation
1200 K Street, NW
Washington DC 20005-4026
Website: *http://search.pbgc.gov*

National Association of Unclaimed Property Administrators
(To search each state database)
Website: *www.unclaimed.org*

Action Checklist

SAYING GOOD-BYE	To Do By	Completed
Be aware of clues of the letting go process	_____	❑
Create quality time—reminisce	_____	❑
Record and write down stories	_____	❑
Fill out an heirloom book	_____	❑
Help your elder mend severed relationships		
letter writing	_____	❑
telephoning	_____	❑
visiting	_____	❑
keeping journals	_____	❑

Help elder attain milestones
    family events   _____ ❏
    important projects   _____ ❏
    personal goals   _____ ❏

Remind yourself that your elder's withdrawal
   is not rejection   _____ ❏

Make end-of-life plans with your elder
    hospice   _____ ❏
    nutritional and respiratory life support decisions _____ ❏
    funeral arrangements _____ ❏
    living wills _____ ❏
    durable power of attorney for health care _____ ❏
    physician directives _____ ❏
    review *Managing Death's Details* section _____ ❏
    review *Legal Matters* chapter _____ ❏

Offer gifts of presence, comfort, and small joys _____ ❏

Call upon the assistance of
    clergy _____ ❏
    social worker _____ ❏
    hospice nurse _____ ❏

Make arrangements to stay overnight _____ ❏

Review your elder's advance directives (if any)
   with medical staff _____ ❏

Ask hospital counselors for support and guidance _____ ❏

Manage your elder's pain _____ ❏

Consider hospice _____ ❏

Consider bereavement support _____ ❏

Watch for excessive behavior patterns _____ ❏

MANAGING DEATH'S DETAILS

Review Communicaring chapter before talking about
   funeral planning _____ ❏

Become familiar with funeral options _____ ❏

Plan for organ or body donation _____ ❏

Secure vital statistics _____ ❏

Discuss funeral arrangements and costs
    get written itemized list up front _____ ❏
    ask about all charges _____ ❏
    for state requirement laws, request written proof _____ ❏

Shop around for funeral merchandise and services _____ ❏

Have a plan to cover funeral expenses
    social security _____ ❏
    veterans administration _____ ❏
    prepayment plans _____ ❏
    life insurance _____ ❏
    burial trusts _____ ❏
    savings accounts _____ ❏
    traveler's insurance _____ ❏

Incorporate plans as part of letter of instruction
  in your elder's will _____ ❏

Notify others of the death
    telephone _____ ❏
    death notice _____ ❏
    obituary _____ ❏

Settle financial affairs
    secure sources of your elder's income _____ ❏
    purchase multiple copies of death certificate _____ ❏
    collect documentation to close up the estate _____ ❏

Retain attorney _____ ❏

Maintain detailed notes on all financial interactions _____ ❏

Locate missing documents and assets _____ ❏

Tie up loose ends
    what to keep _____ ❏
    what to give away _____ ❏
    what to sell _____ ❏
    what to auction off _____ ❏
    what to donate _____ ❏
    transfer titles _____ ❏
    lock up property _____ ❏
    file final tax returns _____ ❏
    store records _____ ❏

· 14 ·

DOCUMENTS LOCATOR

The Documents Locator

Quick. *What's Dad's Social Security number? Where does Mom keep the title documents to her house? Do they have a will? Who has power of attorney? Does your elder have supplemental health insurance? Does heart disease run in the family?*

Discovering what legal documents already exist, knowing where they're stored, and producing them on demand is an inevitable responsibility in the eldercare process. *The Documents Locator* is an invaluable planning tool that, when completed, will help you avoid the trauma, expense, and inconvenience of having to scramble around looking for important papers under stressful emergency conditions. Having done so in advance allows family members peace of mind, especially in unfortunate cases when elders may be incapacitated and not able to advise you of any answers.

The sooner you complete this section of *The Planner,* the better. The content is extensive, so be realistic on how long it will take you to complete this process. Do a small portion of the Documents Locator at a time. Store original documents in a safe location that is accessible day and night, seven days a week. Keep copies of originals in your elder's file. Also, make sure key family members and advisers have copies of this information and related documents. Review your documents file every three to six months for possible revisions and updates.

PIN NUMBERS / ACCESS CODES

Bank by phone_____

Debit cards _____

Online banking _____

Computer _____

Websites_____

Cash station_____

Voice mail _____

E-mail address _____

E-mail access code _____

Property_____

PERSONAL BANK ACCOUNTS

Account name and number_____

Names on account_____

Bank _____

Telephone _____

Type of account _____

Location of account documents _____

Need for second signature _____

Power of attorney in place_____

Account name and number_____

Names on account_____

Bank _____

Telephone _____

Type of account _____

Location of account documents _____

Need for second signature _____

Power of attorney in place_____

AUTOMATIC BILL PAYING

Name of store and service _____

Contact name _____

Telephone _____

Date payment deducted _____

Bank and account number _____

Name of store/service _____

Contact name _____

Telephone _____

Date payment deducted _____

Bank and account number _____

ELECTRONIC FUNDS TRANSFER ACCOUNT (ETA)

Account name and number _____

Names on account _____

Bank _____

Telephone _____

PERSONAL LOAN

Name(s) on loan _____

Loan number _____

Bank _____

Telephone _____

Type of loan _____

Location of loan papers _____

OUTSTANDING LIEN AGAINST PROPERTY

Name(s) on loan _____

Loan number _____

Bank _____

Telephone _____

Location of loan papers _____

PAID LIENS AGAINST PROPERTY

Name(s) on loan _____

Loan number _____

Bank _____

Telephone _____

Location of proof of payment papers _____

Name(s) on loan _____

Loan number_____

Bank _____

Telephone _____

Location of proof of payment papers _____

INSTALLMENT LOANS

Name(s) on loan _____

Loan number_____

Bank _____

Telephone _____

Location of loan papers_____

Name(s) on loan _____

Loan number_____

Bank _____

Telephone _____

Location of loan papers_____

BUSINESS BANK ACCOUNT

Bank _____

Telephone _____

Location of account documents _____

Business name on account _____

Account number _____

Type of account_____

Need for second signature _____

Power of attorney in place_____

BUSINESS LOAN

Name(s) on loan _____

Loan number_____

Type of loan_____

Bank _____

Telephone _____

Location of loan papers_____

CREDIT UNION

Union name_____

Telephone _____

Name on account(s) _____

Type of account(s)_____

Account number(s) _____

Location of documents _____

FOREIGN BANK ACCOUNT

Name(s) on account _____

Account number _____

Type of account_____

Bank _____

Telephone _____

Location of account papers _____

COMPANY PENSION

Name on pension _____

Reference number _____

Dates of employment _____

Company name_____

Telephone _____

Location of pension papers _____

RETIREMENT ACCOUNTS

Name on account _____

Account reference number _____

Type of account_____

Bank _____

Telephone _____

Location of account documents _____

Name on account _____

Account reference number _____

Type of account _____

Bank _____

Telephone _____

Location of account documents _____

SAVINGS CERTIFICATES

Depositor _____

Certificate number _____

Bank _____

Telephone _____

Location of certificates _____

Depositor _____

Certificate number _____

Bank _____

Telephone _____

Location of certificates _____

SAVINGS BONDS

Bond held by _____

Type of bond _____

Bond series number _____

Location of bond _____

Bond held by _____

Type of bond _____

Bond series number _____

Location of bond _____

STOCK CERTIFICATES

Stockholder(s) _____

Stock name _____

Stock number _____

Broker _____

Telephone _____

Location of stock documents _____

Stockholder(s) _____

Stock name _____

Stock number _____

Broker _____

Telephone _____

Location of stock documents _____

SAFE-DEPOSIT BOX

Box holder _____

Has access to box _____

Telephone number _____

Box number _____

Bank _____

Telephone _____

Key location _____

CASH-ON-HAND

Location _____

Location _____

Location _____

HOME SAFE

Has access to safe _____

Telephone _____

Location of combination or key _____

BUSINESS SAFE

People with access to safe _____

Telephone _____

Telephone _____

Location of combination or key _____

WILL

Will of _____

Attorney _____

Telephone _____

Location of original will papers_____

People with copies of will papers _____

Telephone _____

TRUST

Established by _____

Trust for_____

Attorney _____

Telephone _____

Location of original trust papers_____

People with copies of trust papers_____

Established by _____

Trust for_____

Attorney _____

Telephone _____

Location of original trust papers_____

People with copies of trust papers_____

LIVING WILL

Will of _____

Attorney _____

Telephone _____

Location of original living will _____

People with copies of living will _____

Telephone _____

DURABLE POWER OF ATTORNEY

Given to _____

Telephone _____

Attorney _____

Telephone _____

Location of original document _____

People with copy of papers _____

DURABLE POWER OF ATTORNEY FOR HEALTH CARE

Location of original document _____

People with copies of the document _____

Agent _____

Telephone _____

Agent _____

Telephone _____

Agent _____

Telephone _____

LETTERS OF INSTRUCTION

Written by _____

Location of original documents _____

Telephone _____

People with copy of documents _____

Telephone _____

FUNERAL INSTRUCTIONS

Arranged by _____

Funeral home _____

Telephone _____

Location of instruction papers _____

People with copies of instructions_____

Telephone _____

DONOR ARRANGEMENTS

Donor name _____

Donor bank _____

Telephone _____

Location of donor papers _____

AUTOPSY ARRANGEMENTS

Location of autopsy papers _____

Organization _____

Telephone _____

SOCIAL SECURITY

Name of beneficiary _____

Social Security number _____

Location of Social Security card _____

MILITARY DISCHARGE PAPERS

Veteran name _____

Service number _____

Discharge papers location _____

INCOME TAX FILINGS

Name of taxpayer _____

Tax identification number _____

Tax adviser _____

Telephone _____

Location of tax records _____

PASSPORT

Name on passport _____

Passport number _____

Location of passport _____

DRIVER'S LICENSE

Name on license _____

License number _____

State license issued _____

License renewal date _____

CHARGE ACCOUNTS

Account name _____

Account number _____

Name on account _____

Location of card _____

Account name _____

Account number _____

Name on account _____

Location of card _____

Account name _____

Account number _____

Name on account _____

Location of card _____

MEDICARE/MEDICAID

Name of beneficiary _____

Claim number _____

Is entitled to _____

Effective date _____

MEDICAL INSURANCE POLICY

Subscriber's name _____

Contract number _____

Group number _____

Insurance company _____

Telephone _____

LONG-TERM CARE INSURANCE POLICY

Name on policy _____

Policy number _____

Insurance company _____

Insurance agent _____

Telephone _____

Location of policy _____

LIFE INSURANCE POLICIES

Name on policy _____

Policy number _____

Insurance company _____

Insurance agent _____

Telephone _____

Location of policy _____

Name on policy _____

Policy number _____

Insurance company _____

Insurance agent _____

Telephone _____

Location of policy _____

ANNUITIES

Name on annuity _____

Insurance company _____

Contract number _____

Location of papers _____

DISABILITY INSURANCE POLICY

Name on policy _____

Policy number _____

Insurance company _____

Insurance agent _____

Telephone _____

Location of policy _____

HOME OWNER'S INSURANCE POLICY

Name on policy _____

Policy number _____

Insurance company _____

Insurance agent _____

Telephone _____

Location of policy _____

REAL ESTATE INVESTMENT INSURANCE POLICY

Name on policy _____

Policy number _____

Insurance company _____

Insurance agent _____

Telephone _____

Location of policy _____

RENTER'S INSURANCE POLICY

Name on policy _____

Policy number _____

Insurance company _____

Insurance agent _____

Telephone _____

Location of policy _____

BUSINESS INSURANCE POLICY

Name on policy _____

Policy number _____

Insurance company _____

Insurance agent _____

Telephone _____

Location of policy _____

LIABILITY INSURANCE POLICY

Name on policy _____

Policy number _____

Insurance company _____

Insurance agent _____

Telephone _____

Location of policy _____

AUTO / VEHICLE INSURANCE POLICIES

Policy holder _____

Vehicle insured _____

Registration number _____

Insurance company _____

Insurance agent _____

Telephone _____

Location of title _____

Policy holder _____

Vehicle insured _____

Registration number _____

Insurance company _____

Insurance agent _____

Telephone _____

Location of title _____

VALUABLES INSURANCE POLICY

Policy holder _____

Item insured _____

Policy number _____

Insurance company _____

Insurance agent _____

Telephone _____

Location of policy _____

VEHICLE OWNERSHIP

Vehicle _____

Make and model _____

Serial number _____

Where purchased_____

Telephone _____

Name on title_____

Location of title papers _____

Vehicle _____

Make and model _____

Serial number _____

Where purchased_____

Telephone _____

Name on title_____

Location of title papers _____

REAL ESTATE OWNERSHIP DOCUMENTS

Property address _____

Owner _____

Telephone _____

Co-owner _____

Telephone _____

Bank or mortgage company _____

Telephone _____

Location of documents _____

Property address _____

Owner _____

Telephone _____

Co-owner _____

Telephone _____

Bank or mortgage company _____

Telephone _____

Location of documents _____

CEMETERY PLOT

Owner _____

Plot intended for _____

Cemetery _____

Plot location _____

Telephone _____

Location of plot deeds _____

MAGAZINE AND NEWSPAPER SUBSCRIPTIONS

Name of publication _____

Sent to _____

Name of publication _____

Sent to _____

Name of publication _____

Sent to _____

CLUB MEMBERSHIPS

Organization _____

Telephone _____

Organization _____

Telephone _____

MEMBERSHIP CARDS

Account name _____

Account number _____

Name on account _____

Location of card _____

Account name _____

Account number _____

Name on account _____

Location of card _____

RELIGIOUS AFFILIATION

Name of church/temple/place of worship _____

Address _____

Clergy person _____

Telephone _____

BAPTISM RECORDS

Baptismal name _____

Date of baptism _____

Church _____

Telephone _____

Baptism records location _____

BAR/BAT MITZVAH RECORD

Date of bar/bat mitzvah _____

Synagogue _____

Telephone _____

Records location _____

ITEMS IN STORAGE

Stored in name of _____

What is being stored _____

Storage company _____

Telephone _____

Location of storage documents _____

ITEMS—REPAIRED/RESTORED/CLEANED

Item owner _____
Item description _____
Shop name_____
Telephone _____
Claim ticket location _____

Item owner _____
Item description _____
Shop name_____
Telephone _____
Claim ticket location _____

ITEMS BORROWED

Item description _____
Lent to _____
Telephone _____

ITEMS ON ORDER

Ordered for _____
Item description _____
Order reference number _____
Shop name_____
Telephone _____
Expected order date_____
Location of paperwork _____

PERSONAL CONTRACTS/AGREEMENTS

Names on contract _____
Telephone _____
Nature of agreement _____
Location of paperwork _____

MEDICAL HISTORY

History of _____

Birth date_____

Location of records _____

BIRTH RECORD

Name at birth _____

Birth date_____

Place of birth _____

Birth certificate location _____

ADOPTION PAPERS

Adoption name _____

Adopted by _____

State of adoption _____

Adoption agency _____

Telephone _____

Location of paperwork _____

NATURALIZATION PAPERS

Citizen name _____

Place of naturalization_____

Location of papers_____

MARRIAGE LICENSE

Names on license_____

Marriage date _____

State license issued _____

License location_____

DIVORCE DECREE

Names on decree _____

Divorce date _____

State divorce granted _____

Decree location _____

SCHOOL RECORDS

Student name _____

School _____

School location _____

Telephone _____

Dates attended_____

Graduation date _____

Diploma location _____

Student name _____

School _____

School location _____

Telephone _____

Dates attended_____

Graduation date _____

Diploma location _____

Student name _____

School _____

School location _____

Telephone _____

Dates attended_____

Graduation date _____

Diploma location _____

EMPLOYMENT HISTORY

Employee name_____

Dates of employment _____

Company_____

Company address _____

Telephone _____

Employee name _____

Dates of employment _____

Company_____

Company address _____

Telephone _____

Employee name _____

Dates of employment _____

Company_____

Company address _____

Telephone _____

MOTHER'S HISTORY

Mother's name at birth _____

Date of birth _____

Place of birth _____

Birth certificate location _____

Mother's name at death_____

Cause of death_____

Date of death _____

Location of death _____

Burial location_____

Death certificate location _____

FATHER'S HISTORY

Father's name at birth _____

Date of birth _____

Place of birth _____

Birth certificate location _____

Father's name at death_____

Cause of death_____

Date of death _____

Location of death _____

Burial location _____

Death certificate location _____

DEPENDENTS

Name _____

Date of birth _____

Location of birth certificate _____

Name _____

Date of birth _____

Location of birth certificate _____

Name _____

Date of birth _____

Location of birth certificate _____

Name _____

Date of birth _____

Location of birth certificate _____

GROWN CHILDREN—NO LONGER DEPENDENTS

Name _____

Date of birth _____

Address _____

City/State/Zip _____

Telephone _____

Name _____

Date of birth _____

Address _____

City/State/Zip _____

Telephone _____

Name _____

Date of birth _____

Address _____

City/State/Zip _____

Telephone _____

Name _____

Date of birth _____

Address _____

City/State/Zip _____

Telephone _____

PET HISTORY

Name of pet _____

Breed _____

Date of birth _____

Sex _____

Animal hospital _____

Telephone _____

Name of pet _____

Breed _____

Date of birth _____

Sex _____

Animal hospital _____

Telephone _____

HOME INVENTORY (fixtures, furniture, equipment, appliances)

Item description _____

Model number _____

Purchase price _____

Value of item today _____

Location of receipt _____

Location of warranty _____

Is promised to _____

PERSONAL ITEMS INVENTORY (clothes, books, photos, mementos)

Item description _____

Purchase price _____

Value of item today _____

Location of receipt _____

Is promised to _____

VALUABLES INVENTORY (collections, jewelry, artwork, antiques)

Item description _____

Serial number _____

Purchase price _____

Value of item today _____

Location of receipt _____

Is promised to _____

BUSINESS INVENTORY (fixtures, furniture, equipment, appliances)

Item description _____

Model number_____

Purchase price _____

Value of item today _____

Location of receipt _____

Location of warranty_____

Is promised to _____

FAMILY PETS

Name of pet_____

Is promised to _____

Name of pet_____

Is promised to _____

Action Checklist

DOCUMENTS LOCATOR	To Do By	Completed
Complete the Documents Locator	_____	❑
Make copies of original documents	_____	❑
Store original documents in safe place	_____	❑
Maintain 24-hour access to original documents	_____	❑
Keep in safety-deposit box		
stock certificates	_____	❑
securities and bonds	_____	❑
certificates of deposit	_____	❑
titles to property and vehicles	_____	❑
deeds	_____	❑
bills of sale—major purchases and valuables	_____	❑
appraisals of property and valuables	_____	❑
retirement bank account records	_____	❑
company pension records	_____	❑
contracts and legal agreements	_____	❑
naturalization papers	_____	❑
Duplicate and distribute copies of these documents to key family members and family attorney		
proof of insurance	_____	❑
letters of instruction	_____	❑
durable power of attorney	_____	❑
durable power of attorney for health care	_____	❑
living will	_____	❑
the Documents Locator	_____	❑
Keep in fireproof box at home		
birth certificates	_____	❑
death certificates	_____	❑
marriage licenses	_____	❑
divorce decrees	_____	❑
financial records	_____	❑
passports	_____	❑
insurance policies	_____	❑
wills	_____	❑
letters of instruction	_____	❑
durable power of attorney	_____	❑

durable power of attorney for health care _____ ❏
military discharge papers _____ ❏
income tax returns for past six years _____ ❏
property tax receipts _____ ❏
warranties _____ ❏

ELDERCARE GOALS CHART

The most effective goal setting is specific, realistic, and written.

GOALS   **GOAL ACHIEVED**

1. _____ ❏

2. _____ ❏

3. _____ ❏

4. _____ ❏

Prioritize and list what you need to do to accomplish each goal.

GOAL 1.   Completed   **GOAL 2.**   Completed

Call _____ ❏   *Call* _____ ❏
_____ ❏   _____ ❏
_____ ❏   _____ ❏

Write _____ ❏   *Write* _____ ❏
_____ ❏   _____ ❏
_____ ❏   _____ ❏

Meet _____ ❏   *Meet* _____ ❏
_____ ❏   _____ ❏
_____ ❏   _____ ❏

Buy _____ ❏   *Buy* _____ ❏
_____ ❏   _____ ❏
_____ ❏   _____ ❏

Read _____ ❏   *Read* _____ ❏
_____ ❏   _____ ❏
_____ ❏   _____ ❏

GOAL 3.	Completed	GOAL 4.	Completed
Call _____	❏	*Call* _____	❏
_____	❏	_____	❏
_____	❏	_____	❏
Write _____	❏	*Write* _____	❏
_____	❏	_____	❏
_____	❏	_____	❏
Meet _____	❏	*Meet* _____	❏
_____	❏	_____	❏
_____	❏	_____	❏
Buy _____	❏	*Buy* _____	❏
_____	❏	_____	❏
_____	❏	_____	❏
Read _____	❏	*Read* _____	❏
_____	❏	_____	❏
_____	❏	_____	❏

ORGANIZATIONS INDEX

AAA Foundation for Traffic Safety, 1440 New York Avenue, NW, Suite 201, Washington, DC 20005, (202) 638-5944, Fax: 202-638-5943

Administración del Envejeciente Administration on Aging, 330 Independence Avenue, SW, Washington, DC 20201, (202) 619-7501, Fax: (202) 260-1012

AARP, 601 E Street, NW, Washington, DC 20049, (800) 424-3410

AARP Grandparent Information Center, 601 East Street, NW, Washington, DC 20049, (202) 434-2296

ABLEDATA, 8401 Colesville Road, Suite 200, Silver Spring, MD 20910, (800) 227-0216, (301) 608-8998, TTY: (301) 608-8912, Fax: (301) 608-8958

Administration on Aging, 330 Independence Avenue, SW, Washington, DC 20201, (202) 619-7501, Fax: (202) 260-1012, TTY: (202) 401-7575

American Associaĭof Homes and Services for the Aging (AAHSA), 901 E Street, NW, Suite 500, Washington, DC 20004-2011, (202) 783-2242, Fax: (202) 783-2255

American Bar Association, 750 N. Lake Shore Drive, Chicago, IL 60611, (312) 988-5000

American Board of Medical Specialties, (800) 776-2378

American Dietetic Association, 216 W. Jackson Boulevard, Chicago, IL 60606-6995, (312) 899-0040

American Health Assistance Foundation (AHAF), 15825 Shady Grove Road, Suite 140, Rockville, MD 20850, (800) 437-2423, (301) 948-3244, Fax: (301) 258-9454

American Health Care Association (AHCA), 1201 L Street, NW, Washington, DC 20005, (202) 842-4444, Fax: (202) 842-3860

American Heart Association, 7272 Greenville Avenue, Dallas, TX 75231, (800) 242-8721

American Institute of Certified Public Accountants (AICPA), 1211 Avenue of the Americas, New York, NY 10036-8775, (212) 596-6200, Fax: (212) 596-6213, (888) 999-9256, Fax: (800) 362-5066

American Medical Association, 515 North State Street, Chicago, IL 60610

American Parkinson's Disease Association, 1250 Hylan Boulevard, Suite 4B, Staten Island, NY 10305-1946, (800) 223-2737, (718) 981-8001, Fax: (718) 981-4399

American Red Cross, 1621 N. Kent Street, 11th Floor, Arlington, VA 22209, (703) 248-4222

American Trauma Society, 8903 Presidential Parkway, Suite 512, Upper Marlboro, MD 20772, (800) 556-7890, (301) 420-4189

Americans for Better Care of the Dying (ABCD), 2175 K Street, NW, Suite 820, Washington, DC 20037, (202) 530-9864, Fax: (202) 467-2271

The Anger Clinic, Mitch Messer, 111 N. Wabash, Suite 1702, Chicago, IL 60602, (312) 263-0035

Assisted Living Federation of America, 10300 Eaton Place, Suite 400, Fairfax, VA 22030, (703) 691-8100, Fax: (703) 691-8106

BenefitsLink, Inc., 1014 East Robinson Street, Orlando, FL 32801, (407) 841-3717, Fax: (407) 841-3054

BR Anchor Relocation Consultants, 7213-A Market Street, Suite 342, Wilmington, NC 28411-9448, (910) 256-9598, Fax: (910) 256-9579

Brookdale Center on Aging of Hunter College, 425 E. 25th Street, New York, NY 10010, (212) 481-4426, Fax: (212) 481-5069

CareQuest, Inc., 583 D'Onofrio Drive, Suite 103, Madison, WI 53719, (800) 833-2524, TTY relay: (800) 947-3529

Catholic Charities USA, 1731 King Street, Suite 200, Alexandria, VA 22314, (703) 549-1390, Fax: (703) 549-1656

Center for Work and The Family, 910 Tulare Avenue, Berkeley, CA 94707, (510) 529-0107 in California, (301) 309-0870 in Maryland, Fax: (925) 376-3766

Certified Financial Planner Board of Standards, 1700 Broadway, Suite 2100, Denver, CO 80290, (888) 237-6275, (303) 830-7500, Fax: (303) 860-7388

Children of Aging Parents, 609 Woodburne Road, Suite 302A, Levittown, PA 19057, (800) 227-7294

Choice In Dying, 1035 30th Street, NW, Washington, DC 20007, (202) 338-9790, Fax: (202) 338-0242

Christmas in April, 1536 Sixteenth Street, NW, Washington, DC 20036-1402, (202) 483-9083, Fax: (202) 483-9081

Close-Up Program for Older Americans, 44 Canal Center Plaza, Alexandria, VA 22314-1592, (800) 256-7387, (703) 706-3300

Community Transportation Association of America, 1341 G Street, NW, Suite 600, Washington, DC 20005, (202) 628-1480, Fax: (202) 737-9197

Consumer Information Center, Pueblo, CO 81009, (888) 878-3256

Consumer Coalition for Quality Health Care, 1275 K Street, NW, Washington, DC 20005, (202) 789-3606

Continuing Care Accreditation Commission, 901 E Street, NW, Suite 500, Washington, DC 20004, (202) 783-7286, Fax: (202) 783-2255

Corporation for National Service, 1201 New York Avenue, NW, Washington, DC 20525, (202) 606-5000, TDD: (202) 634-9256

Council on Family Health, 1155 Connecticut Avenue, NW, Suite 400, Washington, DC 20036, (202) 429-6600

Department of Veteran Affairs, 810 Vermont Avenue, NW, Washington, DC 20420, (800) 827-1000, (202) 273-5771, Fax: (202) 273-5716

Direct Marketing Association, Attention: Mail Preference Service, P.O. Box 9008, Farmingdale, NY 11735; Attention: Telephone Preference Service, P.O. Box 9014, Farmingdale, NY 11735

The Eden Alternative, 742 Turnpike Road, Sherburne, NY 13460, (607) 674-5232, Fax: (607) 674-6723

Eldercare Locator, (800) 677-1116

Employee Services Management Association, 2211 York Road, Suite 207, Oak Brook, IL 60521, (630) 368-1280, Fax: (630) 368-1286

Equal Employment Opportunity Commission, 1801 L Street, NW, Washington, DC 20507, (800) 669-4000, (202) 663-4900, TDD: (800) 669-6820

Families USA Foundation, 1334 G Street, NW, Washington, DC 20005, (202) 628-3030, Fax: (202) 347-2417

Federal Trade Commission, Consumer Response Center 240, Washington, DC 20580, (202) 382-4357

Funeral and Memorial Societies of America (FAMSA), P.O. Box 10, Hinesburg, VT 05461, (802) 482-3437

Generations United, 440 First Street, NW, Suite 310, Washington, DC 20001-2085, (202) 662-4283, Fax: (202) 408-7629

Gray Panthers, 733 15th Street, NW, Suite 437, Washington, DC 20005, (800) 280-5362, (202) 737-6637, Fax: (202) 737-1160

Growth House, San Francisco, (415) 255-9045

Health Care Financing Administration (HFCA), 7500 Security Boulevard, Baltimore, MD 21244, (410) 786-3000

Health Insurance Association of America (HIAA), 555 13th Street, NW, Washington, DC 20004, (202) 824-1600

HMO Facts, 6853 SW 18th Street, Suite 110, Boca Raton, FL 33433, (toll-free) (877) 466-3228, (561) 361-9165, Fax: (561) 361-1049

Hospice Association of America, 228 Seventh Street, SE, Washington, DC 20003, (202) 546-4759, Fax: (202) 547-9559

Insurance Institute for Highway Safety, 1005 N. Glebe Road, Suite 800, Arlington, VA 22201, (703) 247-1500, Fax: (703) 247-1588

Institute of Certified Financial Planners (ICFP), 3801 E. Florida Avenue, Suite 708, Denver, CO 80210, (800) 322-4237, (303) 759-4900, Fax: (303) 759-0749

Insurance Information Institute, 111 William Street, New York, NY 10038, (800) 331-9146, Fax: (212) 791-1807

Internal Revenue Service, (800) 829-1040

International Association for Financial Planning (IAFP), 5775 Glenridge Drive, NE, Suite B-300, Atlanta, GA 30328-5364, (800) 945-4237, (404) 845-0011, Fax: (404) 845-3660

International Foundation of Employee Benefit Plans, 18700 W. Bluemound Road, P.O. Box 69, Brookfield, WI 53008-0069, (414) 786-6710, Fax: (414) 786-8670

Joint Commission on Accreditation of Healthcare Organizations (JACHO), One Renaissance Boulevard, Oak Brook Terrace, IL 60181, (630) 792-5000, Fax: (630) 792-5005

Leadership Council of Aging Organizations, 8403 Colesville Road, Suite 1200, Silver Spring, MD 20910-3314, (888) 3-SENIOR

Legal Services Corporation, 750 First Street, NE, 10th Floor, Washington, DC 20002-4250, (202) 336-8800

Licensed Independent Network of CPA Financial Planners (LINC), P.O. Box 1559, Columbia, TN 38402-1559, (800) 887-8358, Fax: (615) 242-4152

Little Brothers—Friends of the Elderly, 954 W. Washington Boulevard, 5th Floor, Chicago, IL 60607, (312) 829-3055, Fax: (312) 829-3077

Managing Work & Family, Inc., 912 Crain, Evanston, IL 60202, (847) 864-0916, Fax: (847) 475-2021

Meals on Wheels Association of America, 1414 Prince Street, Suite 202, Alexandria, VA 22314, (800) 999-6262, (703) 548-5558, Fax: (703) 548-8024

Medicare Hotline, (800) 638-6833

Medicare Rights Center Hot Line, (888) 466-9050

Mr. Long-Term Care, Martin K. Bayne, 151-A Eastwood Drive, Clifton Park, NY 12065-4299, (518) 383-5989, Fax: (518) 371-1418

National Academy of Elder Law Attorneys, 1604 N. Country Club Road, Tucson, AZ 85716, (520) 881-4005, Fax: (520) 325-7925

National Accessible Apartment Clearinghouse, 201 N. Union Street, Suite 200, Alexandria, VA 22314, (800) 421-1221, Fax: (703) 518-6141

National Adult Day Care Services Association, c/o National Council on the Aging, 409 Third Street, SW, Washington, DC 20024, (800) 424-9046, (202) 479-1200, Fax: (202) 479-0735

National Aging Information Center, Administration on Aging, 330 Independence Avenue, SW, Room 4656, Washington, DC 20201, (202) 619-7501, Fax: (202) 401-7620, TTY: (202) 401-7575

National Indian Council on Aging, 10501 Montgomery Boulevard, NE, Suite 210, Albuquerque, NM 87111-3846, (508) 292-2001

National Institute on Aging (NIA), c/o National Institutes of Health, Bethesda, MD 20892, (800) 222-2225, TTY: (800) 222-4225

National Insurance Consumer Help Line, (800) 942-4242

National Mental Health Association, 1021 Prince Street, Alexandria, VA 22314-2971, (800) 969-6642, TTY: (800) 433-5959

National Library Service for the Blind and Physically Handicapped Hotline, (800) 424-9100

National Network of Estate Planning Attorneys, 410 17th Street, Suite 1260, Denver, CO 80202, (800) 638-8681

National Pacific/Asian Resource Center on Aging (NAPCA), Melbourne Tower, 1511 Third Street, Suite 914, Seattle, WA 98101-1626, (206) 624-1221

National Resource and Policy Center on Housing and Long Term Care, 321 E. 25th Street, Baltimore, MD 21218, (800) 677-7472

National Safety Council, 1121 Spring Lake Drive, Itasca, IL 60143-3201, (800) 621-7619, (630) 285-1121, Fax: (630) 285-1315

National Senior Citizen Law Center, Washington, DC Office, 1101 14th Street, NW Suite 400, Washington, DC 20005, (202) 289-6976, Fax: (202) 289-7224, Los Angeles Office, 2639 S. La Cienega Boulevard, Los Angeles, CA 90034, (310) 204-6015, Fax: (310) 204-0891

North American Securities Administrators Association (NASAA), 10 G Street, NE, Suite 710, Washington, DC 20002, (888) 846-2722, (202) 737-0900

Older Women's League, 666 11th Street, NW, Suite 700, Washington, DC 20001, (800) 825-3695, (202) 783-6686, (202) 783-6689

Pension and Welfare Benefits Administration (PWBA), 200 Constitution Avenue, NW, Washington, DC 20210, (202) 219-8771 (documents), (202) 219-8776 (benefit questions)

Pension Benefit Guaranty Corporation, 1200 K Street, NW, Washington, DC 20005

Pharmaceutical Research and Manufacturers of America, (800) 762-4636

Securities and Exchange Commission (SEC), Office of Investor Education and Assistance, Mail Stop 2-13, 450 Fifth Street, NW, Washington, DC 20549, (800) 732-0330, (202) 942-7040, Fax: (202) 942-9634

Silvercare Productions, Joy Loverde, 1560 N. Sandburg Terrace, Suite 2509, Chicago, IL 60610, (312) 642-3611, Fax: (312) 642-8110

Social Security Administration, Office of Public Inquiries, 6401 Security Boulevard, Room 4-C-5 Annex, Baltimore, MD 21235, (800) 772-1213, TDD: (800) 325-0778

Society of Financial Service Professionals, 270 Bryn Mawr Avenue, Bryn Mawr, PA 19010-2195, (888) 243-2258, (610) 526-2500, Fax: (610) 527-4010

State Representative (Name), United States House of Representatives, Washington, DC 20515

State Senator (Name), United States Senate, Washington, DC 20510

U.S. Consumer Product Safety Commission, Consumer Hotline: (800) 638-2772, Consumer Hotline for TTY: (800) 638-8270

U.S. Department of Housing and Urban Development (HUD), 801 N. Capitol Street, NE, Washington, DC 20002, (202) 523-4400, Fax: (202) 523-4399

Visiting Nurse's Association, 11 Beacon Street, Suite 910, Boston, MA 02108, (617) 523-4042, Fax: (617) 227-4843

Volunteers of America, 110 South Union Street, Alexandria, VA 22314-3324, (800) 899-0089, Fax: (703) 684-1972

Well Spouse Foundation, 610 Lexington Avenue, Suite 208, New York, NY 10022-6005, (800) 838-0879, (212) 644-1338

Work & Family Connection, 5197 Beachside Drive, Minnetonka, MN 55343, (800) 487-7898, (612) 936-7898, Fax: (612) 935-0122

WEBSITE INDEX

AAA Foundation for Traffic Safety
www.aaafts.org

AARP (American Association of Retired Persons)
www.aarp.org

ABLEDATA
www.abledata.com

Access America for Seniors
www.seniors.gov

Administracion Del Envejeciente
www.aoa.dhhs.gov/espanol

Administration on Aging
www.aoa.dhhs.gov

Intergenerational Programs
www.aoa.dhhs.gov/aoa/webres/intergen.htm

Volunteer Programs
www.aoa.dhhs.gov/aoa/eldractn/voluntr.html

Alzheimer's Association
www.alzheimers.org

American Association of Homes and Services for the Aging (AAHSA)
www.aahsa.org

American Bar Association
www.abanet.org

American Dietetic Association
www.eatright.org

American Health Assistance Foundation (AHAF)
www.ahaf.org

American Health Care Association
www.ahca.org

American Heart Association
www.americanheart.org

American Institute of Certified Public Accountants (AICPA)
www.aicpa.org

American Medical Association
www.ama-assn.org

American Parkinson's Disease Association
www.apdaparkinson.com

American Red Cross
www.redcross.org

American Trauma Society
www.amtrauma.org

Americans for Better Care of the Dying (ABCD)
www.abcd-caring.com

Arthritis Foundation
www.arthritis.org

Assisted Living Federation of America
www.alfa.org

BenefitsLink, Inc.
www.benefitslink.com

Better Business Bureau
www.bbb.org

BR Anchor Relocation Consultants
www.branchor.com

National Funeral Directors Association
www.nfda.org

National Guardianship Association
www.guardianship.org

National Health Information Center
www.nhic-nt.health.org

National Highway Traffic Safety Administration
www.nhtsa.dot.gov

National Hospice Organization
www.nho.org

National Indian Council on Aging
www.nicoa.org

National Institute on Aging (NIA)
www.nih.gov/nia

National Mental Health Association
www.nmha.org

National Network of Estate Planning Attorneys
www.netplanning.com

National Resource and Policy Center on Housing and Long Term Care
www.aoa.dhhs.gov/Housing/SharedHousing.html

National Safety Council
www.nsc.org

National Senior Citizen Law Center
www.nscla.org

North American Securities Administrators Association (NASAA)
www.nasaa.org

National Committee to Preserve Social Security and Medicare
www.ncpssm.org

National Council of Senior Citizens
www.ncscinc.org

Older Women's League
http://pr.aoa.dhhs.gov/aoa/dir/207.html

Pension and Welfare Benefits Administration (PWBA)
www.dol.gov/dol/pwba/public/guide.htm

Pension Benefit Guaranty Corporation
search.pbgc.gov

Securities and Exchange Commission (SEC)
www.sec.gov

Senior Law
www.seniorlaw.com

Senior Options
www.senioroptions.com

Seniors-Site
www.seniors-site.com/home/sitemap.html

Silvercare Productions—Joy Loverde
www.elderindustry.com

Social Security Administration
www.ssa.gov

Society of Financial Service Professionals
www.financialpro.org

U.S. Consumer Product Safety Commission
www.cpsc.gov

U.S. Department of Housing and Urban Development (HUD)
www.hud.gov

Visiting Nurse's Association
www.vnna.org

Volunteers of America
www.voa.org

Well Spouse Foundation
www.wellspouse.org

Work & Family Connection
www.workfamily.com

WORKSHEET INDEX

SUBJECT INDEX

ABOUT THE AUTHOR

With expertise based on personal experience, JOY LOVERDE speaks and conducts workshops on elder-care-related topics for business and community events. Uniquely combining the concepts of planning and communication, she arms her audiences with the tools they need to lessen the economic and emotional burdens of caring for aged loved ones. Now in its second edition, *The Complete Eldercare Planner* is widely used by family members and professionals, and is endorsed by the White House Conference on Aging, Alzheimer's Association, Society for Human Resource Management, and the American Counseling Association, among many others.

Joy Loverde founded Silvercare Productions, a Chicago-based consulting firm, in 1989. Silvercare creates and implements effective work/life eldercare programs for corporations and associations. Joy also serves as a consultant to attorneys, financial planners, clergy, health care providers, administrators, and other members of the fast-growing eldercare advisory industry.

Joy's monthly columns appear in websites and publications such as CareGuide, Benefits Link, and *Today's Chicago Woman,* and she frequently contributes work/life articles for trade publications including TEC International Organization of CEOs and the *American Compensation Association Journal.* She is regularly interviewed on television, radio, and Internet programs including the *Today* Show, Fox News Channel, Mr. Long-Term Care, OnHealth Live, *Right on the Money,* and Women-Connect. During her career, she has been quoted in the *Chicago Tribune, Elder Law News,* and *HR Magazine,* among others. *USA Today* ran a four-part series on her planning approach to eldercare.

Joy participates in organizations such as Boomer Agenda, International Center for Eldercare Advocacy, Joint Civic Committee of Italian-Americans, Chicago Fund on Aging and Disability, and the Today's Chicago Woman Foundation. She is a member of the faculty for Eden Across America and is the international eldercare spokesperson for the Employee Services Management Association. A constant advocate for the prevention of elder abuse, Joy established a monthly support group for caregivers of elders for family members to receive Joy's individual attention and expert advice from local professionals.

When she's not on the road with eldercare workshops, you'll find her skiing and Rollerblading with her daughter, Bonnie, and family. Joy is a long-distance caregiver for her elderly mother, and is married to family law attorney, David Schultz. Joy resides in downtown Chicago.

If you are interested in Joy Loverde's eldercare programs and consulting services, please call (312) 642-3611 and visit her website *www.elderindustry.com.*